The BRITISH PORTRAIT

1660–1960

'Mrs Montague and her Sister decorating a Bust of Handel', by William Beechey, 1802, 95 x 57 ins. (241.5 x 145cm). It was in larger-scale portraiture such as this that Beechey used his inventive powers to full effect (Private collection)

The BRITISH PORTRAIT
1660–1960

with an introductory essay by
Sir Roy Strong

and contributions from
Brian Allen, Richard Charlton-Jones, Kenneth McConkey,
Christopher Newall, Martin Postle, Frances Spalding
& John Wilson

Antique Collectors' Club

British Library Cataloguing-in-Publication Data
A catalogue record for this book is available from the British Library

Printed in England on Consort Royal Satin from Donside Mills, Aberdeen, by the Antique Collectors' Club, Woodbridge, Suffolk IP12 1DS

The Antique Collectors' Club

The Antique Collectors' Club was formed in 1966 and quickly grew to a five figure membership spread throughout the world. It publishes the only independently run monthly antiques magazine, *Antique Collecting*, which caters for those collectors who are interested in widening their knowledge of antiques, both by greater awareness of quality and by discussion of the factors which influence the price that is likely to be asked. The Antique Collectors' Club pioneered the provision of information on prices for collectors and the magazine still leads in the provision of detailed articles on a variety of subjects.

It was in response to the enormous demand for information on 'what to pay' that the price guide series was introduced in 1968 with the first edition of *The Price Guide to Antique Furniture* (completely revised 1978 and 1989), a book which broke new ground by illustrating the more common types of antique furniture, the sort that collectors could buy in shops and at auctions rather than the rare museum pieces which had previously been used (and still to a large extent are used) to make up the limited amount of illustrations in books published by commercial publishers. Many other price guides have followed, all copiously illustrated, and greatly appreciated by collectors for the valuable information they contain, quite apart from prices. The Price Guide Series heralded the publication of many standard works of reference on art and antiques. *The Dictionary of British Art* (now in six volumes), *Oak Furniture* and *Early English Clocks* were followed by many deeply researched reference works such as *The Directory of Gold and Silversmiths*, providing new information. Many of these books are now accepted as the standard work of reference on their subject.

The Antique Collectors' Club has widened its list to include books on gardens and architecture. All the Club's publications are available through bookshops world-wide and a full catalogue of all these titles is available free of charge from the addresses below.

Club membership, open to all collectors, costs little. Members receive free of charge *Antique Collecting*, the Club's magazine (published ten times a year), which contains well-illustrated articles dealing with the practical aspects of collecting not normally dealt with by magazines. Prices, features of value, investment potential, fakes and forgeries are all given prominence in the magazine.

Among other facilities available to members are private buying and selling facilities, the longest list of 'For Sales' of any antiques magazine, an annual ceramics conference and the opportunity to meet other collectors at their local antique collectors' clubs. There are over eighty in Britain and more than a dozen overseas. Members may also buy the Club's publications at special pre-publication prices.

As its motto implies, the Club is an organisation designed to help collectors get the most out of their hobby: it is informal and friendly and gives enormous enjoyment to all concerned.

For Collectors — By Collectors — About Collecting

ANTIQUE COLLECTORS' CLUB
5 Church Street, Woodbridge, Suffolk IP12 1DS, UK
Tel: 01394 385501 Fax: 01394 384434
—— or ——
Market Street Industrial Park, Wappingers' Falls, NY 12590, USA
Tel: 914 297 0003 Fax: 914 297 0068

Contents

Measurements are given height by width; portraits are oil on canvas unless otherwise stated.

The British Obsession
An Introduction to the British Portrait

The portrait was a child of the renaissance. It was an expression of a reordering of the universe to one that was fundamentally man centred. Renaissance thought placed man at the centre of a ladder of ascent to God where he was lower than the angels but above the beasts. Through the exercise of his intellect he was uniquely able to place himself attune to higher spheres and, at the same time, control the physical world of nature which God had given him. Renaissance art looks at the world through man's eyes and no longer, as in the middle ages, through God's. The lines of vision, as reordered through the invention of scientific and aerial perspective, radiate from man.

It was out of this huge revolution that the portrait was born. Its driving force, first in fifteenth century Italy, and later in the rest of Europe, through the sixteenth century, was humanism. And because of this portraiture arrived in the British Isles quite suddenly, complete like Minerva springing fully armed from the head of Jove. There was no slow emerging process. Although there had been a handful of predecessors, in the main royal marriage portraits, to all intents and purposes British portraiture begins with Holbein's introduction by Erasmus to the humanist scholar Sir Thomas More in 1526-27. The portrait was a natural expression of early Tudor humanism which, once established, was not only to gain momentum down the centuries but to gather to itself other motivations, above all those connected with ancestry, dynasty and propaganda. Only in the twentieth century have these motives, under the impact of two world wars and the technological society, been shaken and the tradition of the portrait been shattered and reformed.

But for four centuries the British were obsessed by portraiture more than any other European country. Every visiting foreign painter from Van Dyck to John Singer Sargent found that their fate was to act as a face-painter. Every native artist knew that any aspiration to be otherwise was doomed to failure. Some, like Joshua Reynolds, tried to lift portrait painting on to a higher plane by assimilating to it elements of history painting, others, like George Romney, were reduced to frustration while, in an extreme case, Benjamin Robert Haydon was driven insane.

Why is it that the British are so obsessed with portraits? An obsession that extended not only to their own portrait but also collecting those of friends, preserving ones of their forebears, assembling collections of distinguished sitters, both dead and alive, cutting portrait prints out of old books to mount into huge 'grangerised' histories and founding, in 1856, what was the first National Portrait Gallery in the world. I cannot pretend fully to explain that phenomenon. One element was certainly the rejection of religious images at the reformation together with the spread of Puritan sensibilities which eliminated virtually all religious subject matter until the Victorian period and rendered classical subjects open to the charge of licentiousness on account of nudity. An over-conscious sense of caste and of dynasty must certainly also have provided an impulse, for portraits run in tandem with that other passion — which often ran to megalomania — genealogy, and, indeed, the two usually were finally to combine on the sitter's tomb which incorporated both face and armorial bearings.

All of this is a potent reminder that portraits were an expression of class and status. We have virtually no visual records of the mass of the population at all. British portraits give us the likenesses above all of the aristocratic and gentry classes extending out as time progressed to include the professions, such as clerics and writers, and to the middle classes. It is only today, with the advent of inexpensive photographic equipment and processing, that the portrait has become the prerogative of Everyman. But the camera's lens in the hands of an amateur cannot any longer control the image as the painter's brush had done in previous centuries, where a combination of the demands of the sitter and the conventions of the age preconditioned the result. And that is what sets the pre-photographic era apart.

To read British portraiture it is essential to understand what those demands and conventions were and how they changed, for portraits belong not only to the history of art in this country but to a wider canvas of historical evidence. The analysis of who sat and why and at what age tells us much about the attitudes of a past society. The decision to depict a husband and wife together or a family as a group or a child on its own is material for the social historian. What they wore and the setting with which the sitters and the painter framed them can be even more revealing. The British portrait in these aspects remains as yet a relatively uninvestigated phenomenon. Looking at portraits in terms of the history of painting is, therefore, only part of a much richer tapestry of allusion, symbol and sign. And it is to that wider perspective that I would like to devote this introductory essay.

THE SITTERS

British portraiture can be conveniently divided up into three main categories: the single portrait, the family portrait and, a special category, child portraiture. In addition to these figures and combinations of figures, one can add a series of set motifs which make up reiterating themes over the centuries: landscape and the world of nature, sport and animals, and pride of possession. Inevitably to separate the figures from their background is a distortion but it will enable us to draw out more forcefully what it is that is peculiar to British portraiture as it evolved over five centuries down to the present day. Inevitably, too, in considering that duration of time, about four centuries, almost as a single swathe, one must concentrate on generalisations and not dwell on the exceptions.

The Single Sitter

Surprisingly little is known about the occasion which prompted a person to sit for a portrait. Statistically it would seem reasonable to conclude that the painted portrait belonged to a steadily expanding market until the advent of the camera and the collapse in confidence which so dramatically affected the establishment classes with the First World War. Most country house portrait collections seem to atrophy at that moment not only in response to what was an irreversible shift in the power and prestige of the landed classes but also because of an inability on the part of those classes to accept the modernist movement with the fervour that, in previous centuries, they had embraced every other style.

By 1600 the practice of sitting for one's portrait, which had been an innovation of the 1530s, was an accepted attribute of upper class life. One of the few glimpses into motive appears in the autobiography of Thomas Whythorne, a musician, who sat for his portrait more than once. He records the very basic fact that a looking glass only returned one's present image. Therefore '. . . diverse do cause their counterfeits to be made to show how time doth alter them from time to time', and he goes on to dwell on the fact that such images recording the passage of time acted as a *memento mori*. That essentially medieval attitude was to march hand in hand with the new renaissance belief in the enhanced status of man the human being.

The various portrait formats for a single sitter, however, developed remarkably quickly. The single portrait was already well established by the Elizabethan period, both head and shoulders and the three-quarter-length. The full-length, however, was a rarity until the last decade of the century when the fashion returned producing the long series of costume pieces that remain the glory of late Elizabethan and Jacobean portraiture. Portraits of husband and wife painted as a pair, a formula introduced by Holbein during his first visit to England, were taken up and continued by Hans Eworth in a long series stretching to the close of the 1560s (Plates 3 and 4) when they fell from fashion

Reality and Rank

In Tudor and Jacobean portraiture the spirit of northern renaissance realism was married to the presentation of the sitter as an icon of rank and class

PLATE 1
Hans Holbein
Sir Henry Guildford, 1527
Searching realism aligned to a record of rank in which the sitter holds the staff of his office as Comptroller of the Royal Household and wears the collar of the Order of the Garter. There is a pendant portrait of his wife
(Royal Collection: Windsor Castle)

only to be revived in the work of Gheeraerts and others at the close of the century. Costume in these early pictures emphasised rank as indeed did the introduction of wands of office or batons of command (Plates 1, 2 and 6 and Colour Plate 1). The painter depicted precisely what he saw which presupposes the loan of what was worn to the studio, for the records of dress are exact. Looking through the surviving portraits from 1525 to 1625 of single adults it

PLATE 2
Artist unknown
William Cecil, Lord Burghley, late 1570s
A mechanical workshop portrait depicting Burghley as both
Garter Knight and holding the rod of Secretary of State. (See
also Colour Plate 1)
(National Portrait Gallery, London)

PLATES 3 and 4
Hans Eworth
James Stuart, 1st Earl of Moray and his wife, Agnes Keith, 1561
An early instance of portraits of husband and wife, painted to
commemorate their marriage on 8 February 1561/62
(Private collection)

PLATE 5 (above)
Robert Peake the Elder
Sir Edward Grimston, 1591
The sitter holds a *memento mori* in the form of a skull epitomising the role of the portrait as a reminder to the onlooker of the transitory nature of human life
(Private collection)

PLATE 6 (above right)
Hieronimo Custodis
Sir John Parker of Ratton, 1589
The sitter as emblem raising his sword in defence of his motto: Pro Fide et Patria
(Royal Collection: Hampton Court)

is difficult to draw any conclusions that a particular age was favoured for sitting, but that a variety of circumstances could lead to a decision to sit, ranging from marriage, greater affluence, the whim of fashion or the demands of friendship. We can catch this in a rare glimpse of someone asking for a portrait of a friend in the letter from Viscount Howard of Bindon in April 1609 to Sir Robert Cecil when he requests a portrait of Cecil in Garter robes (a status symbol) 'to be placed in the gallery I lately made for the pictures of sundry of my honourable friends, whose presentation thereby to behold will greatly delight me to walk often in that place where I may see so comfortable a sight'.

Any visit to a country house collection will corroborate the fact that the period running from the reign of Charles I to the accession of the Hanoverians saw a huge proliferation of the portrait. In the presentation of the sitter there was a dramatic change away from the reality of the previous period to what

PLATE 7
William Larkin
Lucy Harington, Countess of Bedford, c.1615
Wearing a coronet and peeress's robes, a fashion revived at the coronation of James I
in 1604
(Gripsholm Castle, Sweden)

Rank and Symbol

In portraiture of the Stuart age, running from the reign of Charles I to that of George I, reality gave way to idealisation of feature as the sitter was made to respond to the dictates of the aesthetics of the age which demanded an assimilation to heroic types

PLATE 8
Anthony Van Dyck
Philip, 4th Lord Wharton, 1632
Lord Wharton poses as a shepherd in Arcady reflecting the romantic pastoral conventions of love etiquette at the Caroline court
(National Gallery of Art, Washington, D.C.)

PLATE 9
Michael Wright
*Margaret Onley, Mrs.
George Vernon, c.1660*
Flowers and fruit are
always symbolic, as in
this portrait of a wife
concealing her
pregnancy in the folds of
her dress, her fertility
symbolised in the
pomegranates she holds
(National Trust:
Sudbury Hall)

Jonathan Richardson described in 1715 as 'raising the Character'. Idealisation
was not flattery but a response to the accepted aesthetic demands of the age.
Hence, from Van Dyck onwards, the tendency was for the sitter to be attired
in mythological dress or some version of antique costume. Such guises could,
however, be of serious intent or at least would begin as such. Lely's Countess
of Grammont appears as St. Catherine, renowned both for her wisdom and her
faith, a choice no doubt reflecting the aspirations of the sitter. Mrs. Pepys,
however, was led to sit in exactly the same guise merely because she had seen
a lady of title similarly posed. This tells us everything about her fashionable
snobbery and nothing about her character. In sharp contrast Pepys's own
portrait by a minor artist, John Hayls (Plate 11), provides us with the fullest
account that we have of the motives which led an ambitious young man to sit.

PLATE 10
William Dobson
Colonel Richard Neville,
c.1645
A royalist commander
depicted in armour with
gun and helmet before
him, a battle raging in
the distance and the
figures of Mercury
(speed) and Mars (war)
in relief above him
(National Portrait
Gallery, London)

That occurred in 1666 and the choice of Hayls was financial as much as anything, for Pepys could not have afforded the prices charged by the court painter, Lely. He sat a dozen times. The robe he posed in, an Indian one, was hired for the occasion. The portrait began with a landscape background but Pepys forced Hayls to paint this out after both of them had spent an hour looking at pictures in Whitehall Palace. The paper he holds contains his own setting of a lyric by Davenant put in at the sitter's behest.

This rare instance of a fully documented account of the dialogue between a sitter and a painter cannot have been unique. It is a cautionary tale which should prevent anyone studying the portraits of this seemingly vacuous period from merely dismissing their contents as empty and meaningless. Van Dyck's

COLOUR PLATE 1
Artist unknown
*William Cecil, Lord Burghley,
late 1570s*
18⅞ x 13¼ ins.
(48 x 34cm)
In early portraits
costume and symbols of
office emphasised rank
and status
(National Portrait
Gallery, London)

PLATE 12
Peter Lely
Sir Thomas Isham, c.1678
An instance of 'raising'
the sitter by attiring him
in pseudo-antique
costume
(Lamport Hall)

PLATE 11
John Hayls
Samuel Pepys, 1666
The diary describes the evolution of the portrait with a
hired Indian gown and the introduction of a musical
setting by Pepys of a verse by Davenant
(National Portrait Gallery, London)

PLATE 13
John Closterman
*Anthony Ashley, 3rd Earl of
Shaftesbury, c.1700-1701*
An instance of a portrait with a
highly elaborate programme of
allusions at the behest of the
sitter. This starts from his
classical garb as a philosopher
holding a book to his heart and
opens out to a complex
exposition of his ethical beliefs
in the books ranged near him
(National Portrait Gallery,
London)

portrait of Lord Wharton attired as a shepherd (Plate 8), is a serious reflection
of the preoccupation by the Caroline court with neoplatonic love ethics, just
as at the turn of the century John Closterman's full-length of Anthony Ashley,
3rd Earl of Shaftesbury (Plate 13), is the most complex statement of the Earl's
philosophical aspirations in which every object and gesture is meant to be read.
The Stuart aesthetics of portraiture were overwhelmingly preoccupied with the
sitter as symbol, as soldier, gentleman, Garter Knight, beauty, cleric, lady of
rank. The 'raising' alluded to by Richardson referred to such an idealisation
which went on to embrace the face and figure which was also made to
approximate to a period ideal, with the result that three centuries later almost

The Motions of the Mind

Concern with the interpretation of the psychology of the sitter becomes an over-riding concern in the formulae which evolved for portraits from the middle of the eighteenth century onwards

PLATE 14
William Hogarth
George Arnold, c.1740
35⅝ × 27⅞ ins. (90.5 x 53cm)
The antithesis of the idealised symbolic presentation of a sitter, recording instead the almost raucous reality of a retired merchant and collector. (See also Colour Plate 30)
(Fitzwilliam Museum, Cambridge)

any Lely lady can masquerade as a mistress of Charles II.

If the sitter in the seventeenth century was invested with an heroic stature by, for example, being attired in antique dress and Roman armour, even though he sported a wig, the eighteenth century represented a profound shift in attitude away from such a stance. To paraphrase Alexander Pope, man's

PLATE 15
Joshua Reynolds
The Reverend Laurence Sterne, 1760
Reynolds's use of dramatic chiaroscuro heightens the character of his famous sitter making him, as a contemporary wrote, 'in as facetious a humour as if he would tell you a story of Tristram Shandy' (National Portrait Gallery, London)

PLATE 16
Thomas Gainsborough
The Hon. Harriott Marsham, early 1760s
The painter, making use of his flickering brush technique, draws out the introspective nature of his sitter (Barber Institute of Fine Arts, Birmingham)

best study was man rather than his acts. The heroics of the previous century seemed hollow in the age of enlightenment. Reflecting the drift of contemporary poets, writers and playwrights there was an increased concentration on the psychological motives of the individual. Richardson's *Pamela* or Gray's 'Elegy in a Country Churchyard', in which ploughmen are identified with the heroes of the past, reflect that the age of heroism had passed. This literary preoccupation with the psychological workings of the human mind found its counterpart exactly in the greatest portrait essays of Gainsborough and Reynolds and, in varying degrees of success, in the work of a mass of other portrait painters. We have only to look at Reynolds's portrait of the writer, Laurence Sterne (Plate 15), or Gainsborough's rendering of The Hon. Harriott Marsham (Plate 16), to know their concern was with catching the inner being and rendering everything else on the picture's surface incidental

23

Fancy Dress

The fashion for wearing fancy dress was a feature of much eighteenth century portraiture

PLATE 17
Johan Zoffany
John, Lord Mountstuart, c.1763-64
The fashion for sitters to be painted wearing a version of Van Dyck costume, which began in the 1740s and lasted forty years, appears in the work of most painters of the period
(Collection of the Earl of Harrowby)

PLATE 18
Joshua Reynolds
The Hon. Mrs. Edward Bouverie of Delapré and her child, 1770
Reynolds's attempt to lift portraiture into the realm of history painting included
turning clothes into classical draperies, a fashion also adopted by other painters such
as Romney and Cotes
(Private collection)

to that aim. Although the old set pieces continue, such as the peer in his robes,
and a penchant for fancy dress in the Van Dyck cavalier style (Plate 17), the
overwhelming majority of eighteenth century portraits are first and foremost
records of people and attempts to catch on canvas the motions of the mind. As
a result, whereas there is a high degree of approximation of feature between
the sitters in portraits in the age of Lely and Kneller, that cannot be said of
those from Hogarth onwards and in that elementary observation one catches
what separates the two centuries. Even Reynolds's attempt to lift the art of
portrait painting by marrying it with history painting (Plate 18) is in no way
a return to the symbolism of the past but a vehicle whereby to expand the
sitter's character. That phase, the greatest in British portrait painting, ended
with the death of Sir Thomas Lawrence in 1830.

The Collapse of Conventions

Iconographically the period from 1830 to 1914 is sterile, reworking the inherited repertory of the previous century. Only in the work of the Pre-Raphaelites and in the sunset glory of the Edwardian era is there any forward looking innovation to meet the challenge of the camera

PLATE 19
Thomas Phillips
Michael Faraday, 1841-42
The reworking of a
formula already over
half-a-century old
(National Portrait
Gallery, London)

PLATE 20
William Holman Hunt
Henry Wentworth Monk, 1858
A highly esoteric Pre-Raphaelite portrait
almost overloaded with symbolic
allusions to the sitter's reading of the
Book of Revelation, from the trance-like
glance to the 'sea of glass' behind him
(National Gallery of Canada, Ottawa)

26

PLATE 21
John Singer Sargent
Lady Agnew, c.1892-93
Photography amongst other things was responsible for this new spontaneity of vision
(National Gallery of Scotland, Edinburgh)

Shortly after that date we enter the photographic era and are faced by material on such an enormous scale that generalisations become difficult if not impossible. What we witness down to our own day is the gradual collapse of the conventions of painted portraiture as it had existed from the renaissance. The iconographic innovation of the Victorian period, which was explosive in terms of genre painting, history painting and the revival of religious art, on the whole rarely arose above recycling the inherited formulae of previous centuries. Where it did produce excitement, as in the case of the few portraits by the Pre-Raphaelite painters (Plate 20), that came from the shared intensity of a closed circle anticipating a situation which in our own age has produced new directions for the portrait in the work of the Bloomsbury circle or that which centres on David Hockney. The Edwardian era brought one last burst of visual rhetoric in the grand manner but after 1914 it was dead and hollow. After 1914, too, the structure of society in which the portrait flourished was dislocated. Between 1830 and 1914 that society in which portraiture was a norm of expression, although dented, remained unassailed but its purpose became increasingly meaningless as its motivation could so much more easily be fulfilled by the serried ranks of silver framed photographs which covered the surfaces of Victorian and Edwardian drawing rooms.

The British portrait was an expression of an hieratic society which believed in its right to rule. The spread of the franchise and the collapse of the old class system through the twentieth century went hand in hand with the decline of

Innovation and Informality

Having released the painter from any need to perform the functions of a camera, and as a result of the huge social changes after 1914, the iconography of portraiture has gone through collapse and renaissance

PLATE 22
Graham Sutherland
Somerset Maugham, 1949
An interpretation of a major literary figure with an honesty inconceivable fifty years before (Tate Gallery, London)

PLATE 23
David Hockney
'My Parents', 1977
With inherited
conventions obliterated,
the artist has been
released to make a
moving statement on his
parents. (See also
Colour Plate 3)
(Tate Gallery, London)

the portrait. Suddenly the majestic images hung in country houses ceased or, at the best, continued apologetically in canvases which eschewed grandeur and were hung in an obscure passage. The reluctance to sit for a portrait, which was so striking a feature from 1914 onwards, was another symptom of the loss of nerve of a class.

This phenomenon, however, must be set side by side with another, the release of the painter from producing icons and, thanks to the camera, photographs in paint (Plates 22 and 23 and Colour Plate 3). After a period of loss of will and dislocation both painter and sitter during the last thirty years have entered upon a new relationship. It is based on the rediscovery of portraiture as painting. The painter, no longer boxed in by the constraints of his predecessors, is able to concentrate on his sitter's character as never before. Whereas the nineteenth century in the main lived off a recycling of iconographic formats from previous ages, the twentieth has swept them away exploring a new informality of presentation. As a result the last decades of the century will be seen to have been probably the most extraordinarily innovative in the history of British portrait painting since the eighteenth century.

PLATE 24
Marcus Gheeraerts
Barbara Gamage, Countess of Leicester and her children, 1596
The family as painted genealogy with little emotional relationship displayed
(See also Colour Plate 7)
(Private collection of Viscount De L'Isle)

The Family

One of the earliest and still persistent themes in British portraiture is the family. Portrait painting coincides with what are now recognised to be the centuries of the family. No such emphasis existed in medieval thought and it was only at the close of the fifteenth century that depictions of the family began to appear in the guise of a husband and wife flanked by their offspring kneeling as donor figures in an altarpiece. Throughout the sixteenth century and on until our own, which is witnessing the dissolution of the conjugal family concept, the family group had a vigour as a formula for portraiture. In addition those groups vividly recorded the changing patterns of relationship within that tightly knit unit: the rise of the father as the monarch of his family which reached its apogee in the Victorian age, the decline in the status of women, which reached its nadir during exactly the same period, and the gradual recognition and delight in childhood as a separate period of life.

That was certainly not true in the sixteenth century as can be seen, for example, in Marcus Gheeraerts's group of Barbara Gamage, Countess of Leicester, and her children painted in 1596 (Plate 24 and Colour Plate 7). What we see is family pride of a kind which is akin to witnessing a genealogical tree made flesh, the future countess extending her hands to rest on her two

PLATE 25
David des Granges
The Saltonstall Family,
c.1637
Domesticity arrives: a
husband leads his
children to his wife's
bedside
(Tate Gallery, London)

PLATE 26
Peter Lely
The Carnavon Family, c.1659
Even amidst the trappings of baroque grandeur there is a tender interplay between the
Countess and her children
(Private collection)

PLATE 27
Johan Zoffany
The Family of John, 3rd Duke of Atholl, 1765-67
The ducal pair with their family informally indulge in sports and pastimes from fishing
to tree climbing in the grounds of their estate
(Blair Castle)

boys while the girls flank the male heir. Forty years later the atmosphere begins
to be very different in David des Granges's group of the Saltonstall Family
where the father takes his son by the hand and leads him to his wife's bedside
(Plate 25). Later in the century Lely's family groups, however grand, register
a similar warmth in relationship established by gesture and pose between
parents and children (Plate 26). By the time that we get to the conversation
pieces of the eighteenth century that delight in children has found full
expression in groups in which the parents preside over their offspring engaged
energetically in fishing, tree climbing or playing with a dog (Plate 27). With
a few exceptions in the nineteenth century the family group was to be taken
over by the camera whose mechanical lens was far more able to record the
gradual evolution of a family in terms of multiple images and at far less cost.
Such a development was to apply equally to children's portraiture.

Children

The earliest separate portrait of a child in English portraiture must be Holbein's rendering of the two year old Edward VI which was presented to his father as a New Year's gift on 1 January 1539. Although the young prince holds a rattle, to all intents and purposes what we see is the picture of a miniature adult wearing clothes which, but for what would have been skirts to the ground, were identical to those worn by Henry VIII. This picture was a precursor of what was established by the close of the sixteenth century as a separate portrait genre. Portraits were an expensive commodity in the Tudor period, the prerogative of the aristocratic, the gentry and gradually the rich merchant classes, and the fact that it was thought worth bestowing money on recording the likeness of a person whose survival to adulthood was dubious is an index of a change of attitude to childhood unknown in the middle ages. The emergence of the separate and group child portrait away from the family group and the mother and child reflects a new belief in the importance of that phase of life.

So in 1563 Hans Eworth records Henry Stuart, Lord Darnley and his brother, Charles, Earl of Lennox, then only six and wearing the skirts to the ground which were the norm for a boy until he was breeched at seven (Plate 28). Forty years later, at the turn of the century, Robert Peake catches the young 4th Earl of Bedford, in the newly breeched phase of his childhood, holding a hawk on his left wrist and a hood in the other hand, with two hounds in attendance (Plate 29). Moving down a generation in the same Russell family we witness this interest in children reflected in the Earl's decision to have all six of his painted by an exceedingly rare portrait painter, Johann Priwitzer, in 1626-27 (Plate 30). In these portraits the children are still essentially miniature adults, as they are in Van Dyck's group portraits of the children of Charles I in the 1630s, although in the famous 1637 group posed around an enormous mastiff we encounter a new motif which was also to have a vigorous life in child portraiture down to the studio photographers of the twentieth century. On the extreme right the two year old Princess Elizabeth can be seen cradling the naked Princess Anne who had been born on 17 March of that year (Plate 31).

In that nudity we witness an innovation whose roots lay in the revival of the antique putto in the renaissance and also in the nudity which spread into scenes of the infant Christ and other holy children during the later middle ages and renaissance. This was to become a standard formula for infant child portraiture for over a century. In the early Lely portrait of William, 6th Earl of Pembroke he is depicted naked, bar an appropriately placed piece of drapery, at the foot of a tree trunk patting his dog's head (Plate 32). Even if the nudity is not total it is substantial in the long series of portraits of children in vaguely antique costume which form a distinctive iconographic category in the Lely and Kneller periods.

Children

The emergence of separate portraits of children by the close of the sixteenth century documents the rise in the recognition of childhood as a distinctive period of life

THES BE THE SONES OF THE RIGHTE HONERABLE PEEPLLE OF LENOXE AND THE LADYMA PGARETZ GRACE COVNTYES OF LENOXE AD AN GWYSE

AN° DO
M·D·LXII

HENRY STEWARDE LORD DARNL AND DOWGLAS, AETATIS SVAE X

CHARLLES STEWARDE HIS BROTHER, AETATIS SVAE VI

PLATE 28
Hans Eworth
Henry Stuart, Lord Darnley, and his brother Charles, later Earl of Lennox, 1563
The six year old boy is a miniature adult apart from the skirts of his robe
(Royal Collection)

34

PLATE 29
Robert Peake the Elder
*Francis, 4th Earl of Bedford,
c.1600*
The picture depicts the boy
shortly after he would have been
breeched at seven and looking
like a small adult
(Woburn Abbey)

Something else happens in the seventeenth century which was to affect child
portraiture — the development of children's clothes. If we turn to Michael
Wright's portrait of the children of the 3rd Earl of Salisbury painted c.1668-69
we see the future 4th Earl, aged about two, attired in a costume very different
from what a boy would have worn earlier in the century (Plate 33). It is a low-
cut lace-edged dress with full sleeves and with a headdress topped with a forest
of pale blue ostrich plumes. The dress is far more effeminate than that in the
Eworth portrait a century before in which an adult male doublet merely tops
a long plain skirt. Gradually boys' costume was being effeminised until often
it becomes impossible in eighteenth and nineteenth century portraits to tell
whether a child is a boy or girl before the age of four or five.

PLATE 30
Johann Priwitzer
Lady Diana Russell, 1627
One of a set of six portraits of the 4th Earl of
Bedford's children reflecting the new interest in
childhood as a phase of life
(Woburn Abbey)

PLATE 31
Anthony Van Dyck
The Family of Charles I, 1637
Groups of children without their parents are
further manifestations of the emergent cult of
childhood. The nude baby to the right is an
innovation
(Royal Collection)

PLATE 32 (above)
Peter Lely
William, 6th Earl of Pembroke, c.1645
Responding to the influence of the putto it became customary to depict very young children nude *à l'antique* (Wilton House)

PLATE 33 (above right)
Michael Wright
Lady Catherine Cecil and James, 4th Earl of Salisbury, c.1668-69
By the mid-seventeenth century distinctive children's clothes emerged for boys. There was no such categorisation of dress for girls (Hatfield House)

PLATE 34 (right)
William Hogarth
The Graham Children, 1742
(See Colour Plate 2 overleaf)

No such categorisation of girls through dress in childhood was called for because their status was low, staying at home and, if educated at all, in receipt of instruction at the hands of governesses. Girls continued to be little women, for their journey to adulthood was never punctuated by the stages which affected their brothers' one to manhood which was marked by breeching at seven, school or service in a noble household, university and the Grand Tour. Each of these phases could evoke a portrait. In the case of a girl there were no such distinctive events until marriage. It is not until the Victorian period that girls develop types of dress which were in any significant way different from those worn by their mothers.

COLOUR PLATE 2
William Hogarth
The Graham Children, 1742
63¾ x 71¼ ins. (162 x 181cm)
The development of the child portrait reflected a growing realisation of the importance
of childhood — here shown as a joyous time, although the Cupid bearing the Scythe
of Time on the clock reminds the onlooker of its transitoriness
(National Gallery, London)

COLOUR PLATE 3
David Hockney
'My Parents', 1977
72 × 72ins. (183 × 183cm)
During the last thirty years portraiture has seen a new relationship between painter
and sitter, in which the artist has been able to concentrate on the personality of his
sitters
(Tate Gallery, London)

THE SETTING

The background surrounding a sitter on an empty canvas or panel offered space to develop the statement made through countenance and costume. It was not until the second decade of the seventeenth century that the handling of that space began to be in accordance with the renaissance norms whereby the picture frame, like a proscenium arch, opened on to a world governed by scientific perspective which the sitter inhabited (Plate 37). Before that date virtually all backgrounds were circumscribed (Plate 35). In the main they are areas of opaque colour, generally in the early Tudor period blue and later, in the Elizabethan age, a shade of beige or brown. Occasionally there is an inset emblematic scene or a coat of arms. This treatment of background space is typical of Holbein, Hans Eworth, George Gower and Marcus Gheeraerts, and pertains to a sense of vision still essentially medieval and polycentric, one which continued to have vigour in provincial portraiture until the middle of the next century. It should not be forgotten that the fact that a sitter was able accurately to record his age inscribed on his portrait was new in itself. Medieval people had only the vaguest notion of what age they were and such exactitude in inscriptions is an expression of a concept of man in time which is essentially renaissance.

Space in early portraits is never more than shallow and confined. Eworth's few full-lengths place a sitter amidst marble columns and architecture, but in the main he rarely extends beyond a folded curtain suspended behind a sitter. In the Elizabethan period any sense of location is reduced to the abstract: a table to one side on which to rest a hand, parts of a chair and a swag of curtain. Only in the last decade of the sixteenth and the first of the seventeenth century does a greater sense of space open up around the sitter in the full-lengths by Robert Peake, Gheeraerts, William Larkin and John de Critz in which variations are made on the theme of turkey carpet, chair and cushion, table and curtain (Plate 36 and Colour Plate 4).

This only serves to emphasise that from the outset the background of all but the most exceptional portraits is entirely artificial and even if it does contain things that actually existed they are reordered and rearranged. That in itself produces a dichotomy between the reality in the person of the sitter and the artificiality of everything else.

Nature and the Sitter

Portraiture often reflects the Englishman's dialogue with the world of Nature, a dialogue which underwent a great revolution from the sixteenth century onwards. To the middle ages that world was viewed as hostile and untamed. Woods were menacing and abounding in savage beasts, the rivers and seas were dangerous, the mountains threatening. This view was to linger on until the close of the seventeenth century. Celia Fiennes, travelling around England in the reign of William and Mary, still retained much of this medieval outlook.

PLATE 35
George Gower
Richard Drake of Esher, 1577
There is no sense of space behind the sitter: the inscriptions, a coat of arms and a helmet on a shelf have no logical relationship to each other
(National Maritime Museum, Greenwich)

The Invention of Space

The reception of the renaissance norms for the ordering of space within a picture's surface was slow. Until well into the second quarter of the seventeenth century the treatment remained medieval and polycentric

COLOUR PLATE 4
William Larkin
*Dorothy Cary, Lady St.
John, c.1615*
81 x 48⅛ ins.
(206 x 122cm)
The emergence of space:
though still confined, a
sense of space is
achieved by the flanking
curtains
(English Heritage:
Ranger's House,
Blackheath)

42

COLOUR PLATE 5
Artist unknown
The Family of Henry VIII, c.1543-47
74¾ × 140¼ ins. (190 × 356cm)
Portraiture reflects man's dialogue with Nature, and in this, the earliest garden view
in British painting, the seed of one of the great themes in portraiture can be seen
(Royal Collection)

But already, in the Tudor period, new sensibilities were gaining ground. In the background of the group portrait of Henry VIII and his family (Plate 38 and Colour Plate 5) we can see two archways each of which frames an exact record of the recently created Great Garden of Whitehall Palace. No such view figures in any portrait by Holbein or indeed of any of his successors until well into the Elizabethan period. In this picture we are at the beginning of one of the great themes in British portraiture.

The garden was an intermediate stage in man's dialogue with the realm of nature. The renaissance garden epitomised man's subjugation of Nature by the powers of Art as well as man's reordering of Nature in accord with the Divine Order as it prevailed before the Fall. In addition the garden was a powerful status symbol as the land around the country's palaces and manor houses was transformed into an earthly paradise for the delectation of the owner harnessing the elements and defying the seasons. Thus the garden is one of the earliest of all attributes to appear in British portraiture as both symbol and reality.

In the background of a portrait of Lettice Newdegate at Arbury Hall dated 1606 we see three knots stretching away towards an arbour shaped like an igloo (Plate 39). Thirty years later Arthur, Lord Capel, and his family are grouped before a backcloth of their newly created Italianate garden at Much Hadham, Hertfordshire, the epitome of courtly taste as propagated by Inigo Jones with its statuary, fountains, terraces and stairways in the new classical style (Plate 40). In 1673 Michael Wright similarly placed Sir Robert Viner's family before what must be elements of his famous baroque garden at Swakeleys, Middlesex (Plate 41).

PLATE 36
William Larkin
*Dorothy Cary, Lady St.
John, c.1615*
(See Colour Plate 4)
(English Heritage:
Ranger's House,
Blackheath)

By the eighteenth century, and with the revolution of the landscape movement in all its various phases from William Kent through to Repton, the garden ceased merely to be a distant attribute and became the setting in which the owner and his family elected to display themselves in the newly fashionable conversation piece. Edward Haytley's depiction of a Kentish squire, James Brockman, his family and friends, c.1744-46, disposed around what was a temple and a landscape garden with a formal pond, which were actually under construction while the picture was being painted, sums it all up in a formula which was to have vitality throughout the eighteenth century (Plate 42).

Side by side with gardens there was the development of the landscape as a setting for the sitter. The earliest portrait of a British sitter standing in a landscape is Marcus Gheeraerts's fancy dress likeness of Captain Thomas Lee attired as an Irish Knight in the midst of what the artist conceived to be an evocation of Ireland (Plate 43). This is landscape as emblem. Moving on in date we have William Larkin's astoundingly exact rendering of countryside behind the full-length figure of Lady St. John of Bletso, with its village and church spire nestling amidst the hills (Plate 44). But this is an exception which must have been at the behest of the sitter, for the landscape settings which dominate British portraiture from Van Dyck onwards are firmly those of an imaginary Arcadia. This repertory was first established by Van Dyck's portraits of the 1630s of Caroline courtiers, often clothed as shepherds, in which the painter gave visual substance to the pastoral dreamworld of the poets and playwrights of the age and in which couples acted out their amours in the language of neoplatonic preciosity. The nebulous rock formations, trailing trees, symbolic blossoms and spouting fountains set against a romantic twilight became props which continued to have a vitality and a meaning, particularly for women sitters, until well on into the eighteenth century. Reynolds's sitters, for example, remain inhabitants of Arcady.

The landscape movement, however, was to set in motion new sensibilities to the world of nature. Ostensibly it may seem that we are moving out of a classical never-never land into the reality of nature. In truth it was one form of artifice replacing another. Gainsborough's feathery trees set amidst landscapes that seem almost to be backlit by flashes of lightning in the distance, anticipate what the artist's young friend, Uvedale Price, was to categorise as the Picturesque (Plate 47). Only when we move into the middle of the nineteenth century do we for the first time encounter that meticulous fidelity to nature observed which was to be one of the keystones of early Victorian critical appreciation. Millais's famous portrait of John Ruskin standing by what in a letter the sitter describes as 'a lovely piece of worn rock, with foaming water and weeds and moss, and a whole overhanging bank of dark crag' says it all (Plate 48).

What is so striking is that by that period the source of wealth for both the established but above all the new classes was no longer land but industry and commercial endeavour. We find no reflection of that in portraiture. Far from

PLATE 37
George Geldorp
William, 2nd Earl of Salisbury, 1626
The figure is placed in space reordered to the renaissance norms with
the picture frame acting as a proscenium arch leading the eye in
(Hatfield House)

COLOUR PLATE 6
Arthur Devis
'Children in an Interior', c.1742-43
39 x 49¾ins. (99 x 125.5cm)
Interiors in British portraits should rarely, if ever, be read literally and, as here, were
often mocked up by the painter in his studio
(Yale Center for British Art: Paul Mellon Collection)

COLOUR PLATE 7
Marcus Gheeraerts
Barbara Gamage, Countess of Leicester and her children, 1596
80 × 102½ ins. (203 × 260.5cm)
Throughout the sixteenth century the family group was a familiar theme of portraiture, and one which presented a form of family tree
(Private collection of Viscount De L'Isle)

The World of Nature

The portrait encapsulates the long British dialogue with the world of Nature, even if only artificial

PLATE 38
Artist unknown
The Family of Henry VIII, c.1543-47
Through the flanking archways we see an accurate rendering of the new Great Garden of Whitehall Palace, the earliest garden view in British painting. (See also Colour Plate 5). (Royal Collection)

PLATE 39
Artist unknown
Lettice Newdegate, 1606
Behind her stretches a knot garden and an arbour
(Arbury Hall)

PLATE 40
Cornelius Johnson
The Family of Arthur, Lord Capel, c.1639
Nature tamed by Art with a view of the newly created Italianate garden made by the sitter at Much Hadham, Hertfordshire
(National Portrait Gallery, London)

PLATE 41
Michael Wright
The Family of Sir Robert Viner, 1673
The background celebrates the owner's garden at Swakeleys, Middlesex
(National Portrait Gallery, London)

it, for every attempt is made by the sitters to distance themselves from the source of their money. In this way the Edwardian portrait in the heyday before the outbreak of the First World War witnesses a return to Arcadia in portraits which revive the artificial idylls of the eighteenth century grand tradition. The result, as in Sargent's Millicent, Duchess of Sutherland (1904) or Steer's Mrs. Hammersley (1907), is closer to the escapist world of musical comedy and the Gaiety Girl (Plates 49 and 50). After 1914 the dialogue between the sitter and nature was to be far more prosaic.

COLOUR PLATE 8
Edwin Landseer
'Windsor Castle in Modern Times', 1840-45
44¾ × 56⅞ ins. (113.5 x 144.5cm)
The hunt portrait was not confined to open spaces, but could be painted in the drawing room in the shape of the husband returning from the chase bearing his spoils
(Royal Collection)

PLATE 42
Edward Haytley
The Brockman Family and friends at Beachborough Manor, 1744-46
The picture records the creation of the garden with its formal pond and temple
(National Gallery of Victoria, Melbourne)

PLATE 43
Marcus Gheeraerts
Captain Thomas Lee, 1594.
The earliest portrait placing a sitter into a landscape, albeit an imaginary one
(Tate Gallery, London)

PLATE 44
William Larkin
Lady St. John of Bletso, c.1615
The earliest portrait with what appears to be a topographically exact rendering of the English landscape behind the sitter
(Mapledurham House)

PLATE 45
Anthony Van Dyck
Anne, Countess of Clanbrasil, c.1635
The sitter in the imaginary pastoral landscape of Arcadia
(Frick Collection, New York)

PLATE 46
Joshua Reynolds
Anne Dashwood, 1764
Arcadia still reigns through the landscape settings of
the eighteenth century as in this portrait of a bride as
a shepherdess
(Metropolitan Museum of Art, New York)

PLATE 47
Thomas Gainsborough
Lady Brisco, 1776
Gainsborough's land-
scapes anticipate the
Picturesque movement
in landscape gardening
with their use of
dramatic chiaroscuro,
rugged effects and a
waterfall
(English Heritage:
Kenwood House)

PLATE 48
John Everett Millais
John Ruskin, 1854
Pre-Raphaelite fidelity to nature dictated that the subject be painted standing against
a Highland setting which was minutely recorded by the artist
(Private collection)

PLATE 49
John Singer Sargent
Millicent, Duchess of
Sutherland, 1904
The Edwardian return
to Arcady in a last fling
of the Grand Manner
(Thyssen-Bornemisza
Foundation, Lugano)

PLATE 50
Philip Wilson Steer
Mrs. Violet M. Hammersley, 1907
Ruritania rather than Arcadia is evoked in this Edwardian essay after Boucher
(Art Gallery of New South Wales, Sydney)

Dogs

In no other country did dogs occupy quite such a status within the household, hence their uniquely dominant presence in portraiture

PLATE 51
Marcus Gheeraerts
Sir Henry Lee, 1590-1600
Verses commemorate how the sitter's life was saved by his dog, Bevis
(Ditchley Park)

Animals and Sport

If landscape is crucial to the reading of the British portrait, so are animals. Indeed Britain has always had a higher ratio of domesticated beasts per acre than anywhere else in western Europe except The Netherlands. And in no other country do animals figure so prominently in portraits of every kind. So important were they that eventually they gave rise to whole genres of painting:

PLATE 52
Nathaniel Bacon
Self-portrait, c.1625
The faithful dog as a recurring theme in the portrait
(Private collection)

PLATE 53
Attributed to Jonathan Richardson
Alexander Pope, c.1718
The poet with his dog, Bounce, with a collar inscribed
'A. POPE'
(Hagley Hall)

the hunting picture, and the dog, horse and cattle portrait. It is significant that although portraits of animals exist in abundance in Britain few exist of any domestic servants.

No animal is as important as the dog. A pet dog appears nestling at the feet of old Judge More in the famous family group by Holbein, and another minute creature is asleep on the train of Jane Seymour in the same artist's great dynastic wallpainting in the Privy Chamber of Whitehall Palace. Both are now only known through copies but these two creatures were heralds of the

PLATE 54
Hieronimo Custodis
Lady Elizabeth Brydges, 1589
The subject's pet terrier jumps up seemingly from nowhere
(Woburn Abbey)

PLATE 55
Peter Lely
Viscountess Weymouth,
c.1675
The Viscountess caresses
the toy spaniel on her lap
(Longleat House)

innumerable dogs which were to populate British portraiture during the succeeding centuries.

Amongst the earliest of domesticated animals, dogs were originally working animals, needed for the exercise of the chase which in itself was an upper class prerogative. Royalty, together with the aristocratic and gentry classes, revelled in their dogs. A proverb ran, 'he cannot be a gentleman who loveth not a dog'. It is easy to forget that the dogs we see in portraits are also portraits and indeed ones of creatures whose way of life and status often far exceeded that of the servants. Gentlemen's dogs were greyhounds, hounds and spaniels whose ownership was by law confined only to persons above a certain social level.

PLATE 56
Joseph Highmore
Unknown lady, 1738
Another fashionable pet
dog, the pug
(Sheffield City
Art Galleries)

They pertained above all to the hunt. Dogs were also admired for their virtuous qualities which made them within the animal kingdom closest to man. Sir Henry Lee's mastiff, Bevis, saved his life and Gheeraerts was called upon to commemorate both knight and dog accompanied by verses lauding his loyalty and devotion (Plate 51). Alexander Pope sat for the portrait attributed to Jonathan Richardson with one of his 'great faithful Danish dogs', all of which were called Bounce (Plate 53). Faithful hounds looking up to their masters were to be a recurring theme evoking the virtues of loyalty epitomised in the animal and the acreage of land needed for the exercise of the hunt and the shoot.

PLATE 57
Thomas Gainsborough
'The Morning Walk', 1785
The portrait records the late eighteenth century fashion for the Pomeranian
(National Gallery, London)

PLATE 58
Luke Fildes
Queen Alexandra, 1884
Recording again a mutation in fashion with the Queen's passion for Japanese chin
(National Portrait Gallery, London)

Pet dogs, which began to be kept by ladies of rank at the close of the middle ages, were also an indication of class. They did not work and were generally as small as possible and, of course, existed on a diet superior to that normal for the average cottager. We can see one of the earliest in the delightful terrier that jumps up the skirts of Lady Elizabeth Brydges in Custodis's portrait at Woburn (Plate 54). The lap dog that occurs most in portraits is the spaniel which appears as a prop in a long series of portraits in the post-restoration Lely-Kneller period (Plate 55). The other is the pug (Plate 56). Thereafter, as the fashion in breeds changed, they can be followed down to the present day in canvas after canvas. The late eighteenth century cult of the Pomeranian captured in Gainsborough's famous picture 'The Morning Walk' (Plate 57), remains as vividly in the mind as Lukes Fildes's record of Queen Alexandra with one of her beloved Japanese chin sprawled on her lap (Plate 58) or Michael Leonard's of the present Queen with a corgi.

Horse and Hounds

The hunt produced its own quite separate genre but also provided a motif for the portrait with its assertion of land possession

PLATE 59
Robert Peake the Elder
'Henry, Prince of Wales à la Chasse', 1604
The earliest portrait painting incorporating the motif of the hunt
(Royal Collection)

Cats until this century have never enjoyed the status of dogs and so make rare appearances in portraits. Birds, monkeys and other creatures appear but only exceptionally. The dog swept all before it except, of course, the horse. In both instances these creatures reflect a preoccupation which is English, for it was in this country that there first emerged in the seventeenth century a sensitivity to animals as part of God's creation and that they should not be tyrannised or caused to suffer. Ironically such sensitivity on the part of owners

PLATE 60
William Dobson
Endymion Porter, 1643
The sitter holds a gun while a page carries the dead game and the dog looks up at his
master
(Tate Gallery, London)

was extended precisely to those creatures which took part in the hunt. From
Robert Peake's group of 1604 of Henry, Prince of Wales *à la chasse* (Plate 59)
the hunt was to be a vehicle for portraiture, but above all from the early
eighteenth century onwards in the long series of sporting groups by John
Wootton, George Stubbs, James Ward and the succession of artists who

PLATE 61
Francis Hayman
George Rogers with his wife and sister, c.1750
The sitter waves his game at the spectator asserting not only his skill with a gun but
his landed status
(Yale Center for British Art: Paul Mellon Collection)

PLATE 62
Edwin Landseer
'Windsor Castle in Modern Times', 1840-45.
The infant Princess Royal inspects her father's game bag piled up on the carpet
(See also Colour Plate 8)
(Royal Collection)

recorded the hunt into the middle of the Victorian period until the subject
became the property of the camera. It was not a theme confined either to the
open air but could enter the drawing room in the form of the husband
returning from the chase bearing the spoils as, for instance, in Landseer's
'Windsor Castle in Modern Times' (Plate 62 and Colour Plate 8). As a theme
in British portraiture it was to have renewed vitality in this century in the work
of Sir Alfred Munnings, though by the time of his death in 1959 the movement
against the hunt was gaining wide public support.

Pride of Possession

Inevitably portraits incorp-
orate items inserted at the
behest of the sitter, in the
main country houses and
their interiors. The latter
can, however, often be
wholly imaginary

PLATE 63
Robert Peake the Elder
William Pope, 1st Earl of
Downe, c.1605
The sitter celebrates his
creation as Knight of the
Bath and stands with a
courtyard of his house
behind him
(Collection of Viscount
Cowdray)

PLATE 64
Daniel Mytens
Thomas, Earl of Arundel, c.1618
The portrait incorporates a view of the Earl's newly constructed gallery of classical sculpture in Arundel House, London
(National Portrait Gallery, London: on loan to Arundel Castle)

Pride of Possession

Pride of possession is not the strongest of iconographic themes in British portraiture. For all the explosion in building between 1580 and 1620 the idea of including the house in a portrait was rare and Robert Peake's portrait of William Pope is a unique Jacobean instance (Plate 63). A little later the 2nd Earl of Salisbury included Hatfield House in the landscape behind him in his portrait by George Geldorp dated 1626. By then the renaissance norms in placing the figure within its own artificial space was accepted, enabling such views to be included. Daniel Mytens's portraits of the Earl and Countess of Arundel painted eight years before include vistas of the Earl's sculpture and picture galleries (Plate 64). In both instances the views are inset into the background as attributes divorced physically from the sitter rather than providing an architectural framework which they inhabit.

The Arundel portraits are important reminders that interiors in British

PLATE 65
Attributed to Jonathan Richardson
Richard, 3rd Earl of Burlington, c.1717
To the right a view of 'The New Bagnio' built at Chiswick House
(National Portrait Gallery, London)

PLATE 66
Arthur Devis
Robert Gwillym of Atherton and his family, c.1745-46
The artist records the house, Atherton Hall, Lancashire, begun by the sitter's father-in-law and completed by his son-in-law
(Yale Center for British Art: Paul Mellon Collection)

portraits should rarely, if ever, be read literally. In seventeenth century portraits the likelihood of their reality is rare as they are so transparently composed of painter's props — the pillar, the curtain, the flight of steps. It is the conversation pieces of Georgian England which are the snare, for these rooms are in the main as artificial as their Stuart predecessors, constructions from pattern books into which would be inserted furniture and props at the dictates of the sitter. Thus Arthur Devis could set two families in two almost identical interiors with only sight variants. On the other hand he could, if a sitter provided him with the necessary material, paint a room that existed, as

PLATE 67
Arthur Devis
'Children in an Interior', c.1742-43
An instance of an entirely fictitious interior mocked up by the painter in his studio and
repeated by him with only slight variants for another family group. (See also Colour
Plate 6)
(Yale Center for British Art: Paul Mellon Collection)

in the case of Sir Roger Newdegate seated in his Gothick Library at Arbury.
Even in the case of the seemingly topographically exact interiors by Zoffany,
items within a room could be slightly changed or actually invented. This is not
true when applied to houses, even though a painter may be inserting a building
still in the process of erection.

THE BRITISH PORTRAIT

Even a rudimentary survey gives some strong feelings as to the peculiarity of British portraiture and through it the British as they wished to be seen. As pioneers of the democratic process and opponents of the absolutism which was the norm in the rest of Europe until 1789, the rights of the individual were more widely respected here at a much earlier date across a far wider section of society. The absence of revolution, which ensured the continuity of families, as well as the primogeniture system, which simultaneously guaranteed a mobility between classes, also focused attention on the individual and his abilities to rise or fall through his own efforts. The individual therefore, enjoyed a role for several centuries in these islands, a feature not seen elsewhere in Europe until the last century. Perhaps it is also significant that portraiture went into decline in the twentieth century with the rise of socialism which took responsibility away from the individual and invested it in the state. If that line of argument can be accepted it equally explains the revival of portrait painting in an era presided over by a government dedicated to drawing back the boundaries of the state and reinstating the individual.

In addition, as in the case of our landscape painting, British portraits seem inescapably an expression of our literature which also centres on a fascination for the foibles of human character from Chaucer's Prologue to *The Canterbury Tales* to the great novels of the nineteenth century by Dickens, Eliot, Thackeray and Trollope. That fascination for people exlains our tolerance of eccentrics as much it does our love of caricature. The British portrait should not only be read as a monument to past pride and prejudice but as evidence of a people who still believe in and celebrate the rights of the individual to be himself as sacrosanct.

ROY STRONG

PLATE 68
Paul Van Somer
James I, c.1620
94 x 54¾ins.
(239 x 139cm)
(Royal Collection: Holyrood House)

Chapter 1
Lely to Kneller
1650-1723

In the second half of the seventeenth century, the art and development of portraiture in this country was to be dominated by two men, neither of them English. Between them, the careers of the Dutchman Peter Lely and the German Godfrey Kneller almost span the period between the death of Van Dyck and the advent of Hogarth. Both dominated the artistic scene of their day and, commensurate with their positions, both ran large and highly efficient studios which spread their respective styles far beyond London. The mass of portraits thus linked to their names has subsequently done more harm than good to their reputations; but both Lely, in his unrivalled rendering of the languorous elegance of the Restoration court, and Kneller in his portrayals of the personalities of the Augustan age produced sound, and occasionally brilliant works. Both artists were, of course, foreigners, and their success was at the expense of their English contemporaries, but the establishment of their studio practices and the training it afforded native-born painters were to be among their most important legacies to the great age of English painting that lay ahead. It is equally significant, therefore, that it was also with Lely and Kneller that an era of foreign domination of painting came to an end.

There is no more dramatic moment in the history of the evolution of the English portrait in the later Stuart period than the arrival of Sir Anthony Van Dyck at the court of Charles I. The influence and impact of Van Dyck's work for Charles I is of central importance to an understanding of the development of the English portrait in the second half of the seventeenth century. From his youth in Antwerp Van Dyck had been known to the English court, and for a few weeks in the winter of 1620-21 he had been employed by James I. When he returned to London in the spring of 1632, he had been trained in the studio of Rubens and deeply influenced by the work of Titian, artists greatly admired by Charles I, and with his experiences with the aristocracy of Genoa and Flanders he rapidly produced images that epitomise the elegance and cultural sophistication of the Caroline court. By comparison with the static and linear images of the Tudor and Jacobean courts, Van Dyck's vision and delicate sense of colour, and above all his mastery of movement and baroque design on a grand scale, represented a new departure in English art. By contrast with

PLATE 69
Anthony Van Dyck
Charles I, 1636
97¾ x 60½ ins.
(248 x 154cm)
(Royal Collection:
Windsor Castle)

Paul Van Somer's static and sombre portrait of James I (Plate 68), painted around 1620, Van Dyck's portrait of Charles I of 1636 (Plate 69) presents a majestic and penetrating image painted with a supreme elegance of line and Venetian richness of texture that would profoundly affect the future development of the English state portrait. Indeed the impact of Van Dyck's stay in England was to be, in artistic terms, as revolutionary as the era of political upheaval which it preceded. Van Dyck's reputation was international, and after Charles I's execution in 1649 and the sale of his collection, dealers and collectors from all over Europe fought for his work. Among the purchasers was the young Peter Lely, and a quarter of a century later when Kneller came to England he was reported to have had 'a longing to see Sir Anthony Van Dyck's works, being most ambitious of imitating that great master'. The achievements of Van Dyck remained above all those which, for the rest of the century, painters would both strive to emulate and judge themselves against.

Van Dyck died in December 1641, at a time when the Civil War had led this country into one of the most troubled periods in its history, and when the marvellous cultural atmosphere engendered by the court of Charles I was in the process of disintegration. It was at this date, in either 1641 or 1643, that the young Peter Lely (1618-80) came over from his native Holland. The poet Abraham Cowley later wrote that 'a warlike, various, and a tragical age is best to write of, but worst to write in', and indeed it must have been a fearful time for any artist to attempt to work in London. Of other portrait painters working at this date, Cornelius Johnson, for example, had returned temporarily to Holland in October 1643, and William Dobson, the most gifted native-born painter, remained isolated and in increasing poverty at the wartime court at Oxford.

The son of an infantry captain in the garrison town of Soest in Westphalia, Lely had been apprenticed to the Haarlem painter Pieter Frans de Grebber for a period of roughly two years before coming to London. Vertue tells us that when Lely 'came first to England he wrought for Geldorp, who was then in great repute, & had been somewhat concern'd in keeping the King's pictures'. The influence of the painter George Geldorp remains uncertain, but some valuable connection must have been made for, by contrast with Dobson, Lely was fortunate in securing at this early stage the patronage of a group of rich noblemen of moderate political views, including the earls of Northumberland, Leicester and Salisbury, who had remained in London during the war. All had

PLATE 70
Peter Lely
Charles I with James, Duke of York, 1647
49¾ x 57¾ ins.
(126 x 147cm)
(Syon House, Middlesex)

been prominent at court and patrons of Van Dyck in pre-war days and their favour towards Lely and the opportunity it gave him to study the work of Van Dyck was to be of the utmost importance in his first decade in England.

The most important of these early patrons was to be Algernon Percy, 10th Earl of Northumberland. After the King's surrender at Oxford, the young Duke of York, together with the Princess Elizabeth and the Duke of Gloucesterth, had been placed in Northumberland's care, and in 1647 their guardian commissioned a series of their portraits from Lely. The best of these are the portraits of the King and James, Duke of York (Plate 70) and a group portrait of the three children now at Petworth. The dominant influence in the latter is, unsurprisingly, that of Van Dyck, in particular his own royal groups, although the rich tonality and strongly lit forms, and especially the emphasis on the landscape, owe more to Lely's Dutch background. The painting of Charles I and his son James marks one of the rare occasions when the captive King was allowed to see his children. Perhaps as a result of the occasion, the painting has a singular emotional intensity. Lely's friend the royalist poet Richard Lovelace referred to it in his *Lucasta* (1649) as that 'excellent picture' of 'a clouded Majesty...The amazed world', continued Lovelace, 'shall henceforth find None but my Lilly ever drew a Minde', but the degree of psychological interest he so admired remained a disappointingly isolated

PLATE 71
Peter Lely
Henry Sidney, Earl of Romney, 1650
65 x 49ins.
(165 x 124.5cm)
(Private collection of Viscount De L'Isle)

instance in Lely's work. Undoubtedly, however, the technical quality of these works was beyond anything any other painter working in London at this date could have offered. William Dobson, the only English artist capable of matching Lely's work had died the previous autumn and, after the years of Civil War and with the absence of any major figure to occupy the vacuum left behind by Van Dyck, Lely must have sensed that a great opportunity was there for the taking.

The most charming paintings of Lely's early years in England are to be found in a series of portraits of children in pastoral settings. The sitters are

PLATE 72
Peter Lely
'Sleeping Nymphs'
50½ x 56¾ins.
(128 x 144cm)
(Dulwich Picture
Gallery, London)

almost all drawn from the Percy or Sidney families and may well have sat just before 1650 at Penshurst, the seat of the 2nd Earl of Leicester. The best of these are the portrait of the young Henry Sidney as a shepherd (Plate 71) and the 'Little Girl in Green' now at Chatsworth. Both are painted in the arcadian vein that was prevalent in contemporary poetry and in this choice Lely must have been influenced by his friend Lovelace. The canvases do not possess Van Dyck's rich Venetian tones, but the colouring, with its green, greys and pinks, is more subtle than in the pictures painted for Northumberland. The rich pastoral landscape settings also provide a link with another aspect of Lely's career at this date. Lely's earliest biographer Richard Graham records that he initially 'pursu'd the natural bent of his genius in landscapes with small figures and Historical compositions: but finding the practice of Painting after the Life generally more encourag'd...he appli'd himself to portraits'. Though portrait painting was unquestionably the dominant genre in the seventeenth century, to the extent that Lovelace bewailed the predilection of this 'un-understanding land' for 'their own dull counterfeits', Lely did produce a fair number of subject pictures during his early years. The best of these are, perhaps, the 'Music Lesson' signed and dated 1654, and the 'Sleeping Nymphs' (Plate 72). The prototypes and influences are specifically Dutch: Metsu for the former and Poelenburgh for the latter, and such paintings seem to have found a market even during the puritanical years of the Commonwealth. They inspired no imitations but they play an important part in the development of Lely's mature

PLATE 73
Peter Lely
The Perryer Family, 1655
64½ x 89½ ins.
(164 x 227cm)
(Private collection)

style, for a good deal of their richly atmospheric landscapes and sensuality (so evident in the 'Sleeping Nymphs') is carried over into the images of the later Stuart court.

At the beginning of the 1650s Lely received £5 for a head and £10 for a half-length, and by 1654 he was regarded as 'the best artist in England'. His portraits of this date are still somewhat stiff and unconvincingly placed against their backgrounds (Colour Plate 9). A good if rather austere example of his style under the Commonwealth is the portrait group of the Perryer family, signed and dated 1655 (Plate 73). In this despondent group portrait (the earliest known of Lely's three-quarter-length family groups on the scale of life) we can perhaps gain a more accurate reflection of life in these difficult times. The unnecessarily crowded design and the awkwardness of the central figures are representative of Lely's difficulty in establishing a mature portrait style. The extraordinary life-size sculpture bust, which lends the picture a somewhat unreal air, is a common feature of Lely's portraits up to the Restoration, and sculptural props, in particular fountains, remain a constant feature of his designs. Although the Commonwealth could not have represented a propitious time for artistic patronage, Lely was again fortunate in his friends and patrons at this period. The most important of these were Elizabeth Murray, Countess

Elizabeth Murray
Countess of Dysart

of Dysart, and Arthur, Lord Capel (later Earl of Essex), and his young wife Lady Elizabeth Percy, daughter of Lely's early patron, the Duke of Northumberland. Though a friend of Cromwell, the remarkable Lady Dysart not only preserved her seat at Ham House, but also contrived to keep in touch with the exiled members of the royal court. Lely's work for her remains at Ham, and portraits of his patron (Plate 74), or Sir William Compton and the 1st Duke of Rothes are typical of this date. The Capels, and their royalist relations like the Dormers or Stanhopes, were equally important patrons during the interregnum. In portraits such as the Capel Sisters (Metropolitan Museum, New York) or of Lord and Lady Capel (Paul Mellon Collection), as well as those at Ham, the model is still Van Dyck, but we can see the smooth, even finish of the portraits of the earlier 1650s giving way to a more confident, open treatment in which richer impasto and stronger colour replace the more carefully layered tones of his earlier canvases. It was perhaps at this juncture, in portraits such as that of Lady Bellasys (Colour Plate 10) that Lely came closest to the elegance he admired in Van Dyck, and with this and the young 'Shepherd Boy' at Dulwich of c.1658-60, the last of his portraits in an arcadian vein, he produced the most romantic and accomplished of all his canvases on the eve of the Restoration.

PLATE 75
Peter Lely
Self-portrait, c.1660
42½ x 34½ ins.
(108 x 87.5cm)
(National Portrait
Gallery, London)

Lely's practice was not however coloured by political prejudice. He had
already painted his famous image of Oliver Cromwell — presumably soon
after the latter's installation as Lord Protector in 1653 — although he does not
seem to have enjoyed close links with Parliamentarian sitters, who preferred
the more wooden Van Dyckian derivations of the native Robert Walker. Lely
had also made an interesting attempt, together with Gerbier and Geldorp, to
persuade Parliament to commission a scheme to decorate Whitehall with
scenes commemorating its achievements. Though the undertaking was
unsuccessful it demonstrates an adaptability to the changing political climate
which no doubt stood Lely in good stead. More significant, perhaps, was his
friendship with the architect Hugh May, who shared his house in Covent
Garden and whom he accompanied on a trip to Holland in 1656. May's role

PLATE 76
Peter Lely
The Cotton Family, c.1660
62 x 88ins.
(157.5 x 223.5cm)
(Manchester City Art
Galleries)

as a royalist agent was no doubt of considerable significance to both men's careers after 1660. Lely certainly seems to have made a good deal of money during the Commonwealth, for he was prosperous enough to acquire works of art at the dispersal of the royal collections, and at this date he had certainly begun what was to become one of the finest private collections of his day. By the time of his death he owned no less than twenty-five Van Dycks, and his collection of paintings and Old Master drawings fetched over £8,400 during their sales between 1682 and 1694.

By 1660 Lely already had the largest practice of any painter 'in large' in the country. At the Restoration his position was made secure, and in October 1661, he received official recognition of his position as the best painter in London in the form of an annual pension from the Crown of £200 that had formerly been paid to Van Dyck. He was soon painting the chief personalities of the Restoration world, and his personality came to dominate the scene as completely as Van Dyck's had done in the 1630s. These events happily coincided with his complete maturity as a painter (Plate 75). His portrait of the Cotton family (Plate 76) is one of the best examples of his style at the time of the Restoration. Comparison with the Perryer family, painted only five years earlier, shows how quickly Lely had advanced in stylistic terms. His mature style clearly accorded perfectly with the tastes of his patrons, and Lely would use it with only minor variations for the rest of his career.

PLATE 77
Peter Lely
Barbara Villiers, Countess of Castlemaine and Duchess of Cleveland, c.1662-65
49 x 40ins. (124.5 x 101.5cm)
(Royal Collection: Hampton Court)

PLATE 78
Peter Lely
Frances Brooke, Lady Whitmore, c.1665
49 x 40ins. (124.5 x 101.5cm)
(Royal Collection: Hampton Court)

Despite Lely's new status, neither the King nor his consort seem to have been particularly attracted by his style and he was to find far more constant patrons in the Duke of York and his first Duchess, Anne Hyde. Two famous and accessible series of portraits painted for them can be used as examples of Lely's mature Restoration style — the Windsor Beauties at Hampton Court and the Flagmen at Greenwich. The former set, 'a gallery of the Fairest persons at Court', was painted for the Duchess between 1662 and 1665, and as de Grammont records 'in this commission he [Lely] expended all his art; and there is no doubt that he could scarcely have had more beautiful sitters'. The Windsor Beauties were hung in the White Room at Whitehall where they must have made a splendid impression. The sitters are portrayed in an unashamed celebration of beauty and sensuality which displays Lely's powers at their best (Plates 77 and 78). When Pepys saw the set he made his famous comment that they were 'Good, but not like'. But though the Beauties — like many of the fashionable female

PLATE 79 (left)
Peter Lely
Sir John Harman,
c.1666-67
48½ x 39½ins.
(123 x 100.5cm)
(National Maritime
Museum, Greenwich)

PLATE 80 (above)
Peter Lely
Sir Jeremiah Smith,
c.1666-67
50 x 40ins.
(127 x 101.5cm)
(National Maritime
Museum, Greenwich)

portrait types which emanated from them — are no doubt devoid of any psychological insight, they are highly distinguished in terms of both colour and technique. The figures have overcome the awkwardness of Lely's earlier designs and are placed more confidently in the canvas, the modelling is assured and the canvases worked throughout with a rich texture of paint fluently applied in clear and vibrant colours. Their real impact lies not in their likenesses but in the way they capture the atmosphere of a world so well expressed by Alexander Pope:

> In Days of Ease, when now the weary Sword
> Was sheath'd and *Luxury* with *Charles* restor'd,
> Lely on animated canvas stole
> The Sleepy Eye, that spoke the melting soul.
> No wonder then, when all was Love and Sport,
> The Willing Muses were debauch'd at Court.

In these portraits more than anywhere else, Lely provides an unrivalled evocation of the sensuous luxury that was fashionable at the new court of Charles II, and the Beauties, with their uniform languor, sleepy eyes and suggestive dishevelment are the fullest epitome of both this aspect of his work and the world to which it belonged.

The second series, the Flagmen, was commissioned by the Duke of York and represents the flag officers who served under him at the battle of Lowestoft in 1665. The portraits were painted between 1666 and 1667, and placed by the Duke in the Great Chamber of his hunting box at Culford. The nature of the

85

COLOUR PLATE 9
Peter Lely
Elizabeth Bindlosse, 1654
48 x 38¼ ins. (122 x 97cm)
A good example of Lely's three-quarter-length patterns
during the Protectorate. The sitter was the wife of
Francis Bindlosse of Brock Hall in Lancashire
(Private collection)

COLOUR PLATE 10
Peter Lely
Diana Rogers, Lady Bellasys, late 1650s
47½ x 38½ ins. (120.5 x 98cm)
The richly painted landscape, the strong colour and the
confident handling of the draperies make this an
outstanding example of Lely's style on the eve of the
Restoration
(Formerly Sir Francis Dashwood Bt., West Wycombe
Park)

commission in itself represents a fascinating contrast with the mood and types
represented by the Beauties. In spirit the portraits clearly reveal Lely's Dutch
background, and they are closely related in type to those portraits of the
Flagmen's opponents being painted at the same date in Holland by Maes or
Van der Helst. The heads of the Flagmen, which were seen by Pepys when he
visited Lely's studio in April 1666, such as those of Sir John Harman and Sir
Jeremiah Smith (Plates 79 and 80), show a penetration of character as good
as anywhere in Lely's work. The portrait of Smith, in particular, gives an
enduring impression of a dour wind-bitten personality motivated by a deeply
felt Protestant faith and, in terms of character, is perhaps unsurpassed in
Lely's *oeuvre*. It is no doubt a reflection of the increasing pressures of business

COLOUR PLATE 11
Peter Lely
Anne Hyde, Duchess of York, c.1660
71¾ x 56¾ins. (182 x 144cm)
Painted for the sitter's father, the 1st Earl of Clarendon soon after her marriage to the
Duke of York in 1660. Her father exclaimed 'that he had much rather his daughter
should be the Duke's whore than his wife'
(Scottish National Portrait Gallery, Edinburgh)

PLATE 81
Peter Lely
*Mary Bankes, Lady
Jenkinson, c.1660-65*
50 x 40ins. (127 x
101.5cm)
(National Trust:
Kingston Lacy)

that Lely was under by the later 1660s that the draperies and backgrounds of
the Flagmen — unlike those of the Beauties — are of uneven quality and must
have been painted with assistance from the studio.

Nevertheless, though the naval portraits must have represented an
interesting alternative from the demands of fashionable society portraiture, the
quality of the heads of the Flagmen was rarely to be matched again by Lely.
It was later remarked by a contemporary that he had a habit of making his
male sitters appear 'blacker, older and moroser in his draughts than they are'.
Horace Walpole remarked that Lely 'was in truth the ladies' painter', and
certainly his most successful designs from this period are those in which his
sitters were best suited to his rich and colourful style. The portraits of the
Duchess of York (Colour Plate 11); the delightfully erotic Diana, Countess of
Oxford (Paul Mellon Collection), or the portrait of Lady Jenkinson (Plate 81)

all provide good examples of his mature baroque style at its best. Many of the charms of Lely's female sitters were, of course, scarcely concealed in the fashionable attire of night-gowns and shifts, and though it was not quite true, as Marshall Smith claimed in 1692, that Lely 'brought up first the curious *Loose-Dressing* of *Pictures* which most of our Masters have since follow'd', many of his sitters, both male and female, chose to be depicted in less formal dress than that in which they would normally have been seen. Many of these gowns were then easily assimilated into the varieties of pseudo-antique dress (Plate 12) or mythological costume so fashionable in portraiture at this period.

By 1660 Lely's prices had risen to £15 for a head, £25 a half-length and by 1671 these had increased again to £20 and £30 respectively, with £60 being charged for a full-length. Lely's friends the Beales noted in their diary at this date that though Lely 'had raised his rates...he intended to finish every picture with his own hands'. Unfortunately, as has already been seen, even in a commission as important as the Flagmen, the pressures of business did not easily ally themselves with such intentions.

PLATE 82
Peter Lely
Unknown girl, late 1650s
11 x 6¾ins.
(28 x 17cm), black and
red chalk
(British Museum)

To cope with the vastly increased workload Lely required an extensive and highly organised studio organisation in order to produce the required number of portraits as efficiently as possible. When Pepys called with Peter Pett on 20 October 1662, Lely, thinking they had come to arrange a sitting, announced that he would not be at leisure for three weeks. Four years later, when Pepys called again in July 1666 with Sir William Penn, whose portrait was included among the Flagmen being painted for the Duke of York, Lely had to consult his 'table-book' and make an appointment six days later at seven in the morning. Once a sitting had been arranged, and a suitable pose chosen, the head would be painted by Lely from life. That of the Duke of York (Colour Plate 12) represents all that would probably have been done in the presence of the sitter. For important sitters Lely would take his easel to their residence, but the majority would have come to his studio in Covent Garden. Such an arrangement did not always please. When Lely refused to take his easel to the Guildhall to paint a requested series of Judges in 1671, the commission was given instead to John Michael Wright. According to one account given in 1673, at the initial stages Lely would also lightly chalk out the intended pose and lay in the colouring of the hands and garments. Enough drawings survive to indicate the part that they played in the development of a design. A few such drawings were also conceived as independent works, unrelated to a

COLOUR PLATE 12
Peter Lely
James II, when Duke of York, c.1665-66
20¼ x 17¾ins. (51.5 x 45cm)
A useful surviving example of Lely's technique. The canvas (now cut down) appears
as it would have done once sittings had been completed; thereafter the design would
have been completed in the studio. After the Restoration, this represents probably as
much as the pressures of work would normally have permitted Lely to paint himself
(National Portrait Gallery, London)

COLOUR PLATE 13
Willem Wissing
Elizabeth, Countess of Kildare
49½ x 39¾ ins. (125.5 x 101cm)
The sitter was the daughter of Lord Ranelagh and the wife of John, 18th Earl of
Kildare. An outstanding example of Wissing's independent style, perhaps painted on
the occasion of the sitter's marriage in 1684
(Yale Center for British Art: Paul Mellon Fund)

commissioned work on canvas, and that of the young girl in Plate 82 is without doubt one of the most beautiful of these to have survived.

Lely worked extremely hard but the demand for quantities of new portraits inevitably led to the need for assistants to execute the majority, if not the entirety, of a canvas. Demand, was, of course, greatest for portraits of the royal family and the more spectacular court beauties, together with entire sets for important patrons at home and abroad, for example those assembled by the Grand Duke of Tuscany or by Robert, 2nd Earl of Sunderland in the late 1660s and still at Althorp. Lely's ability to find new variations of pose for his sitters was remarkable, but by 1670 he had formalised these poses into a numbered series. His executors' accounts list a series of numbered postures

PLATE 83
Peter Lely
Louise de Keroualle, Duchess of Portsmouth, early 1670s
48 x 40ins. (122 x 101.6cm)
(J. Paul Getty Museum)

PLATE 84
Studio of Lely
Charles II
90 x 54ins. (228.5 x 137cm)
(Private collection)

92

such as '14 halfe lengths outlines' or 'Whole length postures nos. 8 and 1'. An idea of the volume of the output of the studio can be ascertained from the fact that at his death there remained well over one hundred original canvases and an enormous number of copies — of the King, for example, five full-lengths, nine half-lengths and three heads, and ten copies of the Duchess of York. Such a profoundly efficient studio organisation was not new, for Van Dyck had evolved similar methods to meet the demands of his own practice, but the degree of efficiency to which it was taken by Lely was one of his most important legacies to later generations of portrait painters in England.

It seems, however, that both Lely and his patrons were all too aware of the possible implications of such a practice. In December 1677, Lely had to write to the short-tempered baronet Sir Richard Newdegate that his half-lengths of Sir Richard and his wife had been 'from the Beginning to ye end drawne with my owne hands'. Such an attestation is remarkable even for an age which must have been accustomed to multiples as works of art. At a similar date a friend of Sir Thomas Isham warned him that 'I have know Sir Peter Lely change an originall for a coppy, especially to thos that don't understand pictors'. Even for those who did receive originals, it seems that some contemporaries were not too impressed by the artist's ability to catch a good likeness. Pepys, who saw the Duchess of York sitting to Lely in March 1666, doubted the resemblance, 'the lines not being in proportion to those of her face'. As early as 1653, Dorothy Osborne wrote of her own portrait that 'Mr. Lilly will have it that hee never took more pains', but 'that was it I thinke that spoiled it, he was condemned for making the first hee drew for mee a little worse than I, and in making this better hee has made it as unlike as tother'.

It is this charge of lack of character or obvious flattery which has formed the backbone of later criticism of Lely's work. His own industriousness and the licentious nature of much of his fashionable clientele did nothing to lessen this impression. There is little doubt that under the pressures of business his fashionable female portraits become increasingly devoid of character and stereotyped in form. Throughout, however, their colour and execution — particularly when by Lely himself — remain sound. It should perhaps be borne in mind that Lely was, especially with female sitters, as much concerned with the creation of an ideal or fashionable type as with truth to feature. Though it may seem to us a curious feature of women of fashion at this date to desire to be represented as much alike as possible, Lely himself would not have spoken of stereotypes as much as idealised beauties, though even he must have doubted the extent to which such a concept could be ceaselessly applied to courtesans.

Though pressure of work meant an increasingly diminished participation in the majority of his paintings, Lely never grew slack in his practice and constantly refined his technique throughout his career. From the later 1660s his paintwork becomes drier and thinner, and the brilliant colours of the Windsor Beauties fade to more sombre tones, at times almost monochromatic

COLOUR PLATE 14
Godfrey Kneller
Louise de Keroualle, Duchess of Portsmouth, 1684
94 x 58ins. (239 x 147.5cm)
The sitter was sent by Louis XIV to captivate Charles II and hold him to the French interest. By 1671 she had successfully become the King's mistress and was created Duchess of Portsmouth two years later. The King is said to have remarked of this portrait that ''twas the finest Painting of the finest woman in Christendom' (Goodwood House)

COLOUR PLATE 15
Godfrey Kneller
James II, 1684
92¾ x 56¾ins. (235.5 x 144cm)
James is shown as Lord High Admiral; the crown, orb
and sceptre are later additions, no doubt painted in after
his accession. Comparison with the elaborate confection
produced c.1672-73 by Gascars (Plate 90) reveals why
Kneller's simpler and more vigorous approach
succeeded so quickly
(National Portrait Gallery, London)

COLOUR PLATE 16
Godfrey Kneller
William III, c.1700
40 x 36ins. (101.5 x 91.5cm)
A sketch for the enormous canvas of 1701 painted for
the Presence Chamber at Hampton Court, and
considerably more energetic in handling. The picture is
a complex glorification of William III as warrior and
peacemaker after the Treaty of Ryswick in 1697
(Formerly Ray Livingston Murphy, New York)

PLATE 85 (above left)
Studio of Lely
Nell Gwynne, c.1675
49¼ x 39½ ins. (125 x 100.5cm)
(Sotheby's sale 13.7.88,29)

PLATE 86 (above)
John Greenhill
Mary Lyon, c.1674-5
41 x 29ins. (104 x 73.5cm)
(Sotheby's sale 19.2.69,40)

PLATE 87 (left)
Mary Beale
Malbon Corill, 1670s
29½ x 24ins. (75 x 61cm)
(Sotheby's sale 9.12.81,154)

(Plate 83). The Beales found this 'a more misterious scanty way of painting...far more open and free'. The full-lengths of the 6th Duke of Norfolk and his Duchess, painted in 1677 and now at Arundel, are excellent examples of his most formal portraits at this date, and indeed remained the standard pattern for elaborate fashionable portraiture until the end of the century. Even late in life, the confident draughtsmanship and modelling of his own work is distinguishable from that of the studio (Plates 84 and 85), whose work is generally betrayed by its duller tones and simpler drapery patterns, which are at times quite laboured as the pressure of business forced them to become increasingly formalised.

The names of some of Lely's many assistants are known, but few if any attained any independent distinction. After the Restoration perhaps his most valued assistant was John Baptist Gaspars (d.1692), a native of Antwerp who came to England in the 1640s and who painted postures for Lely for many years and later also worked for Riley and Kneller. The backgrounds, flowers and ornaments were often painted by Prosper Henry Lankrink (1628-92), the draperies by Thomas Hawker and Joseph Buckshorn and many others. Of his assistants the most promising native-born painter was certainly John Greenhill (c.1644-76). Greenhill may have enjoyed a few years in independent practice, and certainly included the 1st Earl of Shaftesbury among his patrons after 1673. His independent work remained heavily dependent upon Lely's patterns, and in some instances he used Lely's designs verbatim. His style, however, is generally softer and more rounded, and though it may lack Lely's richness of colour or texture, it is more than the equal of a purely studio piece (Plate 86). His portraits in coloured chalks are amongst the most appealing of their day. One of the very few native-born painters of this period to show real promise, his career was cut short by dissipation and he predeceased his master in 1676.

The most important of Lely's later pupils was Willem Wissing (1656-87), who came to London from Holland in 1676 and took over much of Lely's fashionable practice after his death in 1680. Wissing continued to enjoy patronage, particularly under James II, whose Queen and daughters he painted in an elaborate court style very close to Lely's. Like Greenhill, Wissing died young, in his thirties, having developed an interesting variation on Lely's later style, characterised by a brownish palette, rather frenchified accessories and a large (and much derided) use of exotic flora in his backgrounds (Colour Plate 13). His better works, such as the portraits of Mary II or the young sons of Lord Exeter at Burghley, reveal why he was one of the most patronised artists in his later years; but his death left the way open for Kneller's all too undisputed supremacy.

Lely's friendship with the artist Mary Beale (1633-99) was of considerable interest, for he lent her and her sons paintings from his studio and allowed her to study his technical methods. Beale repeatedly made use of Lely's patterns for her own work, and particularly affected the use of a framing cartouche of

COLOUR PLATE 17 (above left)
Godfrey Kneller
John Crewe, c.1705-10
49 x 38¾ins. (124.5 x 98.5cm)
A fully autograph example of a standard three-quarter-length pattern, which admirably illustrates the vigour of Kneller's brushwork at this, his best, period
(Sotheby's sale 16.11.83,44)

COLOUR PLATE 18 (above)
Godfrey Kneller
Jacob Tonson, 1711
36 x 28ins. (91.5 x 71cm)
Tonson was a successful publisher, and Secretary of the Kit Kat Club. The portrait admirably suggests the character of a man of whom it was said that 'he speaks his mind on all occasions, and will flatter nobody'
(National Portrait Gallery, London)

COLOUR PLATE 19 (left)
Michael Dahl
Self-portrait, 1691
49 x 39ins. (124.5 x 99cm)
Painted only two years after he settled in London, the quality explains why, within a decade, Dahl was the most patronised painter in the capital after Kneller
(National Portrait Gallery, London)

COLOUR PLATE 20
Jonathan Richardson
Edward Rolt and his sister Constantia, 1690s
66 x 48ins. (167.5 x 122cm)
One of the most refined and accomplished examples of Richardson's mature style
(Formerly with Colnaghi, London)

feigned fruit or stone for her half-length portraits (Plate 87). Between 1671 and 1681 her husband's diaries record about 150 portraits (including a number of copies after Lely) with a particular profusion of Anglican divines; the standard of those known varies but mostly offers little more than a close imitation of Lely's manner — deficient in colour and texture and at times indistinguishable from the output of the studio.

After the Restoration, the cosmopolitan nature of and Catholic influences at the court of Charles II and later his brother James II had succeeded in attracting a number of painters from both France and Italy as well as The Netherlands. It was from the ranks of these foreign painters, rather than from the older native painters such as John Hayls or Isaac Fuller, that Lely was to encounter the most rivalry. Very little is known of Hayls or Fuller although both were active over a long period. Pepys was painted by Hayls in 1666, and his diary provides a vivid account of the experience of sitting for a portrait at this time. Sittings began on 17 March 1666, and finished in May, when Pepys paid Hayls £14 for the picture and twenty-five shillings for the frame and pronounced himself 'very well satisfied'. The portrait (Plate 88) is rather coarse in execution, and Pepys was forced to admit that Hayls was much inferior to Lely. Fuller was primarily a decorative painter, but some of his portraits, for example the self-portrait of 1670 in the Bodleian or the portrait of the sculptor Edward Pierce (Plate 89) have a distinct character. Their execution, however, is disappointing, the flesh being very pallid and the draperies marked by an intemperate use of black.

Charles II's admiration for his cousin Louis XIV no doubt made him more sympathetic towards the French painters such as Philippe Vignon or Henri Gascars (Plate 90), but although they enjoyed considerable support at court, their style with its 'Embroidery, fine Cloaths, lac'd drapery, and a great Variety of Trumpery Ornaments' never seriously rivalled Lely and only briefly influenced him.

The most important painters to come to London from the Low Countries — apart from Wissing — were Jacob Huysmans (c.1633-96) and Gerard Soest (c.1600-81). Huysmans, a Catholic and an especial favourite of Queen Catherine of Braganza, arrived in London by 1662. He certainly seems to have considered himself as 'the Queen's painter', and his flamboyant portraits of her as St. Catherine and a shepherdess, both at Windsor, are the fullest epitome of his continental baroque style, employing a full range of flying putti, paschal lambs and quixotic weeds (Plate 91). For a while in the 1660s the Catholic clique surrounding the Queen sought to promote Huysman's virtues as exceeding Lely's, but his cold and liverish tones never managed to endow his sitters with the same fashionable sensuality as did Lely. Soest, who like Lely came from Westphalia to London in the 1640s, also enjoyed good patronage after the Restoration, though seemingly not in court circles. By 1667 he was charging £3 a head as opposed to Lely's £15. His style by this date had become fixed, and is easily recognised by its use of sweeping curves of metallic drapery

PLATE 88
John Hayls
Samuel Pepys, 1666
29¾ x 24¾ins. (75.5 x 63cm)
(National Portrait Gallery, London)

PLATE 89
Isaac Fuller
Edward Pierce, c.1670
49 x 40ins. (124.5 x 101.5cm)
(Yale Center for British Art: Paul
Mellon Fund)

PLATE 90
Henri Gascars
James II, c.1672-73
90 x 64ins.
(228.5 x 162.5cm)
(National Maritime
Museum, Greenwich)

and rather pneumatic hands. His colour, with its range of greys and silver, scarlet, orange and metallic blues, is also very personal. That Soest lacked Lely's brasher high-key style was no doubt to his disadvantage in terms of court patronage. Nevertheless, his best work is sensitive and distinguished and portraits, such as that of Mr. Tipping (Plate 92) or those painted for the 2nd Marquis of Tweedale, suggest that he was perhaps better able than Lely at

PLATE 91
Jacob Huysmans
Edward Henry Lee, later 1st Earl of Litchfield, and his wife Charlotte Fitzroy as children,
c. 1676-77
74¼ x 69½ ins. (188.5 x 176.5cm)
(Private collection)

PLATE 92
Gerard Soest
Mr. Tipping, c.1655
37 x 54ins. (94 x 137cm)
(Tate Gallery, London)

concentrating on the human rather than the social aspects of his sitters.

By far the most interesting of Lely's contemporaries was the London born painter John Michael Wright (1617-94). Alone of his generation, Wright enjoyed a lengthy stay in Rome in the 1640s, where he acquired considerable antiquarian knowledge and also became a Roman Catholic. He returned to London in 1656, and by 1659 was sufficiently successful to be called 'the famous painter' by Evelyn. His style has a rather pale silvery tone and, though his figures are often somewhat flat and lack Lely's solid modelling and sense of composition, Wright retains a greater sincerity in the interpretation of character than Lely achieved (Plate 93). His best works, such as the Colonel Russell of 1659 (Ham House), or the group of the young 4th Earl of Salisbury

PLATE 93
John Michael Wright
Augusta Coventry, 1670s
48½ x 38ins.
(123 x 97cm)
(Sotheby's New York
sale 4.6.87,129)

and his sister (Plate 33), have a frankness and delicacy of painted detail that makes them among the finest portraits of the period. It is doubtful, however, whether any of his contemporaries saw Wright as a serious rival to Lely. Pepys, when he visited his studio in 1662 after that of Lely could only remark, 'Lord! The Difference'. Though the only British painter 'in large' to enjoy royal patronage, Wright never seems to have adapted his style to the prevailing court taste and was consequently never firmly established in court circles. His one portrait of Charles II (Plate 94), however, presents the most remarkable image of the monarch of the whole Restoration period. This semi-hieratic image of the King, enthroned beneath a canopy and flanked by emblematic figures, remains the most unequivocal statement of the restored monarchy.

Wright returned to Rome between 1685 and 1687 when he acted as Steward to Lord Castlemain's vain embassy sent by James II to the Pope, but his absence lost him ground as a fashionable painter and after the expulsion of James II he ended his life in poverty.

When the Florentine Lorenzo Magalotti visited England in 1667-68, of the best artists in the country he mentioned only two, Lely and Samuel Cooper. Though this book is not concerned with the development of the English miniature, mention must be made of Cooper, in whose work we find the finest expression of the personalities of the Restoration world (Plate 95). Cooper was 'esteemed the best artist in Europe' and enjoyed a more international reputation than Lely. Through an early study of Van Dyck, and especially from his travels abroad in Venice and Italy, Cooper turned the miniature into an instrument of analysis of a subtlety and penetration unknown since Holbein and never since surpassed. Though an acute observer of fashion, Cooper was never subservient to its demands, and brings the same seriousness of purpose to his portrayal of sitters as different as the Duchess of Cleveland and Cromwell. He gives us, with a consistency unequalled by any other painter of his day and an honesty matched only by the written work of Pepys, a moving insight into the personalities of a troubled age.

Lely was knighted on 11 January 1680, but died suddenly in November of that same year. Over two decades of unremitting work he had maintained his supremacy over all nis rivals; none of his contemporaries were so consistently successful and his vogue was never seriously undermined. It was later remarked that 'he drew many graceful pictures, but few of them were like', and it has been a common perception of his work that he too readily allowed the consideration of a true likeness to take second place to flattery. But perhaps it was this very ability, so well adapted to the prosaic demands of fashionable portraiture, that ensured his success. His reputation has suffered because it has too often been made to rest on portraits in which he himself played little part, but in those portraits executed by his own hand there is no doubt that his colour and his technical gifts were beyond the reach of any other painter of his day. 'A mighty proud man he is, and full of state', wrote Pepys, but one suspects that Lely himself may have been aware of his limitations. When asked by a friend 'For God's sake Sir Peter, how come you have so great a reputation? You know that I know that you are no painter', his reply was simply, 'My Lord, I know I am not, but I am the best you have'.

When Lely died, no immediate appointment was made to the post of chief painter, and none of his surviving rivals like Huysmans, Wissing or Riley seemed likely to establish himself as the dominant artistic personality. Ironically it was Lely himself who had most clearly perceived who his successor was ultimately to be. Some four years previously the young Godfrey Kneller (1646-1723), newly arrived from Germany, had painted his first important patron, the Duke of Monmouth, and in 1679 he painted the King. Though Lely feigned indifference, the success of this confident young foreigner

PLATE 94
John Michael Wright
Charles II, c.1661
111 x 94¾ins. (282 x 240.5cm)
(Royal Collection: St. James's Palace)

troubled him greatly, to the extent that he reputedly relied upon the daily visits
of his physician to keep him informed of developments. In the event it was not
until five years after Lely's death that the post of chief painter was filled by the
Italian decorative painter Antonio Verrio, whose tenure lasted only until the
Revolution of 1688. By then Wissing and Greenhill had died, Wright had lost
ground by his absence in Rome, and so the office devolved on Riley and
Kneller together, who in December 1688 were jointly 'sworn and admitted
chief painter'.

For John Riley, the tenure of the post was to last only a few years before
his death in March 1691. Though a pupil of Soest, his style is more reminiscent
of Wissing or late Lely, and he employed the latter's posture painter, Gaspars,

in his studio. Before this date he had entered into partnership with John Baptist Closterman, with whom he shared expenses and profits of his full-lengths and half-lengths, for which he charged £40 and £20 respectively. He never painted the new monarchs and it is only with his less illustrious sitters — amongst whom he had a very considerable practice — that a more consistent style can be encountered. Although he could never match Lely's broader sense of design or his facility for handling paint, the showy or vulgar aspects of the latter's style have been drained from Riley's heads and replaced by a more sensitive, almost gentle, depiction of character. His portrait of Mary, wife of Sir Richard Spencer (Plate 96), though characteristically awkward in the placing of the figures, has an engaging modesty about it, and his portrait at Windsor Castle of the nonagenarian servant Bridget Holmes, which is invested with all the panoply of a grand society full-length, is one of the more remarkable portraits of this period. This sobriety of manner was not the least important aspect of his style passed on to his pupil Jonathan Richardson and from there its influence passed on well into the eighteenth century.

PLATE 95
Samuel Cooper
Unknown gentleman,
c.1660
3¼ ins.(8cm) high
(Formerly Holzscheiter collection)

For Kneller, who now assumed the whole office of chief painter, the death of Riley marked the threshold of a career that was to stamp him beyond question as the dominant artistic personality of his age. When he had arrived in England in 1676, Kneller was thirty years old and already experienced in his profession. His father had been an official to Queen Eleanor of Sweden and Chief Surveyor to the city of Lubeck, and this background of public service must have stood him in good stead in later years. He had originally studied under Ferdinand Bol in Amsterdam around 1666, and later travelled to Italy, where he had studied under Maratta in Rome and Bombelli in Venice. It is very significant that Kneller came to England at the invitation, not of a royal patron or member of the court circles, but of John Bankes, a merchant with connections in Hamburg, for it demonstrates that an appreciation of and, importantly, the power to buy works of art and support new painters was no longer the monopoly of the King and court.

Bankes's encouragement was to prove highly important. Kneller's portrait of him was seen and admired by Mr. Vernon, secretary to the Duke of Monmouth, who subsequently commissioned portraits of himself in 1677 (Plate 97) and his master in 1678 (Bowhill House). This initial contact with the court led to an introduction to the King who sat to Kneller for the first time the following year. These first portraits in England remain uncertain in design and unsurprisingly reflect a variety of influences; that of Bankes recalls the work of Bol, while the full-length of Charles II now at Windsor Castle owes everything to Van Dyck. Nonetheless they possess an unpretentious quality that must have been refreshing to his contemporaries after the mannerisms of

Lely and his rivals. Certainly Kneller's success seems to have been immediate. According to Vertue, after he had painted Charles II 'his reputation daily increased so that most Noblemen and Ladies would have their pictures done by him'. A more realistic indicator of this success was his removal to larger premises in Covent Garden in 1682 — thereby following in Lely's footsteps — and his becoming a nationalised Englishman the following year.

Reflecting this new found status, the 1680s mark the emergence of Kneller's mature style. The various and conflicting trends which resulted in his unsteady early work gives way to a new interpretation of the Van Dyck and Lely tradition, vigorous and elegant but also highly naturalistic, a style in which he continued to practise with only minor modification until the end of the century. Initially this style remained heavily influenced by Lely, many of whose poses and gestures he freely borrowed, but there is a readily discernible strength of character in these works that is alien to Lely's practice. His portrait of the Duchess of Portsmouth of 1684 (Colour Plate 14) for example, although it represents one of the most languorous personalities of the age, has a rigidity quite lacking in Lely's depictions of the same sitter (Plate 83). There is no shortage of works which display the range and power of his emerging maturity. The dashing full-length of James II when Lord High Admiral (Colour Plate 15), painted just before his accession, is an excellent example, confident in design and strongly executed throughout. A greater contrast with the foppish and theatrical image produced by Gascars (Plate 90) can hardly be imagined. His portrait of Philip, Earl of Leicester, painted in 1685 and now at Penshurst Place, equally shows the sensitive penetration of character found in Riley's best work. For the new King in 1687 he produced the masterly portrait of Michael Alphonsus Shen Fu-Tsung, the Chinese convert to Christianity, which he himself seems to have considered his masterpiece (Plate 98).

Kneller maintained his position at court after the Revolution of 1688, unlike many foreign and Roman Catholic artists who had flourished under Charles II

PLATE 97
Godfrey Kneller
James Vernon, 1677
29½ x 24½ ins. (75 x 62cm)
(National Portrait Gallery, London)

PLATE 98
Godfrey Kneller
Michael Alphonsus Shen Fu-Tsung, the 'Chinese Convert', 1687
83½ x 58ins. (212 x 147.5cm)
(Royal Collection: Kensington Palace)

110

PLATE 99 (left)
Godfrey Kneller
*Margaret Cecil, Countess of
Ranelagh, c.1690-91*
91½ x 56½ ins.
(232.5 x 143.5cm)
(Royal Collection:
Hampton Court)

PLATE 100 (above)
Godfrey Kneller
*Isabella Bennet, Duchess of
Grafton, 1690*
91¾ x 56½ ins.
(233 x 143.5cm)
(Royal Collection:
Hampton Court)

but had been forced to retire after the flight of James II. The fortuitous combination of Wright's absence in Rome, and the deaths of both Riley and Wissing gave him the undisputed inheritance of the position in society formerly occupied by Van Dyck and Lely. Indeed his relationship with the new King William and his Queen was in many ways to be the apogee of his career as a court painter. His first state portrait of William III, taken from sittings at Kensington in March in 1690, was to be very popular, and the large number of repetitions make it the most successful state portrait between Van Dyck's of Charles I and Ramsay's of George III. It may have been that the new sovereigns felt the need both to justify and emphasise their tenure of the throne, and certainly the 'official' likeness was distributed with methodical efficiency. This and the great equestrian portrait of the King at Hampton Court (Colour Plate 16) marks one of the highpoints of the most enduring reign ever enjoyed by a court painter in this country. Thereafter Kneller was entrusted with the official likenesses of Queen Anne, George I and George II as Prince of Wales, as well as many other minor royal personages. For almost forty years he had a virtual monopoly on official portraits of British sovereigns, and on his likeness would depend the presentation of the monarch to their subjects at home and to governments overseas. Already sent abroad by Charles II to paint Louis XIV in 1684, Kneller also painted visiting ambassadors and heads of state such as Peter the Great (1698) and the Archduke Charles (1703-4). He never shirked the task and his services did not go unrewarded: he was knighted by William III, made a Knight of the Holy Roman Empire and, in 1715, created a baronet. As Addison later wrote:

> Thy pencil has, by monarchs sought,
> From reign to reign in ermine wrought,
> And in their robes of state arrayed,
> The kings of half an age displayed.

By 1690 Kneller was firmly established as the most fashionable and successful painter of his day. There remain a large number of works painted before the turn of the century to confirm his reputation and Dryden's famous comment that 'Some other hand perhaps may reach a Face; But none like thee a finish'd figure place'. Like Lely, many of Kneller's best known works are to be found in certain series of portraits. Shortly after 1690, he painted for Queen Mary a series of full-lengths of her 'principal ladies' (Plates 99 and 100). These hang at Hampton Court and naturally provoke comparison with the Windsor Beauties painted by Lely for the Queen's mother. Kneller's Hampton Court Beauties, however, belong to a politer age. His portraits lack altogether the physical sexual appeal of his predecessor's, and they are noticeably more restrained both in temperament and palette. This has been partly accounted for by moral changes in English society in the 1690s, which included the foundation of societies for the reformation of manners, and certainly one feels that the averted glance of Lady Grafton belongs to a different world from the inviting sleepy-eyed gazes of Lely's courtesans. In terms of the full-length portrait, the Countess of Ranelagh (Plate 99) or the Duchess of Grafton (Plate 100) are among the most refined examples of their kind before the age of Ramsay and Reynolds. Not that Kneller was limited to portrayals of fashionable elegance. His portrait of the Duchess of Marlborough and Lady Fitzhardinge playing cards, painted in 1691 and now at Blenheim Palace, is an admirable study of two of the great ladies of this era. One of the last portraits at the turn of the century is that of the poet, diplomat and patron of the arts, Matthew Prior (Plate 101). The directness of the handling and the tension of the diagonals make this an outstanding piece of incisive portraiture and one of the masterpieces of the period. It would be hard indeed to find any period of comparable variety in Lely's career.

About the turn of the century, perhaps as a result of a renewed contact with the work of Rubens during a trip to Flanders in 1697, Kneller's style begins to change. His handling of paint becomes freer and acquires a new dash and vigour, and this new lightness of touch is coupled with a lighter tonality (Plate

PLATE 101 (left)
Godfrey Kneller
Matthew Prior, 1700
54¼ x 40¼ ins.
(138 x 102cm)
(Trinity College,
Cambridge)

PLATE 102 (above)
Godfrey Kneller
Mrs. Portman, 1715
48½ x 39½ ins.
(123 x 100.5cm)
(Collection of Philip
Mould, Esq.)

102 and Colour Plate 17). This may also have been a response to the more rococo styles of the Italian painters Giovanni Pellegrini and Marco Ricci, brought over from Venice to England after 1708 by the 4th Earl of Manchester. But though in some ways Kneller foreshadows the work of later painters like Vanderbank and Hogarth, he never became a true rococo painter; his style remains to the end tempered by the baroque classicism he had inherited from his travels in Italy. Again taking up a theme from Lely, a good index of his powers at this time is found in the series of naval portraits of Admirals now at Greenwich painted for Queen Anne's consort, Prince George of Denmark. Anne seems to have regarded Kneller with distinctly less enthusiasm than her predecessors, and the commission was not given entirely to Kneller. Perhaps the High Church Tory principles espoused by the new monarch were at odds with Kneller's basic Whig outlook, although political allegiance does not seem to have coloured his work to any great degree. The portraits are somewhat uneven in quality, but an underlying soundness of construction is always apparent. Some, most notably Sir Charles Wager (Plate 103) and Admiral Sir John Jennings, are of high quality, the former having something of the bluff directness found in Lely's portrait of Sir Jeremiah Smith (Plate 80).

The best of Kneller's work after 1700, however, is to be found without question in the Kit Kat series now in the National Portrait Gallery. These forty-two portraits, all but one 36 x 28 inches, were painted between 1702 and

PLATE 103
Godfrey Kneller
Sir Charles Wager, 1710
50 x 40ins.
(127 x 101.6cm)
(National Maritime
Museum, Greenwich)

1717. They represent members of the Kit Kat Club (named after the tavern keeper Christopher Cat) which has been described as 'the Whig party in its social aspect'. The set was presented by its members to the secretary Jacob Tonson in affectionate appreciation of what Vanbrugh afterwards described as 'a Club, and the best Club, that ever met' — and its members were certainly among the most prominent men of literature, politics and the arts of the day.

The size of these portraits was in itself something of a new departure in English portraiture, chosen perhaps for the advantage of showing both head and one hand while at the same time being able to keep the portrait on the scale of life. They are astonishingly simple portrayals. Most of the sitters wear plain perukes and are uniformly set against plain backgrounds, with only the

occasional attributes indicating special honours or concerns. The unpretentious 'gravitas' of Kneller's sitters corresponds closely with the gentlemanly ideals of Augustan society, very different from the quality of *toujours gai* which Addison found so derisive in contemporary French portraiture. Despite the handicap of the equalising frame of the periwig these heads are amongst the most incisive and brilliant Kneller ever painted, and the variety of pose and expression is remarkable (Plates 104 and 105 and Colour Plate 18). Kneller seems to have taken more than ordinary care with his Kit Kat sitters and, quite apart from his technical virtuosity with paint, he reveals a knowledge of the human mind too often dismissed in reckonings of his *oeuvre*. The ambitious and successful Vanbrugh (Plate 104), the elegant patrician Lord Somers, and the dissipated dramatist and essayist Sir Richard Steele (Plate 105), have their characters displayed for us with remarkable variety and liveliness of touch. Perhaps the finest of the group is that of the yeoman-like Tonson himself (Colour Plate 18), painted in 1717, which has an informality and directness that anticipates Hogarth.

The last date on any of the Kit Kat series is 1717, by which date a noticeable decline in quality had set in to much of Kneller's work. The handling of many commissions becomes summary and even perfunctory, and the features of many of his sitters increasingly schematised (Plate 106). It is this basic dichotomy in Kneller's work that prompted some of the more strident criticism from later writers, including Horace Walpole's famous comment that 'where

PLATE 106 (above)
Godfrey Kneller
Unknown lady, c.1708-10
30 x 25ins.
(76 x 63.5cm)
(Present whereabouts
unknown)

PLATE 107 (right)
Godfrey Kneller
Self-portrait, 1685
29¾ x 24¾ins.
(75.5 x 63cm)
(National Portrait
Gallery, London)

he offered one picture to fame he sacrificed twenty to lucre'. The late eighteenth century painter James Northcote added that 'the great mass of his works are such hasty slobbers that they are scarcely fit to be seen'. Kneller (Plate 107) certainly has to be considered one of the most prolific painters this country has ever produced, but the length of his career does not alone explain his enormous output; his extreme dexterity and speed and, of course, his efficient studio have also to be taken into account. There is no doubt that many of Kneller's finest works, particularly those painted at the end of his life, have tended to be swamped when viewed against the background of his vast studio output.

From 1706 until his death Kneller's prices rose to 20 guineas for a Kit Kat, 30 guineas a three-quarter-length and 60 guineas for a full-length. As the most successful painter of his day, Kneller, like Van Dyck and Lely before him, was compelled to pass an increasing proportion of his work to assistants in order to cope with the pressures of business. Having produced an approved likeness from life, Kneller could work up in his studio the complete portrait and, on the basis of the original, organise the repetition of innumerable copies; those of the royal portraits were, for example, charged at £50 a time. Alexander Pope, writing later to Lady Mary Wortley Montagu, gives us a glimpse of these methods, and shows how they had passed on into Kneller's wider practice. '[Kneller] thinks it absolutely necessary to draw the face first, which he says can never be set right on the figure if the Drapery and Posture be finished before. To give you as little trouble as possible, he proposes to draw your face with Crayons, & finish it up, at your own house in a morning; from

PLATE 108
Kneller and Studio
Anne Harrison, 1719
49¼ x 39¾ ins.
(125 x 101cm)
(Sotheby's sale
30.10.85,227)

whence he will transfer it to the Canvas, so that you need not go to his house. This I must observe is a manner in which they seldom draw any but Crown'd Heads'.

In this manner, while Kneller himself may have painted the face, the rest of a canvas as often as not was passed to a multitude of specialist assistants for completion. Plate 108 is an example of a commission typical of its date, where the head is autograph but the remainder probably the work of assistants in the studio. The execution of the draperies is noticeably more ponderous when compared to autograph work of a similar date (see Plate 102). Kneller carried the organisation of the studio to a pitch of efficiency hitherto unequalled. His factory for the production of portraits of William III alone must have been the

equal of Lely's, and the practice it maintained was still being used by Ramsay for George III and Lawrence for George IV. One has to bear in mind, of course, that the idea of studio repetitions (Plate 109) or the reuse of identical patterns for different sitters had already been practised by Van Dyck and Lely, and their impact was rather less alarming to an age accustomed to many such works being painted as conventional pieces of decoration or rhetoric. Unlike Lely, however, Kneller took considerable care over the reproduction of his portraits by the engraver. Though some fine mezzotints after Lely's royal portraits were produced by Abraham Blooteling, he never seems to have established a relationship similar to that of Kneller with John Smith, whose

PLATE 110
Godfrey Kneller
Alexander Pope, 1722
28 ¾ x 24ins. (73 x 61cm)
(Private collection)

popular mezzotints of every one of his royal portraits must have greatly enhanced Kneller's reputation and spread his designs to a far wider audience. Nonetheless, an idea of the output of the studio can be ascertained by the fact that Kneller gave instructions in his will that the unfinished works in his studio were to be completed by his assistant Edward Byng or sold at auction. Although three years elapsed between Kneller's death in 1723 and the sale of the studio, and assuming Byng had been able to finish a good many, there were still some 340 canvases sold in 1726.

An equally cogent reason for the dullness of many of Kneller's later works was probably the lack of stimulating or understanding patrons, and certainly with some sitters one can sense a deliberate slackness that is missing from Lely's work. The reigns of Anne and George I, though not entirely antipathetic towards the arts, no doubt also failed to provide any particularly strong focus or impetus of artistic patronage. But with stimulating patrons from literary and political circles, Kneller's powers showed no sign of waning even at the end of his long life. The portrait of Alexander Pope of 1722 (Plate 110) has a simplicity and sympathy of character that the average studio piece would hardly prepare us for. In contrast, Kneller's relations with his normal landed or aristocratic sitters were perhaps rather less stimulating.

Jonathan Richardson records an example of the apathy and ignorance which no doubt often explains Kneller's lesser efforts. 'Some company, coming to see their son's picture... stood staring about the room to look at it; and then asked

PLATE 111
Michael Dahl
Unknown lady, 1690s
49½ x 39ins.
(126 x 99cm)
(Present whereabouts unknown)

Sir Godfrey where it was, when it was all the while before them. This did not use to be the case with him; and accordingly he was provoked, yet kept his temper; but as soon as they were gone, he turned to Byng, who always attended him on these occasions. "My God, Byng, I did never paint a liker picture than that young lord; but, by God, man, I did put a little sense in his face, and now his friends do not know their fool again" '. Happily Kneller's outstanding works are sufficiently numerous to indicate his real capabilities. His full-lengths and equestrian portraits, for example, show a competence and variety unknown in England since the death of Van Dyck. Unlike Peter Lely, his work provides us with many valuable portraits which concentrate upon the likeness of a historical personality as opposed to their social aspect. 'In the

PLATE 112
Michael Dahl
Sir James Wishart,
engraved 1722
49 x 39 ½ ins.
(124.5 x 100.5cm)
(Private collection)

talent of an exact likeness', wrote Vertue, 'Sr. Godfrey Kneller has excelled most if not all that have gone before him in this art', and at their best his works display a vigour and sympathy for character that rank them amongst the best of the century.

Of his contemporaries Kneller's only serious rival for public patronage was the Swedish painter Michael Dahl (1659-1743). Dahl first came to London in the summer of 1682, but stayed only a couple of years before travelling abroad in France and Italy. He returned to London in March 1689 and decided to settle for good. He had already painted Queen Christina of Sweden while in Rome, and from the start, perhaps via Swedish diplomatic connections, was successful in securing healthy patronage. Vertue attributed this to his personality, describing him as 'a man of great modesty and few words', as compared to the 'Great business and High carriage of Kneller'. In the mid- to late 1690s Dahl worked for the Duke of Somerset, for whom he painted a set of Beauties now at Petworth House, perhaps in conscious rivalry to Kneller. Dahl's patterns are undoubtedly indebted to Kneller's, but his palette is lighter, dominated by a soft greyish tone, and his sitters have a more solid and static appearance (Plate 111). Such a formula was not without some distinction, and the Countess of Pembroke in this set remains a lovely exercise in a silvery-grey tonality.

The self-portrait of 1691 (Colour Plate 19) gives a better indication of Dahl's ability. The brushwork is different to Kneller's, applied in shorter and more careful strokes, with little of the latter's dash or bravura. The colours, maroon and purple-grey against a cool pale grey background, are also quite personal, and some of the passages of paint, for example around the bust to the right, are exceptional and almost anticipate the eighteenth century.

At much the same period Dahl enjoyed the favour of Princess Anne and Prince George of Denmark, and after the accession of the former in 1702, painted a number of royal presentation portraits. These included the large equestrian portrait of Prince George in 1704 at Kensington Palace, and part of the series of Admirals at Greenwich (already mentioned in connection with Kneller) between 1702 and 1708. The portrait of Prince George, painted for the Queen's Guard Chamber at Windsor Castle, is admirably painted but lacks the power of Kneller's William III at Hampton Court. Of the Admirals set, however, Sir Cloudesley Shovell and Sir George Rooke, for example, are amongst his finest works. There is a quieter but somehow more understanding approach to character, which relies upon its own integrity to make its impact and does not recognise the more self-important heroics so well engineered by Kneller. The portrait of Rooke is a lovely exercise in crimson and grey which is distinct from Kneller's richer colouring; indeed it is possible that Dahl's approach may have influenced Kneller in later years.

With Queen Anne's death in 1714, Dahl's period of favour at court seems to have ceased, but his practice amongst the gentry, law and church remained considerable. His later works, such as the Admiral Sir James Wishart, engraved by Faber in 1722 (Plate 112), show no diminution of his powers, and some of his larger groups, such as the Popham family, or the group of Evelyn, 1st Duke of Kingston and friends (Thoresby Castle) show a sound sense of design. Nevertheless his style does not seem to have developed any further, and by the time he retired from painting in 1740 it must have seemed very old- fashioned to the new classes of patron. His presentation remained formal and conventional, but within its limits Dahl was capable of work of real distinction.

An artist who might perhaps have troubled Kneller and Dahl seriously in terms of patronage but for his early death in 1711, was John Closterman (1660-1711). A native of Osnabruck, he studied under de Troy in Paris in 1679 before coming to London in the 1680s. As we have seen, he was employed in

PLATE 113
John Closterman
The children of John Taylor of Bifrons, c.1696
74½ x 107ins. (189 x 272cm)
(National Portrait Gallery, London)

partnership with John Riley painting draperies and accessories until the latter's death in 1691. In the 1690s he worked for a number of important patrons, including the dukes of Somerset and Marlborough, for whom he painted a large family group of 1696-97 at Blenheim Palace, very much influenced by Van Dyck's group of Lord Pembroke's family at Wilton House. To this period also belong two of his finest works, the portrait of Sir Christopher Wren belonging to the Royal Society, and the children of John Taylor of Bifrons of 1696 (Plate 113).

In 1698 Closterman travelled to Spain and Italy in the company of James, later 1st Earl Stanhope and Lord Ashley, later the 3rd Earl of Shaftesbury. The influence of Rome, and of antique sculptural forms in particular, coloured his work for Shaftesbury after his return to England in 1700. His double portrait of the Earl and his brother of 1701 (National Portrait Gallery) reflects the work of Carlo Maratta and displays a new muted colouring, which Vertue found 'intirely [sic] disagreeable' when compared to his previously 'strong lively manner'. Despite this, Closterman's work for Shaftesbury (Plate 13) which

PLATE 114
Jonathan Richardson
Sir Richard Steele, 1712
29½ in x 24½ ins. (75 x 62cm)
(National Portrait Gallery, London)

reflected closely the philosophical and neoplatonic ideas of his patron, was the
product of one of the most interesting episodes of patronage of this period. His
success as a society painter continued with the full-length of Queen Anne (now
lost) commissioned for the Guildhall in 1702 in the face of competition from
Kneller, Richardson and Lilley, and the hugely baroque equestrian portrait of
the 1st Duke of Marlborough of 1705 now in Chelsea Hospital. Many of
Closterman's ordinary portraits remain slightly perfunctory but his large-scale
figure groups are the finest examples of a genre much neglected since the death
of Van Dyck. At this stage Closterman must have represented a potentially
formidable rival to Kneller, but unaccountably after about 1704, he seems to
have largely given up painting for picture dealing.

Another of Kneller's important contemporaries was Jonathan Richardson
(1665-1745). Richardson was the ablest of the painters who came to
prominence in the last decade of Kneller's life and who flourished after his
death. As the teacher of Knapton and Hudson, who in turn was the first master
of Reynolds, his importance in the lineal descent of the strongest tradition in
English eighteenth century portraiture is always to be acknowledged. Himself
a pupil of Riley, he inherited the latter's quiet manner and sound penetration
of character (Colour Plate 20). There is a certain matter-of-factness about
Richardson's work, but Walpole's comment that 'he drew nothing well beyond
the head' is largely unjustified. Walpole was, however, rather nearer the mark

PLATE 115
Edward Byng
*The Hon. William and
Fulwar Craven, 1702-4*
50 x 39¾ ins.
(127 x 101cm)
(Phillip's sale
11.12.84,36)

when he concluded that 'the good sense of the nation is characterised in his portraits', for his best work has a refreshingly plain directness about it which one senses to be innately English. He was certainly at his best with his male sitters, for example the George Vertue of 1733 (National Portrait Gallery), Sir Hans Sloane of 1730 (Oxford University) or Sir Richard Steele of 1712. The handling of the paint in Richardson's portrait of Steele (Plate 114) is more solid and less vigorous than Kneller's (Plate 105), and their difference in outlook is aptly summed up by Steele himself, who had been painted by Kneller the previous year, and found where Kneller rendered him 'resolute', Richardson portrayed him as 'thoughtful'. We are on far less certain ground with Richardson's female portraits, and the few certain examples suggest a disappointing acquiescence with the prevailing Kneller tradition.

Nevertheless Richardson must have enjoyed an extensive practice, for in

PLATE 116 (above)
Thomas Murray
Sarah Ffarington
48½ x 40ins.
(123 x 101.6cm)
(Sotheby's sale
14.3.84,31)

PLATE 117 (right)
John Medina
*John, 8th Earl of Rothes,
late 1690s*
48½ x 37½ins.
(123 x 95cm)
(Formerly Earl of
Haddington,
Tyninghame)

1718-19 his prices were already 10 guineas a head and 20 guineas a half-length (double those of Dahl) and by 1730 these had doubled. More importantly he had an interesting leaning towards the theory of the arts. His position as critic was based, as was Lely's, not on a personal experience of Italy, but on a particularly impressive collection of drawings which he built up as a substitute. His published writings, in particular his *Theory of Painting* (1715) and *Essay on the Art of Criticism and the Science of a Connoisseur* (1719), probably had a far greater influence than any of his paintings, not least in the way they fired the imagination of the young Joshua Reynolds.

Of the many painters who are known to have assisted Kneller, such as John James Bakker, the elder Marcellus Laroon and Edward Byng (Plate 115), virtually none developed a sufficiently individual style to warrant mention, and only one is illustrated here. The volumes of drawings by Edward and Robert Byng in the British Museum are of interest, for they contain a large number of studies of portraits by Kneller, which no doubt served as a type of pattern book and provide a fascinating indication of the available repertory of designs used by his assistants. Only one of Kneller's pupils, Charles Jervas, later attained any independent distinction, but his career belongs to a later chapter.

Of other Kneller contemporaries, Sir John Medina, Thomas Murray and Thomas Hill produced work of greater merit. Murray was a pupil of Riley, whose style is reflected in his works before 1700, after which they tend to become weaker and rather softer variations of Kneller's manner (Plate 116). He seems to have had a considerable practice, but the fortune he had amassed at his death in 1734 came, according to Vertue, 'rather from usury or improvement of his money...than by the great imployments in painting'. Medina, the son of a Spanish officer who lived in Brussels, came to London in 1686, where he charged £8 for a half-length and £4 for a head. His importance lies more in his career in Scotland after 1688, where he was taken by his patron the 3rd Earl of Leven. His earlier work, such as the portrait of Lord Leven of 1691 (Scottish National Portrait Gallery) is closer to Riley, but once settled in Scotland he maintained an extensive and successful practice (he was knighted in 1706) in a style derived entirely from Kneller, though looser in execution and redder in tone (Plate 117). Frustratingly little is known about Thomas Hill, who worked in a style closer to Dahl, and whose few known works, such as the signed double portrait of the St. Clere children of 1699 at Belchamp Hall, possess a refined tone and considerable distinction.

Richardson was the eldest and most influential of the generation that succeeded Kneller, but many of the younger painters of this period learned their crafts in the Academy in Great Queen Street which Kneller and Richardson were instrumental in founding in 1711. This Academy is not the least remarkable and significant aspect of Kneller's legacy to the eighteenth century. Consisting of an informal gathering of some sixty members, each subscribing a guinea a head, it met to provide for and discuss the interests of professional (and some amateur) painters. As a body it was hitherto unique in this country, and certainly very different from the French Academy developed by Colbert and Le Brun for harnessing the best talents to the service of the crown and for propagating an 'official' theoretical line.

Kneller was unanimously elected as first Governor, and held the post until he was replaced by Thornhill in 1718. Thereafter the Academy lasted only a couple of years, but the idea would, of course, reach fruition in the age of Reynolds. In many respects, its very existence is one of the best indications of the way the artistic climate had changed from the court-orientated bias of the early Stuart period. Changes in taste were no longer principally dependent upon the taste of the court, and patronage was provided from a far wider cross-section of society. The impressive art collections of Lely and Richardson, and the theories of Richardson or Lord Shaftesbury are testament to the increasing movement of both ideas and works of art outside of the court. Foreign influence, particularly from the immigration of painters like Lely and Kneller, remained, of course, the keynote of the period, and a truly independent native spirit in painting had yet to emerge. The Academy would prove to be one of its sources. 'From this school', wrote George Vertue, who was one of the Academy's earliest members, 'many young genius [sic] have distinguished themselves & given great hopes of becoming Flourishing men in this kingdom'. Among these young men was William Hogarth.

RICHARD CHARLTON-JONES
Department of Old Master Paintings, Sotheby's

PLATE 118
John Vanderbank
*'John Dodd, M.P. of
Swallowfield, Berks.', 1739*
94 x 57¾ins.
(239 x 147cm)
(Private collection)

Chapter 2
The Age of Hogarth
1720-1760

One of the clearest indications of the rising status of the painter in early eighteenth century England is the description left to us by the great poet Alexander Pope of a visit paid to Sir Godfrey Kneller just days before his death in 1723: 'I think I never saw a scene of such vanity in my life', wrote Pope. 'He was lying in his bed and contemplating the plan he had made of his own monument...He said he would not like to be among the rascals at Westminster. A memorial there would be sufficient and [he] desired me to write an epitaph for it'.

Kneller's career, however, was hardly typical. When he died in 1723 the London art world was still in a relatively primitive state and there were few opportunities for a young artist to obtain a sound training. Kneller's own Academy, if that is not too grand a term to describe the life class which met at his Great Queen Street house from 1711, was never comparable to the type of organised art school that existed all over Europe. The opportunities to see great art were severely limited and there was nothing comparable in England to the paintings and sculpture accessible in churches and palaces on the Continent, while few collections of any note existed in London, or the country at large, since the disposal of Charles I's collection during the Commonwealth. The knowledge gained by all but a handful of artists who had travelled abroad was based on written description or prints and copies of works of art. In the years immediately before 1720, Jonathan Richardson's treatises were just beginning to be published and they were to have a profound effect both in helping to elevate the status of the artist as well as educating the aesthetic sensibilities of the gentleman.

At the time of Kneller's death, artists were still restricted by a hopelessly inadequate system of patronage that frequently left them dependent on the support of one or a small group of individuals who made the artist part of the household. But the days of the great cultural Maecenaes, like Lord Burlington or the Duke of Chandos, were already numbered by the 1720s and for the up-and-coming generation the challenge was to gain access to the new type of patron that emerged in significant numbers in the second quarter of the eighteenth century: the professional men — bankers, lawyers, physicians and clergymen in particular, whose occupations had flourished since the late seventeenth century and who entered the market for portraits with unrestrained enthusiasm! During the period under discussion in this chapter, the distinction between the aristocratic and middle classes had greatly lessened, both socially and culturally. Unlike on the Continent, the English aristocracy often entered and sprang from commercial and industrial life while the middle class could (and often did) rise socially by purchasing estates and acquiring titles and seats in the House of Commons.

Indeed, the increased frequency with which Parliament met after 1689 may well have had some bearing on the growing popularity of portrait painting. The solid patronage provided by over five hundred Members of Parliament and their wives and families undoubtedly boosted the income of the portrait painters of Kneller's generation as well as swelling the audience for theatre and fuelling the market for the new upper-class housing developments in the Piccadilly and St. James's area. Daniel Defoe tells us in the 1720s that the magnetic attraction of the stock market was also 'one of the principal causes of the prodigious conflux of the nobility and gentry from all parts of England to London, more than was ever known in former years'. The boom in portraiture is but one component of a wider economic upsurge.

Just prior to Kneller's death, and at the beginning of his notes on living British painters, George Vertue, that prolific chronicler of the London art world of the early and mid-eighteenth century, provides us with a list of those painters then in the public eye. Of the new names, the most significant to emerge were John Vanderbank (1694-1739) of whom Sir Thomas Prendergast could write in recommendation: 'I think there is no other in London who comes *so near* deserving the name of a painter' (Plate 118); Enoch Seeman (c.1694-1745), and the young Joseph Highmore (1692-1780). A year later Vertue noted the appearance of a young Scotsman John Smibert (1688-1751) who left for the New World in 1728. This new generation, in which we should also include Charles Jervas, evolved under the lengthy shadow of Kneller. John Bunce, however, thought at least one of this new generation a match for Kneller when he wrote in 1726:

> No more let Britain for her Kneller grieve;
> In Highmore see a rising Kneller live,
> Whose happy pencil claims as high a name
> If equal merit challenge equal fame.

Perhaps it is a sad indictment of British portrait painting in the 1720s that Kneller was seen by most as the exemplar, but his stylistic mannerisms had dominated portraiture for much of the previous half century. Kneller formulated, as David Piper so aptly put it, the Augustan face, 'a polite and urbane mask'; plump male features lurking beneath the ordered trusses of a wig, women's faces an unblemished oval perched on the sort of long necks so redolent of the idealised beauties of Italian renaissance mannerist painters like

PLATE 119
Jonathan Richardson
George Vertue, 1733
29½ x 24½ ins.
75 x 62cm)
(National Portrait
Gallery, London)

Parmigianino. It is an art devoid of even the slightest glimmer of humour.
Gentility must be enhanced and preserved at all times, stressing the somewhat
impersonal public role of the polite, well-bred gentleman. An observant
Frenchman, the Abbé le Blanc, who lived in London from about 1737 to about
1744, was particularly struck by this extraordinary standardisation in
portraiture:

> At present in London the portrait painters are more numerous and more
> unskilful than ever they were. Since Mr. Vanloo came hither, they strive
> in vain to run him down; for nobody is painted but by him. I have been
> to see the most noted of them; at some distance one might easily mistake
> a dozen of their portraits for twelve copies of the same original. Some
> have their heads turned to the left, others to the right; and this is the most
> sensible difference to be observed between them. Excepting the single

131

countenance or likeness they have all the same neck, the same arms, the same colouring, and the same attitude. In short these pretended portraits are as void of life and action as of design in the painter.

Perhaps the best way to attempt to understand early eighteenth century ideas about portraiture is to examine the writings of the portrait painter and art theorist Jonathan Richardson (c.1665-1745). This is not because Richardson's ideas are particularly original, they can be traced back directly through seventeenth century French sources to the sort of Italian renaissance theory which had conferred a graceful dignity on portraiture. Other theorists of Richardson's generation, like William Aglionby, shared Richardson's essentially moral approach to the genre, suggesting that the role of the portrait painter was to pass on to posterity the virtues of the great. 'A portrait-painter', wrote Richardson, 'must understand mankind, and enter into their characters, and express their minds as well as their faces; and as his business is chiefly with people of condition, he must think as a gentleman, and a man of sense, or it will be impossible to give such their true, and proper resemblances'. Within limits, an element of flattery was acceptable. 'The business of painting', he writes, 'is not only to represent nature, but to make the best choice of it: nay to raise, and improve it from what it was commonly, or even rarely seen, to what never was, or will be in fact, though we may easily conceive it to be. As in a good portrait, from whence we conceive a fitter opinion of the beauty, good sense, breeding, and other qualities of the person than from seeing themselves, and yet without being able to say in particular it is unlike: for nature must ever be in view'.

While Richardson does not go as far as to claim that portraiture is on a par with history painting, he infers that portraits by a great painter can approach the highest category reserved for the history painter. Richardson constantly stresses the role of the imagination over mere mechanical copying of nature. For him the great portrait painter's task was 'thus to raise the Character: To divest the unbred Person of his Rusticity, and give him something at least of a Gentleman. To make one of a moderate Share of good Sense appear to have a competency, a Wise man to be more Wise, and a brave Man to be more so...is absolutely necessary to a good Face-Painter...'

Richardson's own portraiture (Plate 119) can hardly be said to correspond to his theory since, in his smaller head and shoulders portraits in particular, there is, surprisingly, a remarkable, almost literal honesty which is at odds with his writing. Like his contemporary Sir James Thornhill, who occasionally painted portraits (Colour Plate 21), Richardson was good at catching a likeness in a solid, unpretentious way — a trait that seems to have led to greater success with male portraits.

The idea of 'politeness' in portrait painting could persist as long as the outward signs of gentility, dress and deportment, remained the paramount signal of social distinction although, as we shall see, by mid-century the conventions of representation suffered a sort of identity crisis when confronted by a class of person unused to sitting for a portrait. An art form previously reserved for commemorating the great increasingly became a vehicle for personal vanity.

In England the portrait painter had long been able to benefit from the apparent limitations of public taste. As late as 1755, William Hogarth's friend the Swiss miniaturist André Rouquet, albeit in a rather scathing manner, could summarise the position of the portrait painter thus:

> A portrait painter in England makes his fortune in a very extraordinary manner. As soon as he has attained a certain degree of reputation, he hires a house fit for a person of distinction; then he assumes an air of importance and superiority over the rest of his profession, depending less on his personal abilities to support this superiority, than on the credit of some powerful friend, or some women of quality, whose protection he has purchased, and which he sometimes courts not much to his honour. His aim then is not so much to paint well, as to paint a great deal; his design is to be in vogue, one of those exclusive vogues which for a while shall throw into his hands all the principal portraits that are to be drawn in England. If he obtains this vogue, to make a proper use of it, he is obliged to work extremely quick, consequently he draws a great deal worse, by having a great deal more business. Fashion, whose empire has long ago subverted that of reason, requires that he should paint every face in the island, as it were, against their will, and that he should be obliged to paint much worse than he would really chuse, even by those who employ him. He thinks of nothing but of monopolising the whole business, and imagines himself a very clever fellow in stupidly expressing an insolent compassion for some defect in politics or abilities, which he humbly pretends must be the cause of the bad success of his brethren; from whence he takes occasion carefully to publish that they are quite neglected, and affects in appearance to wish them a better fate. Thus I have seen it practised in late instances. And yet I do not pretend but that there are vogues in consequence of merit only, but these are very rare. A stock of assurance and affectation will enable a man to make the best of a small share of abilities, and even to supply their place where they happen to be wanting.
>
> We cannot say that the public are really the dupes of all the puerilities which we have been here exposing; no, they are only dupes to the fashion which they follow, even with reluctance: it is the fashion that carries them to a painter of whom they have no great opinion, to engage him out of vanity to draw their picture, which they have no occasion for, and which they will not like when finished. But the women especially must have their pictures exposed for some time in the house of that painter who is most in fashion...

Other commentators noted that portrait painters were frequently dependent for their success on the patronage of an important sitter who could instantly establish a reputation for the painter in society. Writing in the mid-1740s, Robert Campbell, author of *The London Tradesman,* a sort of guide book for parents thinking of apprenticing their offspring, hit out at this iniquity in a few paragraphs devoted to portrait painting:

> The good Face-Painter must have the Name of having travelled to *Rome;* and when he comes Home, he must be so happy as to please some great Personage, who is reputed a Connoisseur, or he remains in Continual Obscurity. If he should paint a Cobbler, with all the Beauties of Art, and the most glaring likeness, he must paint only Cobblers, and be satisfied with their Price; but if he draws a Duke, or some Dignified Person, though his features should prove so strong that the mere Signpost Dauber could not fail to hit the likeness, he becomes immediately famous and fixes what Price he pleases on his Work...

One of the few new men who had been to Rome, although the results are hardly apparent in his work, was Charles Jervas (c.1675-1739) who had not only studied under Kneller in the 1690s but was to succeed his former master as Principal Painter to the King in October 1723. Jervas's success seems to have been largely due to his friendship with the current shining lights of the literary world; Steele, Pope and Swift in particular had encouraged his modest talents. His portraits (Plate 120) are remarkably standardised and unimaginative and perhaps the most flattering remark a modern commentator on his work can offer is that his glossy drapery painting was of above average quality, the result of careful studying and copying of Van Dyck.

In October 1737 George Vertue wrote at length about the new informal mode of portraiture, in the form of the conversation piece as we now call it, which had begun to infiltrate English fashion in the later 1720s. The earliest usage of the term 'conversation piece', which derives from *conversazione* (informal group gatherings), can be found as early as 1706 when Bainbridge Buckeridge used the term to describe small-scale genre pictures by Marcellus Laroon, and Vertue's description of the genre still seems entirely appropriate today when he wrote of 'small figures from the life in the habits and dress of the Times. well disposed gracefull and naturall easy actions suteable to the characters of the persons and their portraitures'.

The conversation piece broke from the rigid formality of much early eighteenth century portraiture. The sitters are frequently shown with their family and friends and, in this sense, they are private rather than public images. In early eighteenth century England private life became increasingly focused on the 'natural' realm of the family and this may account for the increased naturalism in portrait painting, particularly in these intimate conversation pieces. The gentleman who sat for a traditional full-length portrait had hitherto been limited to a very small number of 'proper' postures which upheld the essential dignity befitting someone in public life. In effect,

PLATE 120
Charles Jervas
Portrait of a lady, possibly Elizabeth, Duchess of Bridgwater, c.1710
53 x 61¼ ins.
(134.5 x 156cm)
(Private collection)

this negated the necessity of treating the sitter's body with any degree of individuality. It is almost as if the face, or 'mask', did not need to correspond particularly closely to the reality of the bearer. But, for the private domain, an entirely new visual vocabulary began to emerge. This is illustrated primarily by the sitters' desire to be seen engaged in everyday activities with family and friends. This type of portrait becomes increasingly a means of focusing on the sitters' world because the figures in conversation pieces are reduced in scale — almost miniaturised — and are set back in the picture space by comparison to the traditional portrait. This inevitably results in the viewers' attention being shifted from the face to the immediate environment and possessions of the sitter.

It cannot be claimed that the genre was new in European art. Prototypes abound, even in England, from Holbein's 'Sir Thomas More and his Family' of 1529 to numerous seventeenth century Dutch examples by artists like Ter Borch and Metsu. In fact Vertue was well aware of this venerable tradition when he related the new fashion in the 1730s to 'conversations, done over a hundred years ago — by Teniers, Brower, Breugil, Watteau and some of the Flemish Masters of the Schoolars of Rubens, Vandyke, and indeed some painters lately here'.

It was via the small sporting pictures, with portraits of huntsmen scattered in the foreground, that a tradition of posing the figures in an active outdoor context gradually took root. The growth in informality was undoubtedly boosted by the gradual pervasiveness of the French rococo style. A taste for all

135

things French had reached epidemic proportions by 1738 when a correspondent of the *London Magazine* complained that 'the ridiculous imitation of the French is now become the epidemical distemper of this Kingdom'.

A decade earlier artists like Philip Mercier (?1689-1760), German born but of French Huguenot origin, had broken new ground in England with works like 'Viscount Tyrconnel with his Family in the Grounds of Belton House' of 1725-26 (Plate 121) in which the spectator enters the private world of a family at leisure. Although works like this inevitably invite comparison with the elegant *fête-galante* of the Frenchman Watteau and his followers (Plate 122), it is significant that the inhabitants of Mercier's pictures are real people with their property and not the hedonistic members of the most ethereal realm of the French rococo.

Few native painters gave themselves over more wholeheartedly to the French style than Hogarth's enigmatic contemporary Bartholomew Dandridge (1691-c.1755). Vertue made great play of Dandridge's ability 'to dispose the groopes & lights and shades to very great advantage' and this can be seen in the delightful Price Family portrait of about 1730 (Plate 123) which is painted with an assured, almost impressionist brushwork, every bit as free as Hogarth's liveliest touch and about as close to the transient effect of the school of Watteau as any English painter ever gets.

About this time William Hogarth (1697-1764) also launched his career as a painter of conversation pieces. By 1729 Vertue tells us of Hogarth's 'daily success' and 'great reputation in that way'. Much of Hogarth's success lay in his ability to create episodes that resembled scenes from plays or novels. To Hogarth the world was a stage — 'my Picture was my Stage and men and women my actors who were by Means of certain Actions and expressions to Exhibit a dumb show' he later wrote.

From Vertue's remarks we can also deduce why Hogarth was so successful. The portrait of the Wollaston Family of 1730 (Colour Plate 22) was described by Vertue as 'really a most excellent work containing the true likeness of the persons, shape aire & dress — well disposd. genteel, agreable — & freely painted & the composition great variety & Nature'. Hogarth clearly succeeded, where his contemporaries like Charles Philips (1708-47) and Gawen Hamilton (1697-1737) (Plate 124) failed, in his ability not only to catch 'the true likeness' but also in the skill of arranging a large and complex group so as to avoid the sense of a monotonous row of heads arranged along the same plane. In the Wollaston Family Hogarth places the two groups, one at a card table, the other at a tea table, and engages the viewers' attention at precisely the moment when Mr. Wollaston, apparently explaining the progress of the card game to the ladies to his left, invites a servant to bring another chair to the table in order that one of the standing gentlemen to his right might join in. These moments of action — the 'variety & Nature' of which Vertue writes — were Hogarth's speciality and mark him out from his more mundane contemporaries. Hogarth, as we shall later see, never aspired towards what he called 'the

PLATE 121
Philip Mercier
*'Viscount Tyrconnel with his
Family in the Grounds of Belton
House'*, 1725-26
25½ x 29¾ins. (65 x 75.5cm)
(National Trust: Belton House)

PLATE 122
Philip Mercier (after Watteau)
'The Lesson in Love', c.1722
18¼ x 23¾ins.
(46.5 x 60.5cm), etching.

137

PLATE 123
Bartholomew Dandridge
The Price Family, c.1730
40¼ x 62½ ins.
(102 x 159cm)
(Metropolitan Museum
of Art, New York)

common portrait' and the conversation piece undoubtedly gave him 'more scope for fancy' as he put it. In the hands of other less distinguished practitioners the conversation piece remained the liveliest alternative to the traditional portrait.

Hogarth's friend Francis Hayman (1708-76) was another artist particularly successful in anglicising the French *fête-galante,* modifying it to suit the English propensity for portraiture. The portrait of Samuel Richardson and his family (Plate 125) was painted by Hayman towards the end of 1740, that is to say soon after the publication of the author's phenomenally successful *Pamela, or Virtue Rewarded.* Although the poses here recall Van Dyck, the shimmering and highly individual virtuoso handling of the women's clothes is a good example of the skill of a painter who had no recourse to the specialist skills of the drapery painter. Hayman's compositional formula, which served him consistently for the next decade, consisted essentially of disposing the figures in the near foreground under the umbrella of a tree with an imaginary landscape backdrop. Figure groups, like the young girls in the left foreground of the Richardson family, are only a short remove from the indolent, languid figures of Watteau's or Lancret's pastorals, but distilled into an unmistakably English idiom through the influence of his friend Hubert-François Gravelot (1699-1773).

Gravelot was no portrait painter but his not inconsiderable influence was felt in London in the field of draughtsmanship where his energies as a teacher, both at his own school and at the St. Martin's Lane Academy, made a

PLATE 124
Gawen Hamilton
'The Brothers Clarke with
other Gentlemen taking
Wine', early 1730s
32½ x 45½ ins.
(82.5 x 115.5cm)
(Yale Center for British
Art: Paul Mellon
Collection)

considerable impact on the painfully inadequate native tradition of figure drawing. There is, however, one extraordinary conversation piece in which he had a hand and it must be one of the most hybrid works ever painted. The picture in question, now at Ickworth, is 'Augustus Hervey taking leave of his Family' (Plate 126).

Although begun in Paris in 1750 (Gravelot had recently returned to his native land from London) it was soon abandoned by him after he admitted having problems with it in a letter to Lady Hervey who appears on the extreme right with her son, Augustus. Not only did Gravelot employ an assistant for the architectural elements within the picture but he also persuaded the Swiss painter Jean-Etienne Liotard (1702-89), who came to England three years later, to work up the four figures on the left. In view of Lord Hervey's patronage of the marine painter Dominic Serres a few years later, it has been convincingly suggested that the ship in the background is his work. At Lady Hervey's request the picture was apparently sent to her in London unfinished early in 1751 and, perhaps on Gravelot's recommendation, Hayman was commissioned to complete the two figures on the right: Augustus Hervey, later 3rd Earl of Bristol, and the seated figure of his mother Lady Hervey, better known by her maiden name Molly Lepell. These two figures are markedly

PLATE 125
Francis Hayman
Samuel Richardson and his family, c.1740-41
30 x 40ins.
(76 x 101.5cm)
(Private collection)

PLATE 126 (below)
H.F. Gravelot,
J.E. Liotard, F.
Hayman and others
'Augustus Hervey taking leave of his Family',
c.1750-51
39 x 49ins.
(99 x 124.5cm)
(National Trust:
Ickworth)

different in handling from the group to the left and are characterised by Hayman's softer modelling which is quite unlike Liotard's metallic finish. The result, not surprisingly, is a most unsatisfactory composition. The group as a whole lacks the cohesion of a good conversation piece but, if nothing else, it confirms that some artists were prepared to work piecemeal when the necessity arose.

Collaboration of this kind was probably a great deal more common than we imagine and we shall explore the role of the drapery painter a little later. But if further evidence about collaboration is required then it is provided by a correspondent in a London newspaper in 1766 who provides some fascinating observations on this intriguing subject: 'It is customary to employ brother artists to finish particular parts of their performances. Mr. Lambert, for instance, never painted the figures in his own landscapes; Mr. Hayman's backgrounds have frequently been executed by a variety of hands'.

The young Thomas Gainsborough (1727-88) is one of those who occasionally painted backgrounds for Hayman in the mid-1740s although by the end of that decade he was making his own considerable contribution to the genre. Works like the Gravenor Family (Colour Plate 23) despite their indebtness to Gravelot, and particularly Hayman, show how swiftly the younger artist grasped the essential principles of this fashionable genre.

If any painter can be said to have made the conversation piece his own it is Arthur Devis (c.1711-87) whose paintings form one of the most extraordinary surviving repositories of eighteenth century manners. More than any of his contemporaries, Devis's compositions rely on a self-conscious display of polite postures. Although his contemporaries like Thomas Hudson and Joseph Highmore were, as we shall see, also acutely aware of behavioural mannerisms, no painter relied so consistently on mannered bodily attitudes as Devis. Many of Devis's awkwardnesses can only be explained by his over reliance on the use of small wooden dolls, or 'lay' figures as they were commonly known. These mannequins were a standard prop for many artists in the mid-eighteenth century, their prime purpose being a support for drapery. Vertue, for instance, tells us that in 1723 Dandridge had a number of these aids for composing his conversation pieces. Although Devis's doll does not survive, its size can be deduced as about thirty inches tall from a surviving set of clothes (Plate 127). The advantage of using these figures is that they relieved both artist and sitter from the tedium of numerous studio sittings, but they could never be, as they became with Devis, an adequate substitute for the study of the human anatomy from the life-class model.

Devis applied his postures to his sitters regardless of rank, and the moral benefits of decorum — the outward display of good breeding — is the essential ingredient in his success. The repertoire of genteel gestures employed by the 'polite' classes underwent little change throughout the first half of the eighteenth century and the task of instilling this discipline was the prime responsibility of the dancing master who treated his charges almost as if they

PLATE 127
Clothes for 'lay' figure belonging to Arthur Devis
(Harris Museum and Art Gallery, Preston)

were lay figures whose bodies could be distorted into any variety of attitudes, given sufficient practice. In *The Art of Dancing,* published in 1735 by Kellom Tomlinson, the author issues the following piece of advice: 'Let us imagine ourselves, as so many living Pictures drawn by the most excellent Masters, exquisitely designed to afford the utmost Pleasure to the Beholders: And, indeed, we ought to set our Bodies in such a Disposition, when we stand in Conversation, that, were our Actions & Postures delineated, they might bear the strictest Examination of the most critical judges'.

It is precisely this impersonal approach to the physiognomy of the human form which enabled so many painters to resort to both lay figures and drapery painters with impunity. The gentleman was, effectively, how he presented himself.

Another of these much-in-demand dancing masters, François Nivelon, published in 1737 a fascinating etiquette book, with engraved illustrations after designs by Dandridge, entitled *The Rudiments of Genteel Behaviour.* Its aim, as stated by the author, was to provide 'the Method of Attaining a Graceful Attitude, and Agreable Motion, an easy air and a genteel Behaviour' or to widen the chasm between the aspiring gentleman and the 'rude Rustick'. In Nivelon's book, and in others like it, can be found careful descriptions of precisely the genteel attitudes that appear in works by the fashionable portrait painters. For instance, William Orde presenting his step-mother with a pheasant in Devis's picture from the mid-1750s (Colour Plate 24) can be paralleled in the text and illustrations of Nivelon's book. Similarly, in the slightly earlier portrait of Mr. and Mrs. Hill (Plate 128), the standing figure of Mr. Hill is, as Ellen D'Oench has observed, borrowed directly from

Dandridge's illustration in Nivelon (Plate 129), wherein the gentleman is advised to take great care with his feet: 'The Feet are of great Importance to the Air, Grace, and Motion of the human Figure; if they are turn'd inwards, the Hipps will seem heavy and misplaced, but if turn'd outwards will appear firm, yet light and easy'.

Unlike the conversation pieces by Hogarth, the sitters in pictures by Devis do not appear to 'converse'; instead these staid, property-owning types present themselves and, just as important, their possessions, in real or, as is often the case, in imaginary domestic settings.

Devis, surprisingly, was still active in the 1760s when regular public exhibitions of works by living painters had begun, but his works must have looked increasingly anachronistic at a time when Reynolds and Gainsborough had long cast off the exaggerated mannerisms of fashionable posture which Reynolds dismissed in his third *Discourse* as 'practised to disguise nature, among our dancing masters, hair-dressers, and tailors'. One reviewer, signalling the change in taste, dismissed Devis's portrait of a gentleman exhibited at the Free Society in 1762 remarking 'Dog like a Pig. Leather-Breeches the principal object'. In the same year at the more distinguished rival exhibition of the Society of Artists, the German-born Johan Zoffany first exhibited his work in London in the form of a theatrical conversation piece of 'David Garrick in "The Farmer's Return"'. Zoffany, later Francis Wheatley, Henry Walton and a host of others were to keep the conversation piece an enduring fashion throughout the remaining years of the century.

While the conversation piece was no short-lived fashion the market was still dominated by the productions of more traditional portraitists like Thomas Hudson (1701-79), the son-in-law of Jonathan Richardson. From about 1740 to about 1760 Hudson was probably the most consistently successful portrait painter in England; the heir to the tradition of portrait painting established in England by Van Dyck and continued by Lely and Kneller.

Born in Devon, Hudson came to London in the 1720s to work with Richardson; by 1725 he had married his master's daughter and on his father-in-law's retirement seems to have inherited many clients. These early years of Hudson's career are not well documented although, significantly, in October 1740 the young fellow-Devonian Joshua Reynolds began his apprenticeship in Hudson's studio. Soon after, Reynolds could write to his father of Hudson's lack of fame.

Fashionable portraiture in London at that time seems to have been dominated by the Frenchman to whom the Abbé le Blanc has already drawn our attention, Jean-Baptiste Van Loo (1684-1745) who had previously worked in the south of France, Turin and Rome. Thanks to George Vertue, Van Loo's time in London is well-documented. He arrived in December 1737 on a purely speculative visit since, as Vertue says, he apparently had 'no importunate invitations from any Nobleman or grandee of Court'. Within a few months 'a most surprising number of the people of first Quality sat to him'. This is perhaps a source of bemusement to the modern viewer since Van Loo's work is not even typically French, devoid as it is of the characteristic facility and grace of the best French painting of the time as exemplified by Nattier, Perronneau or La Tour. Perhaps it is because so many subsequent artists, like Hudson, adopted Van Loo's smoother textures that we are inclined to see his style as not so radically different. Van Loo probably consciously anglicised his style into what the late Sir Ellis Waterhouse aptly described as Richardson 'seasoned with a little of the high French affectation'. Van Loo's ability to strike a more convincing likeness must also have been part of his appeal to the London audience. He is at his best in portraits like that of Horatio, Lord Walpole (Plate 130) which contrasts with his more formal portrait of the 1st Viscount Galway (Plate 131). Both have a more urbane air than either Richardson or Vanderbank were capable of producing. Van Loo returned to France in October 1742 because of ill-health but some indication of the esteem in which he was held in the highest quarters was, according to W.T. Whitley, evidenced by the Prime Minister, Sir Robert Walpole, telling Van Loo late in 1739 that he would have appointed him King's Painter in place of the recently deceased Charles Jervas had there not been an Act of Parliament prohibiting foreigners from government office. In the event William Kent, surprisingly, was given the job.

The competition from abroad faced by the new generation of native born painters like Hudson was not confined to a solitary Frenchman. A number of modestly distinguished Italians had begun to try their luck in England from the

PLATE 130
Jean-Baptiste Van Loo
Horatio, Lord Walpole, c.1740
50 x 40ins. (127 x 101.5cm)
(Wollaston Hall)

PLATE 131
Jean-Baptiste Van Loo
John Monckton, 1st Viscount Galway, c.1740
94 x 58ins. (239 x 147.5cm)
(Christie's sale 14.7.1989, 90)

1730s. As the market for large-scale decorative painting began to diminish, at least in part due to the ascendant Palladian style in architecture and interior decoration, the Venetian Giacomo Amigoni (c.1682-1752), for instance, who was in England between 1729 and 1739, increasingly took to portraiture as his compatriot Guiseppe Grisoni (1699-1769) had done before him. Amigoni was patronised by Queen Caroline and her son Frederick, Prince of Wales. The latter would have found Amigoni's high-key Venetian palette in keeping with his taste. Amigoni's spirited three-quarter-length of the prince in the Royal Collection demonstrates the way the artist introduced elements from decorative painting like the flying putti towards whom the Prince gestures. A more sober but equally impressive example of his talent is the portrait of the antiquary and amateur artist Sir Charles Frederick (Colour Plate 25). This sitter had a particular penchant for Italian portraitists and it was he who persuaded Andrea Casali (c.1700-84) to come to England. Casali had been a pupil of Trevisani in Rome before his arrival in London in 1741. Although better known as a history painter, he was capable of producing competent

PLATE 132 (above)
Andrea Casali
Portrait of a gentleman,
probably the husband of
Margaret, 3rd daughter of
William Sloper, c.1738
50 x 40ins.
(127 x 101.5cm)
(Robinson & Fisher sale
23.9.1937, 196)

PLATE 133 (above right)
Andrea Soldi
Sir Robert and Lady Louisa
Smyth with their son,
Hervey, c.1738-39
61¼ x 49½ins.
(155.5 x 125.5cm)
(Yale Center for British
Art: Paul Mellon
Collection)

portraits that appealed to the well-travelled English gentleman. He had painted some English travellers in Rome before his departure and surviving examples correspond well with Vertue's estimate of his portraits as 'thoroughly and strongly painted rather with Italian colouring or complexion than English' (Plate 132). Casali remained in England longer than most foreign painters, not returning to Rome until 1766.

Another distinguished Italian portraitist was the Florentine Andrea Soldi (c.1703-71) who had a flourishing business as a portrait painter in London for about a decade from 1735. Vertue considered his works 'equal to any others' and noted with surprise that between April and August of 1738 he had 'above thirty portraits large and small begun' and was giving Van Loo a run for his money. Soldi's vanity seems to have curtailed his activities since he ran into considerable debt in 1744: 'the singular affectation of thinking himself above the dignity of a painter' seems to have struck Vertue, used to the relatively low status of the portrait painter in mid-eighteenth century London, as his greatest weakness. However, his portraits are often powerful characterisations with strong colouring and firmness of modelling which must have marked him out as an attractive alternative to the more austere native productions. The group portrait of Sir Robert and Lady Louisa Smyth with their son Hervey, c.1738-39 (Plate 133) is an excellent example of Soldi at his fashionable best.

London seems to have exerted a powerful attraction to European portrait

PLATE 134
Barthélémy Du Pan
Frederick, Prince of Wales, c.1743
34 x 28½ ins. (86.5 x 72.5cm)
(Sotheby's sale 13.7.1966, 295)

PLATE 135
John Faber (after Hudson)
Joseph Van Aken, c.1745-49
12⅜ x 9¾ ins. (31.5 x 25cm), mezzotint engraving

painters in the years either side of 1740 and the London public had never been so spoiled for choice. In this context a few other names are worth mentioning briefly.

The Swiss Barthélémy Du Pan (1712-63) was in England by 1743 and is best known for the enormous royal conversation piece of the children of Frederick, Prince of Wales and Princess Augusta of 1746 which now hangs at Windsor Castle. Although Mercier had injected a note of informality into royal portraiture a decade earlier, no artist had ever attempted to do it on such a grand scale. A number of other smaller royal portraits by him survive (Plate 134).

Later in the century Switzerland was to provide several distinguished Royal Academicians: the painters Henry Fuseli and Angelica Kauffmann and the chaser George Michael Moser who became the Academy's first Keeper. It was almost certainly Moser who persuaded the German-born painter, architect and illustrator Carl Marcus Tuscher (1705-51) to come to London in 1741. Tuscher has emerged from obscurity with the identification of the only two highly idiosyncratic portrait groups known from his English period. The authorship of Burkat Shudi and his family of 1742, acquired by the National Portrait Gallery in 1985, had long puzzled art historians but it is certainly by the same hand as the small picture of Tuscher's friend George Michael Moser and his wife (Colour Plate 26) which was seen and admired by George Vertue in 1742. Tuscher's ability to strike 'a great likeness' (Vertue), his hard-edged realism and dynamic colouring, doubtless the product of his cosmopolitan training in Nuremburg, Rome and Florence, should have stood him in good stead had he decided to stay, but in 1743 he was lured to Copenhagen where he spent the remainder of his short career in the service of King Christian VI.

Within a year of Tuscher's departure Thomas Hudson had established himself as the leading portraitist in London with, as Vertue wrote 'the fullest or a great run — of employment'. Hudson's practice was undoubtedly boosted by the departure of Van Loo and the insolvency of Soldi and he was soon seen by Vertue as supplying 'the want of Sr. G. Kneller'. Under pressure of work Hudson, like Kneller, resorted to the extensive use of the drapery painter. In particular Hudson employed, first, Joseph Van Aken (1699-1749) and later his brother Alexander (1701-57) who had both come to England from Antwerp in the early 1720s (Plate 135). Joseph had first established his reputation painting fascinating genre pictures, but in the mid-1730s had begun to specialise in drapery painting. Vertue noticed his activities in 1737 and by 1739 he was working for a number of artists including the Lancashire portrait painter Hamlet Winstanley (1694-1756) who sent his unfinished canvases down to London for completion by Van Aken.

What little evidence we have about studio practice in the mid-eighteenth century suggests that the portrait painter sketched the attitude of the sitter on to the canvas in monochrome paint, completed the face and hands before passing it on, unfinished, to the drapery painter. To the eighteenth century patron the fact that most of Hudson's canvases were completed by Van Aken seems not to have been a cause for concern. If anything, Van Aken's skills as a painter of silks, satins, velvet and embroidery were seen to enhance the final product. As late as 1766 a correspondent in the press makes it clear that the drapery painter's role was an open secret: 'It is well known that Mr. Hudson, Mr. Cotes and several other painters of the first reputation seldom, if ever, finish an atom more than the face of their portraits, notwithstanding that the drapery of their pictures — which is generally the production of indigent excellence — acquired them such uncommon approbation from the public'.

In a letter to his friend William Jackson, Gainsborough even suggested that drapery painting was as lucrative as portrait painting: 'There is a branch of Painting next in profit to Portrait and quite in your power without any more drawing than I'll answer for your having, which is Drapery & Landskip backgrounds. Perhaps you don't know that whilst a Face painter is harassed to death the drapery painter sits and earns 5 or 6 hundered a year, and laughs all the while'.

Hudson's portrait of Grace Parsons, later Mrs. Lambard, signed and dated 1742 (Plate 136) demonstrates the finely tuned skills of the drapery painter at their slickest (Plate 137). A number of drawings by Van Aken survive which show the care he took in fitting the posture to the completed head. In some cases these drawings are preparatory, although the highly finished one

PLATE 136
Thomas Hudson
Grace Parsons, later Mrs. Lambard, 1742
50 x 40ins. (127 x 101.5cm)
(The Drapers' Company, London)

PLATE 137
Detail of Plate 136 showing drapery painting
probably by Van Aken

reproduced in Plate 138 seems to be a record of the composition that could be
used again for repetitions of the same pose. The dearth of drawings of this kind
by other artists is puzzling since the practice was presumably common.

Typical of Hudson's male portraiture in the 1740s is Walter Edwards
Freeman (Plate 139) whose pose is a more dynamic variation on the standard
hand-in-coat posture so often employed by him and used with such regularity
by Arthur Devis. This is the type of portrait which Horace Walpole tells us was
preferred by country gentlemen 'content with his [Hudson's] honest
similitudes, and with the fair tied wigs, blue velvet coats, and white satin
waistcoats, which he bestowed liberally on his customers'.

Hudson's faces are tediously consistent and the more subtle task of
penetrating character usually evades him. This may be partly laziness since he
was capable on occasions of more, as in the portrait of Charles Erskine, a
Scottish lawyer who was made a barrister at Lincoln's Inn (Plate 140). Painted
about 1747/48, this is an essay in the style of Rembrandt whom Hudson, like
many of his generation, admired and collected. It is possible here that Hudson
was responding to similar pictures done at this time by his former pupil
Reynolds (Plate 141).

Hudson was also a great admirer of Van Dyck. Some of his earliest and most
ambitious groups, like Walter Radcliffe and his family of 1741-42 (Colour
Plate 27), are directly indebted to Van Dyck, in this instance to the great

COLOUR PLATE 21
James Thornhill
Alice Selwin, c.1715-20
30 x 24½ ins. (76 x 62cm)
Although Sir James Thornhill only occasionally painted portraits, he presented his
sitters in a straightforward and sympathetic manner
(Private collection)

COLOUR PLATE 22
William Hogarth
The Wollaston Family, 1730
39 x 49ins. (99 x 124.5cm)
Vertue wrote of the painting: '... a most excellent work containing the true
likeness of the persons, shape aire & dress... & freely painted & the composition
great variety & Nature'
(Private collection: on loan to Leicester City Art Gallery)

Pembroke family group from the double cube room at Wilton House, which
Hudson almost certainly knew through the original or at least via Bernard
Baron's engraving.

Many of Hudson's portraits also conform to the fashion for 'Van Dyck'
dress worn at masquerade or fancy-dress parties. The Duchess of Ancaster of
1757 (Plate 142) wears the type of dress derived from the full-length portrait
by Rubens of his sister-in-law Susanna Fourment which was owned in the
1740s by Sir Robert Walpole. Since the portrait was thought to be by Van
Dyck the dress acquired its curious misnomer. This portrait also had a
remarkable influence on many of Hudson's contemporaries, from Vanderbank
to Ramsay, and we find an amusing contemporary reference as early as 1742

PLATE 138 (above)
Joseph Van Aken
*Costume sketch for a lady in
'Rubens Costume',
c. mid-1740s*
18¼ x 11⅞ ins.
(46.5 x 30.5cm), black
and white chalk
(National Gallery of
Scotland, Edinburgh)

PLATE 139 (right)
Thomas Hudson
*Walter Edwards Freeman,
1746*
49¼ x 39¼ ins.
(125 x 99.5cm)
(Sotheby's sale
23.11.1977, 16)

when Horace Walpole, in a letter to Sir Horace Mann, records seeing at the Duchess of Norfolk's masquerade 'quantities of pretty Vandykes, and all kinds of old pictures walked out of their frames'.

Despite visiting France and The Netherlands in 1748 and Italy in 1752, Hudson's style remained largely unchanged; although it might be said that 'Benn's Club of Aldermen' of 1751 — a group of London aldermen with Jacobite sympathies — is a development from the convivial, small-scale genre groups of Laroon or Hogarth, it clearly owes something to the life-size group portrait painted in seventeenth century Holland. An awareness of the French rococo style is confined, in Hudson's case, to the occasional introduction of some rustic elements and a lighter mood in some of his portraits of women and children (Plate 143), but this probably owes as to much to Mercier's 'fancy' subjects as more direct sources.

In 1751 when Vertue visited Hudson's studio he noted that he had more employment 'than any portrait painter in London' and he was to maintain his success throughout the early and middle years of the decade when he took on more pupils including the young Joseph Wright of Derby (1734-97) and John Hamilton Mortimer (1740-79).

Hudson's later years showed a marked decline in his practice, as Horace Walpole put it 'The better taste introduced by Sir Joshua Reynolds put an end to Hudson's reign'. Many of those families who had formerly employed

PLATE 140 (left)
Thomas Hudson
Charles Erskine, 1747/48
30 x 25ins. (76 x 63.5cm)
(Scottish National
Portrait Gallery,
Edinburgh)

PLATE 141 (above)
Joshua Reynolds
'Boy Reading', 1747
31 x 25ins.
(78.5 x 63.5cm)
(Private collection)

Hudson turned to Reynolds, often first sending their children to sit to the younger artist. The variety and sophistication of Reynolds's style from the later 1750s increasingly made Hudson's work look outdated, and he virtually retired in the early 1760s to his house at Twickenham to enjoy the fruits of three decades of successful hard work.

Apart from Hudson, one of the most distinguished painters of the reign of George II was Joseph Highmore (1692-1780). Highmore's career begins some time before Hudson made any impact and a number of modest portraits by him from the 1720s in the Kneller mould survive (Plate 144). By the 1730s he was working in a variety of different manners but works like Mrs. Sharpe and her child of 1731 (Plate 145) seem to justify Vertue's remark that Highmore's portraits were characterised by 'extream likeness'. Perhaps the summit of Highmore's ambitions in the 1730s is the enormous group portrait of the Family of Lancelot Lee of 1736 (Colour Plate 28). Whilst the compositional formula still echoes Dandridge, the delicate pastel colouring and the languid poses owe much to what Highmore saw during a visit to Paris in 1734.

Highmore's posthumous reputation probably owes more to the set of twelve painted illustrations to Richardson's novel *Pamela* which he executed in the mid-1740s than to his distinction as a portraitist, but we should not underestimate the extent to which he helped to challenge Augustan formality in genial portraits like that of the Misses Kenrick (Plate 146). Perhaps Highmore's most extraordinary portrait is 'Mr. Oldham and his Friends' (Plate 147), probably painted sometime before 1740. There is an almost rude

COLOUR PLATE 23
Thomas Gainsborough
The Gravenor Family, c.1747
35½ x 35½ ins. (90 x 90cm)
The young Gainsborough occasionally
painted backgrounds for Francis
Hayman in the mid-1740s, and this
group portrait shows how quickly he
grasped the principles of group
portraiture from the older artist
(Yale Center for British Art: Paul
Mellon Collection)

COLOUR PLATE 24
Arthur Devis
'William Orde's Return from the Shoot',
c.1754
37 x 37⅜ ins. (94 x 95cm)
A group portrait illustrating the
'Graceful Attitude, and Agreable
Motion' which were so characteristic
of Devis's conversation pieces
(Mr. and Mrs. Paul Mellon,
Upperville, Virginia)

COLOUR PLATE 25
Giacomo Amigoni
Sir Charles Frederick, mid- to late 1730s
41½ x 42¾ins. (105.5 x 108.5cm)
An impressive example of the work
of this Venetian painter who
worked in England in the 1730s
and was patronised by royalty
(Leger Galleries, London)

COLOUR PLATE 26
Carl Marcus Tuscher
*George Michael Moser and his wife,
1742*
29 x 29ins. (73.5 x 73.5cm)
The portrait was seen and admired
by Vertue who commented on
Tuscher's ability to strike 'a great
likeness'
(Geffrye Museum, London)

PLATE 142
Thomas Hudson
Mary Panton, Duchess of
Ancaster, c.1757
94 x 54ins. (239 x 137cm)
(Private collection)

PLATE 143
Thomas Hudson
*Lady Essex and Lady Mary
Kerr, daughters of the 2nd
Duke of Roxburghe, early
1750s*
54½ x 66½ ins.
(138.5 x 169cm)
(Private collection)

directness about this portrait that reminds us that Highmore had also travelled in the Low Countries in 1732 where he would have seen seventeenth century Dutch works of this kind.

One branch of portrait painting that had become popular by the 1740s was crayon or pastel painting. As Vertue noted in 1742: 'Crayon painting has met with such encouragement of late years that several Painters those that had been to Italy to Study as Knapton Pond Hoard &c. for the practice of painting in Oyl found at their return that they could not make any extraordinary matter of it, turnd to painting in Crayons and several made great advantages of it...the painters finding it much easier in the execution than Oil colours'.

The fashion may owe something to the popularity of the Grand Tour since so many travellers had sat in Venice to Rosalba Carriera, the best known European practitioner of the genre.

Pastels were cheap and quick to produce and reasonably priced so that they were well within the means of the increasingly affluent middle class. As a rule, only two or three sittings were required and the usual price was 5 guineas unglazed or 8 guineas glazed, a clear indication of the high cost of plate glass. From the artists' point of view the speed of execution allowed for a quick financial return and for the patron the sparkling fresh colour set within a splendid gilded frame created a highly decorative item for the more modest interior.

George Knapton (1698-1778) was one of the first fashionable practitioners in crayon. Something of the crayon technique seems to have permeated his

COLOUR PLATE 27
Thomas Hudson
Walter Radcliffe and his family, c.1741-42
126 x 174ins. (320 x 442cm)
Hudson was a great admirer of Van Dyck, and some of his earliest and most
ambitious groups, like this one, are directly indebted to the Flemish artist
(Private collection)

COLOUR PLATE 28
Joseph Highmore
The Family of Lancelot Lee, 1736
93½ x 114ins. (237.5 x 289.5cm)
The delicate pastel colouring and the languid poses of this enormous group
portrait owe much to what Highmore saw during a visit to Paris in 1734
(Wolverhampton Art Gallery and Museum)

PLATE 144
Joseph Highmore
Sir Thomas Heath, 1728
66 x 42ins. (167.5 x 106.5cm)
(Sotheby's sale 11.7.1984, 204)

Mˢ Sharpe and child
postea Mˢ Douglas
Highmore. 1731.

PLATE 145
Joseph Highmore
Mrs. Sharpe and her child,
1731
50 x 40ins.
(127 x 101.5cm)
(Yale Center for British
Art: Paul Mellon
Collection)

works in oil which often have the softer sfumato effects of crayon. Among his
most interesting works are the twenty-three portraits of the convivial members
of the Dilettanti Society to which he was the official painter (Plate 148).

The most talented of the pastellists of this generation was William Hoare
(c.1707-92) who settled in fashionable Bath by 1739. Hoare by no means
confined his output to pastels and he painted in oils some of the leading West
Country families, like his namesakes the Hoares of Stourhead as well as
statesmen like Chesterfield, Pitt and Newcastle which compare well with works
by Hudson. In many cases Hoare took a head and shoulders in pastel which
served as a *modello* for the more formal oil (Plate 149).

In England, however, pastels never achieved the huge success they had in

COLOUR PLATE 29
Allan Ramsay
Margaret Lindsay, the painter's second wife, c.1759-60
30 x 25ins.
(76 x 63.5cm)
Often acknowledged to be Ramsay's greatest work. In his female portraits in the 1750s he achieved an intimacy and delicacy characteristic of work by his contemporaries in France
(National Gallery of Scotland, Edinburgh)

COLOUR PLATE 30 (opposite above left)
William Hogarth
George Arnold, c.1740
35⅝ x 27⅞ ins. (90.5 x 53cm)
Portraits like this, with its bluff, uncompromising directness, explain why so few aristocratic sitters were brave enough to sit to Hogarth
(Fitzwilliam Museum, Cambridge)

COLOUR PLATE 31 (opposite above right)
William Hogarth
William Cavendish, 4th Duke of Devonshire, 1741
29⅞ x 25ins. (76 x 63.5cm)
One of the few 'aristocratic' portraits by Hogarth
(Yale Center for British Art: Paul Mellon Collection)

COLOUR PLATE 32
William Hogarth
*'Captain Lord George
Graham in his Cabin',
c.1745*
28 x 35ins. (71 x 89cm)
Hogarth has here
reverted to the comic
narrative of his small-
scale group portraits
painted over a decade
earlier
(National Maritime
Museum, Greenwich)

PLATE 146
Joseph Highmore
*Martha, Elizabeth and
Mary Kenrick, daughters of
Dr. Kenrick, Vicar of
Hambledon, c.1740*
58 x 94¼ins.
(147.5 x 240cm)
(Sotheby's sale
11.7.1990, 29)

PLATE 147
Joseph Highmore
*'Mr. Oldham and his
Friends', c.1740*
41½ x 51ins.
(105.4 x 129.5cm)
(Tate Gallery, London)

164

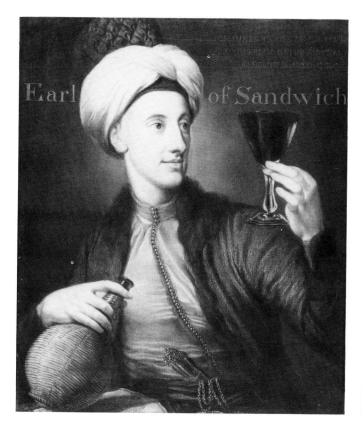

PLATE 148 (left)
George Knapton
*John Montague, 4th Earl of
Sandwich, 1745*
30 x 25ins. (76 x 63.5cm)
(Society of Dilettanti,
London)

PLATE 149 (above)
William Hoare
*Richard, 6th Viscount
Fitzwilliam, c.1744*
23½ x 17½ins.
(59.5 x 44.5cm), pastel
(Fitzwilliam Museum,
Cambridge)

France, where works by Perronneau and La Tour could rival oils in both size and number at the biennial exhibitions of the Paris Salon, though in the hands of distinguished practitioners like Knapton's pupil Francis Cotes (1726-70) the results could be extremely pleasing (Plate 150).

Early in his career Allan Ramsay (1713-84) occasionally produced pastel portraits although it is not a medium we usually associate with him. Ramsay's early training had been in his native Edinburgh but he studied in London in the early 1730s under Hans Hysing (1678-1753). It is unlikely that Ramsay learnt anything of significance from Hysing and his real training took place in Italy, where he spent two years between 1736 and 1738 studying first in Rome under Francesco Fernandi, called Imperiali, whose style was derived from Carlo Maratta. Ramsay's fellow pupil at this time was the young Pompeo Batoni who, despite never visiting England, later specialised in portraying the suave young British traveller in Rome, and Batoni's style certainly influenced Ramsay's youthful efforts. In Rome Ramsay also attended the French Academy in the Palazzo Mancini in the Corso and in a letter to Mariette, the great collector and connoisseur in Paris, he declared in November 1736 that 'it is at the French Academy alone that Youth can profit in the study of the fine arts'. Moving on to Naples, Ramsay also benefited from a short period in the studio of the ageing history painter Francesco Solimena (1657-1747), now virtually forgotten by all but scholars of Neapolitan baroque painting, but in the 1730s still one of the most famous artists in Europe.

PLATE 150
Francis Cotes
Elizabeth Gunning, later Duchess of Hamilton and Argyll, 1751
29½ x 23ins.
(75 x 58.5cm), pastel
(Christie's sale 6.6.1972, 104)

Perhaps surprisingly, in view of his gravitation towards Imperiali and Solimena, Ramsay never seems to have been interested in pursuing a career as a history painter. His exceptional skills as a draughtsman (Plate 151) might have equipped him well for the challenge but he would have needed no reminding that the history painter in Britain in the 1730s was virtually a redundant species. Nevertheless, at least one drawing survives by Ramsay copied from an historical painting in Solimena's studio in Naples and this suggests, significantly, that Ramsay's interest lay in the delineation of the gracefully disposed isolated human figure rather than in attempting an elaborate and formal baroque composition.

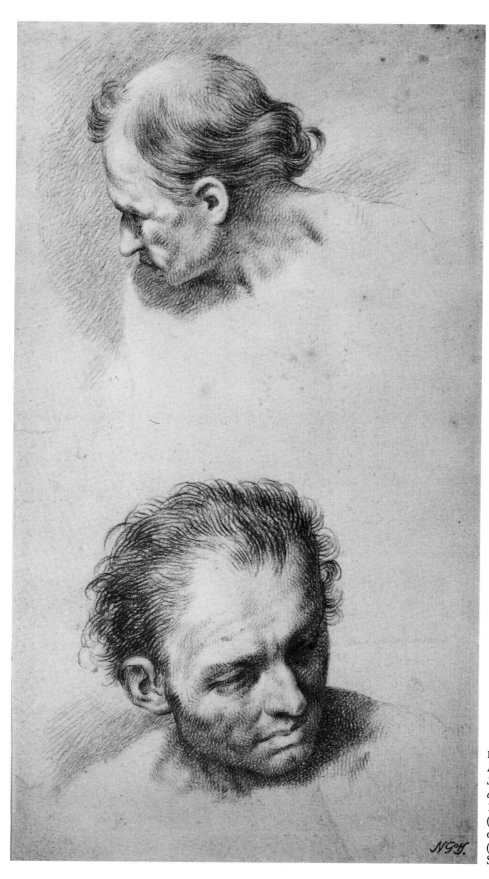

PLATE 151
Allan Ramsay
Study of two male heads,
c.1736
10⅞ x 6¼ ins.
(27.5 x 16cm), red chalk
on buff paper
(National Gallery of
Scotland, Edinburgh)

PLATE 152 (above)
Allan Ramsay
Samuel Torriano, 1738
30 x 25½ ins.
(76 x 65cm)
(Private collection)

PLATE 153 (above right)
Allan Ramsay
*Francis, 2nd Duke of
Buccleuch, 1739*
95 x 58ins.
(242 x 147.5cm)
(Drumlanrig Castle)

Ramsay specifically learnt one Italian technique from Solimena — the use of vermilion for underpainting the face — an effect which Vertue particularly disliked. 'Ramsay still accustomes him self', wrote Vertue, 'to draw the faces in red lines shades &c. finishing the likeness in one red colour or mask before he puts on the flesh Colour, which he proposes as a method to make the flesh clear and transparent'. As Vertue pointed out, this technique was alien to the British tradition and 'rather lick't than pencilld' as he put it.

Something of this break with tradition can certainly be seen in portraits executed by Ramsay about the time of his return from Italy in 1738. The portrait of Samuel Torriano (Plate 152) is so markedly Italianate in colouring and effects of light and so different from the productions of most of Ramsay's British-born contemporaries that, were it not signed, it might have defied attribution.

On his return from Italy in 1738 Ramsay had set himself up as a portrait painter in London, although he also maintained a studio in Edinburgh, and was immediately successful and apparently undaunted by the highly competitive environment in which he had chosen to work. Vertue attributes some of Ramsay's success to what he termed 'the Scotch Interest and favour, appearing in his behalf', noting that eminent and powerful fellow Scotsmen

PLATE 154
Allan Ramsay
The Hon. Francis Charteris
of Amisfield and his wife,
Lady Katharine Gordon
c.1747-48
93½ x 80ins.
(237.5 x 203cm)
(Gosford House)

like the Dukes of Argyll and Buccleuch (Plate 153), 'promoted his interest' so that by the spring of 1740 Ramsay could himself testify to his success in an oft-quoted letter to a friend by brashly stating: 'I have put all your Vanloos and Soldis and Roscos [Ruscas] to flight and now play the first fiddle myself'. Van Loo, Soldi and Rusca had all arrived, to great fanfare in London between 1736 and 1738. Significantly, Ramsay did not even bother to mention his English rivals.

Ramsay's one serious rival into the 1740s was to be Hudson, and there are times when their work can be confusingly similar. This is especially noticeable when they shared the services of the drapery painter Van Aken. Vertue says Ramsay used Van Aken 'at all times' as early as 1739 and, in view of the visual evidence we have to the contrary, rather unfairly suggests that without Van Aken's specialist skills 'he had made but an indifferent progress'. It cannot be denied, however, that c.1750 some of his works have a rather perfunctory

PLATE 155 (above)
Allan Ramsay
Lady Walpole Wemyss, 1754
29 x 24½ins.
(73.5 x 62cm)
(Gosford House)

PLATE 156 (right)
Maurice Quentin de La Tour
Self-portrait, 1751
25½ x 20⅞ins.
(65 x 53cm), pastel
(Musée de Picardie, Amiens)

blandness that places them on a par with Hudson. By 1751, before the ambitious young Reynolds had returned from Italy, Ramsay was quite properly viewed by Vertue as 'much superior in merit' to his contemporaries. He had yet to produce his best work.

Ellis Waterhouse first pointed to Ramsay's adaptation of classical models for portraiture, the most notable example being the full-length of Norman, twenty-second Chief of Macleod of 1747-48. For this Ramsay modified the celebrated Apollo Belvedere, or something close to it, for a portrait of a Scottish gentleman in tartan trews. He was to try something similar with the splendid portrait of the Hon. Francis Charteris of Amisfield and his wife of about the same date (Plate 154).

The robustness of these images from the 1740s gives way in Ramsay's work of the following decade to a more tender, feminine delicacy. He had certainly painted women with success early in his career but by the mid-1750s a more refined and sophisticated style of female portraiture emerges in his hands. In his essay *On Taste,* published in 1755, Ramsay had been fulsome in his praise of the great French pastellist Quentin de La Tour, and we have only to glance at his portrait of Lady Walpole Wemyss of 1754 to see that slight tilt of the head so common in La Tour's work (Plates 155 and 156). Lady Walpole Wemyss had recently married a Frenchman, which no doubt also helps explain the overtly French manner here employed by Ramsay.

The second of Ramsay's four visits to Italy began in 1754 and he spent most of his time in Rome looking at the art of the past. He seems not to have painted

PLATE 157 (left)
Allan Ramsay
Study of hands for the
portraits of George III (as
Prince of Wales), the Duke
of Argyll, and others, c.1757
12⅛ x 9⅛ ins.
(31 x 23cm), red chalk
heightened with
white on buff paper
(National Gallery of
Scotland, Edinburgh)

PLATE 158 (above)
Joshua Reynolds
Anne, Countess of
Albemarle, c.1757
49¾ x 39¾ ins.
(126.5 x 101cm)
(National Gallery,
London)

much, but a number of drawings from this trip survive, some done at the French Academy's life class, while others are copies of frescos by Domenichino and Raphael.

Drawing had always been an important part of Ramsay's routine and in this he differs from most of his British contemporaries. Remarkably few drawings specifically relating to portraits survive by any of the leading artists of the mid-eighteenth century in England but in Ramsay's case we have many, most of them studies of costume or poses and they show the considerable care he took in arranging his figures and exploiting, as Van Dyck had done before him, the expressive possibilities of hands (Plate 157).

This can be seen to particular advantage in what is so often acknowledged to be Ramsay's greatest work: Margaret Lindsay, the painter's second wife, now thought to date from c.1759-60 (Colour Plate 29). This delicate and sensitive image of the young wife surprised while arranging flowers indicates the extent to which Ramsay's stylistic allegiance appears to have transferred from Italy to 'le style Pompadour'. Without recourse here to the drapery painter Ramsay, like Gainsborough at this date, revels in the textural delights of the plum coloured dress and the intricacies of the lace shawl. A comparison with Reynolds's Countess of Albemarle (Plate 158), begun in 1757, shows the astuteness of Horace Walpole's judgement when he wrote to Sir David Dalrymple in February 1759 that Ramsay and Reynolds were his 'favourite painters, and two of the very best we ever had...Mr. Reynolds and Mr.

Ramsay can scarce be rivals; their manners are so different. The former is bold, and has a kind of tempestuous colouring, yet with dignity and grace; the latter is all delicacy. Mr. Reynolds seldom succeeds in women: Mr. Ramsay is formed to paint them'.

Ramsay must have been concerned by the return to London of Reynolds in October 1752, although at the time he was away working in Edinburgh. We can only speculate as to whether Reynolds's presence played any part in Ramsay's decision to return to Italy to refresh his knowledge. Certainly thereafter Ramsay seemed determined to develop a style which would not come into conflict with Reynolds's 'grand manner' bravura. Ramsay's colour becomes more delicate and restrained with the predominance of silvery pastel tones by contrast to Reynolds's Titianesque or Rembrandtesque chiaroscuro.

Within a couple of months of Ramsay's return from Italy in August 1757 he was to receive the most important commission of his career to date, a full-length of the young Prince of Wales (Plate 159). It seems to have been through the offices of the Prince's tutor and close confidante Lord Bute that Ramsay's name had been suggested in royal circles. The pose of the young heir to the throne was adapted rather subtly, as James Holloway has recently suggested, from the Hermes Farnese in the Belvedere Courtyard in the Vatican Museum. The undoubted success of this picture sealed Ramsay's position of favour in the eyes of the future King. When Lord Eglinton later in the 1760s suggested to George III that he might sit to Reynolds, the King is said to have replied curtly 'Mr. Ramsay is my painter, my Lord'.

Ramsay painted the official coronation portrait of George III and its companion of the new Queen Charlotte. He was made King's Painter in 1761 and it was only his dilatoriness in applying for the more senior rank of Serjeant Painter at the time of the accession in 1760 that led to it passing by default to the former holder, George II's tedious image-maker John Shackleton. By the time Ramsay succeeded Shackleton on the latter's death in 1767 Laurence Sterne could wryly remark: 'Mr. Ramsay, you paint only the court cards, the King, Queen and Knave'. This was largely true and, with the exception of a few portraits of close friends like the moral philosopher David Hume of 1766 (Plate 160), the bulk of Ramsay's professional energies in the 1760s were channelled into the highly lucrative production of replicas of royal portraits. By 1770 he had virtually retired to pursue a life of scholarship and a serious accident to his right arm in 1773 put an end to his career as a painter. Ramsay had been a figure of considerable learning who had brought to British painting a much greater degree of sophistication than perhaps any other painter since Van Dyck. Together with Hogarth he pioneered the development of the informal portrait although, unlike Hogarth's, his work did appeal to the world of fashion.

The contribution of William Hogarth to portrait painting in the early 1730s has already been examined. Hogarth painted portraits of various types throughout his career but never thought of himself as a portrait painter in the

PLATE 159 (left)
Allan Ramsay
George III (as Prince of Wales), 1757-58
93 x 58ins. (236 x 147.5cm)
(Private collection)

PLATE 160 (above)
Allan Ramsay
David Hume, 1766
30 x 25ins. (76 x 63.5cm)
(National Gallery of Scotland, Edinburgh)

conventional eighteenth century sense of the term. In fact he derided portrait painting in the scrappy *Autobiographical Notes,* scribbled towards the end of his life, as a branch of art dependent only on 'much practice and an exact Eye...by men of very midling natural parts'. He complained about it being 'engrossed by a very few Monopelisers' (some of whom like Van Loo he specifically identifies), whilst 'others in a superior way more desirving...were neglected' — no doubt meaning himself.

We have seen that most of Hogarth's early portraits were small-scale conversation pieces like the Wollaston Family (Colour Plate 22) and at the end of the 1730s he was still occasionally producing works of this type. However, the more lucrative modern moral subjects, or at least the engravings after them, had liberated him from the time-consuming drudgery of small-scale portraits, which he tells us was not a sufficiently profitable genre for him to pursue energetically. Only occasionally before 1740 did Hogarth paint single figures like the Duke of Cumberland of 1733 (Plate 161), and most of these

PLATE 161 (above)
William Hogarth
*H.R.H. William
Augustus, Duke of
Cumberland, c.1732*
17½ x 13½ ins.
(44.5 x 34.5cm)
(Yale Center for British
Art: Paul Mellon
Collection)

PLATE 162 (above right)
William Hogarth
Unidentified sitter, 1741
29¼ x 24½ ins.
(74.5 x 62cm)
(Dulwich Picture
Gallery, London)

look like renegades from a conversation piece.

After his success with the Rake's and Harlot's Progresses in the mid-1730s Hogarth, somewhat paradoxically, seems to have turned his creative energies towards history painting. It is as if on the death of his father-in-law Sir James Thornhill in 1734, Hogarth felt that the mantle of history painter had descended on his shoulders. The great paintings for the staircase at St. Bartholomew's Hospital, 'The Good Samaritan' and 'The Pool of Bethesda', impressive though they are, were painted in a rather outmoded late baroque style and certainly did not induce the rash of commissions for similar works that Hogarth had hoped would follow.

For the xenophobic Hogarth the arrival in England of the French and Italian portrait painters (the Van Loos, Soldis and Ruscas that Ramsay claimed to have put to flight) undoubtedly fuelled his low opinion of the aristocratic clientele that flocked to them as well as making him all the more determined to show that he was more than a match for them. For the genteel classes at this date it was a safer affirmation of good taste to buy foreign Old Masters and to sit to foreign portrait painters. In this context Hogarth's inscription on the portrait of an unidentified man in a red coat, 'Wm Hogarth Anglus Pinxit 1741' (Plate 162), takes on an added significance at the height of Van Loo's popularity.

A year earlier Hogarth had completed a much more effective riposte against the foreign painters with the unveiling of his portrait of Captain Thomas Coram (Plate 163). This was Hogarth's first 'public' portrait (donated to the

PLATE 163 (above)
William Hogarth
Captain Thomas Coram, 1740
94 x 58ins. (239 x 147.5cm)
(Thomas Coram Foundation, London)

PLATE 164 (above right)
Antonio Verrio, Godfrey Kneller and James
Thornhill
Sir Christopher Wren, c.1724
92 x 70ins. (233.5 x 178cm)
(Sheldonian Theatre, Oxford)

PLATE 165
Detail of Hogarth's portrait of Thomas Coram (Plate
163) showing the vigorous brushwork on the face

Foundling Hospital) and his first on the scale of life. As a deliberate attempt to rally the native portrait painters, it both pays homage to and yet flouts the conventions of the type of baroque court portrait on which it is modelled. Hogarth's challenge, so he tells us, made to him by Ramsay, was to attempt to paint a portrait 'as well as Vandyke'. In reality in 1739/40 the challenge was as much to Ramsay as Van Dyck.

It has been suggested, not unconvincingly, that Hogarth's pictorial source for the Coram portrait was Hyacinthe Rigaud's portrait of Samuel Bernard now at Versailles, or, more likely, Drevet's engraving after it. Nevertheless, there is another possible source nearer to hand in the form of Verrio's portrait of Sir Christopher Wren in the Sheldonian Theatre, Oxford (Plate 164). This picture, which was finished by Kneller and then finally by Hogarth's father-in-law Thornhill in 1724 has a number of striking similarities.

If, in its compositional elements, the Coram portrait follows convention, in its domestication of the French *grand-manière* it is entirely unprecedented. Coram is depicted not in the court dress of a high-born gentleman but in an austere black suit topped by a rather unkempt red great coat. Despite the informal dress, Hogarth formulated a style suitable for portraying a sitter whose rank had been reached through his achievements rather than by birth. The diminutive figure of the elderly Coram seems distinctly ill at ease with his grand surroundings, his short legs dangling nervously above the step. His genial expression is the antithesis of the Augustan mask; his wigless head and puffy complexion captured with a sparkling vivacity — the 'speaking likeness' which Hogarth sought (Plate 165). Here Hogarth's vigorous brushwork on the face, which technically does owe something to the more painterly Kneller tradition, is at odds with the icy smoothness of those descendants of Riley epitomised by Richardson and Hudson. Hogarth never used the drapery painters and resented the success of those whose sole contribution to the canvas was, as he put it, 'contained in an oval about five inches long'. Perhaps a more objective view was put by Reynolds's pupil and biographer James Northcote who wrote: 'The genius of Hogarth was too great, and his public employment too little, to require the assistance of a drapery painter, therefore he might safely point his satire at those who did'.

Hogarth wrote at length about physiognomy in his much-reviled *Analysis of Beauty* which was published in 1753. 'With regard to character and expression', he wrote, 'we have daily many instances that confirm that the face is the index of the mind'. Other observations by Hogarth are equally revealing of his attitude towards portraiture: 'It is by the natural and unaffected movements of the muscles, caused by the passions of the mind, that everyman's character would in some measure be written in his face'. He dismisses the contrived gentility that characterises the work of so many of his contemporaries since 'gravity and solemn looks' are not always 'signs of wisdom...all that the ancient sculptors could do, notwithstanding their enthusiastic endeavours to raise the characters of their deities to aspects of sagacity above human, was to

PLATE 167
Louis-François Roubiliac
Bust of William Hogarth, c.1741
28ins. (71cm) high, terracotta
(National Portrait Gallery, London)

PLATE 166
William Hogarth
Self-portrait, 1745
35½ x 27½ins. (90 x 70cm)
(Tate Gallery, London)

give them features of beauty'. Hogarth acknowledged that everybody would quite properly wish to appear genteel and graceful 'in the carriage of his person', but denies that the dancing and fencing masters are the best means of achieving it: 'Action is a sort of language which perhaps one time or other, may come to be taught by a kind of grammar-rules; but, at present is only got by rote and imitation'.

Hogarth's thoughts on these matters as expressed in his writings surely explain why his portraits so frequently appear unconventional. To his contemporaries they sometimes almost verged on caricature. The appearance of works like George Arnold of c.1740 (Colour Plate 30), with its bluff, uncompromising directness explain why so few aristocratic sitters were brave enough to sit to Hogarth after that date. The future 4th Duke of Devonshire of 1741 is a refreshing exception (Colour Plate 31).

It is not clear at what stage Hogarth's portraits were first criticised and found to be out of tune with the fashionable world. We have Hogarth's own statement in the *Autobiographical Notes* that a 'whole nest of Phizmongers [face painters]' criticised his portraits of women as 'harlots' and his portraits of men as 'charicatures', effectively putting him out of business. In the preface of *Joseph Andrews,* published in 1742, Henry Fielding, defending Hogarth's works against the poet William Somerville's charge that he was a 'burlesque painter', wrote:

> He who would call the Ingenious *Hogarth* a Burlesque Painter, would, in my Opinion, do him very little Honour: for sure it is much easier, much less the subject of Admiration, to paint a Man with a Nose, or any other Feature of a preposterous Size, or to expose him in some absurd or monstrous Attitude, than to express the Affectations of Men on Canvas. It hath been thought a vast Commendation of a Painter, to say his Figures *seem to breathe;* but surely, it is a much greater and nobler Applause, *that they appear to think.*

It has frequently been noted that Hogarth's method of modelling a head in paint has pronounced similarities to the sculptor Roubiliac's busts in terracotta and marble. Louis-François Roubiliac (1702/5-62) had been in England since the early 1730s and was one of the leading teachers at the St. Martin's Lane Academy which had been revived by Hogarth in 1735. The plasticity and general schemata of Hogarth's heads, not least in his celebrated self-portrait, is so close to Roubiliac as to be undeniable (cf. Plates 166 and 167).

By the 1740s portrait sculpture had become exceedingly popular. Robert Campbell, whom we have already encountered writing in the 1740s, noted that 'the taste for Busts and Figures, in these Materials [clay, wax, plaster of Paris etc.] prevails much of late years, and in some measure interferes with Portrait painting. The nobility now affect to have their Busts done in that Way rather than sit for their Pictures, and the Fashion is to have their Apartments adorned with Bronze and Figures in Plaister and Wax'.

The popularity of sculpture in the 1740s should not surprise us since it was in that medium that the first real break with the Kneller pattern of portraiture had emerged. The sculpted portrait had the innate advantage of echoing antiquity in a much more authentic way than painting, a factor that meant much to Englishmen, particularly those of the Burlington circle, who liked to think of themselves as reincarnated Romans. Lord Burlington had imported the Italian Guelfi as early as c.1715 for precisely this purpose, only to replace him with the Fleming John Michael Rysbrack (1694-1770) when he saw that he did a better job (Plate 168). In 1732 Rysbrack had some sixty sitters and only a few years later, in 1738, Vertue noted that none could equal Rysbrack 'for truth of likeness'. The portrait painters had to take notice. Summing up his remarks on the year 1738 Vertue remarked that sculpture 'has of late years made greater advances' than painting.

PLATE 168
John Michael Rysbrack
Bust of James Gibbs, 1726
30ins. (76cm) high,
marble
(Victoria and Albert
Museum, London)

It is probably no coincidence that Hogarth and others like Francis Hayman began to show a serious interest in portraiture just after the unveiling, in the spring of 1738 at Vauxhall Gardens, of Roubiliac's first major success, the seated full-length figure of Handel (Plate 169).

Hayman's small portrait of Joseph Henry of c.1745 (Plate 170) has the same heavy, deeply folded draperies of Roubiliac's Handel and they seem suspended like carved marble. Hayman even employs the sculptor's device of the precariously balanced slipper on Henry's stockinged foot. Roubiliac's skill at modelling draperies was commented on by Vertue in May 1749 after he had seen the Duke of Argyll's monument, recently installed in Westminster Abbey.

PLATE 170
Francis Hayman
Joseph Henry, c.1745
23¼ x 19¼ins. (59 x 49cm)
(Private collection)

PLATE 169
Louis-François Roubiliac
Statue of Handel, 1738
53½ins. (136cm) high,
marble
(Victoria and Albert
Museum, London)

Wrote Vertue: 'the Draperys and foldings truely natural and [he] excells all other in skill and softness of plaits, really more like silk than Marble'.

Hogarth's technique was ideally suited to those who formed the bulk of his clientele. His sitters tended to be from a small circle of friends, relatives and their acquaintances, with a liberal scattering of lawyers and medical men, whom he felt at ease with both ideologically and personally.

During the early 1740s Hogarth was at his most active as a portrait painter although his practice was modest by comparison with the fashionable Ramsay and the fast-riding Hudson. If Hogarth was not successful for the most part in persuading the great to sit to him it was not simply because of his unconventional style but also due to his high prices. Hogarth was at least as pricey as Ramsay and more expensive than most of his contemporaries.

It is worth noting here that the successful portrait painter could expect a sizeable income in the first half of the eighteenth century. Prices rose steadily as the century progressed. Michael Dahl received £44 10s. for his portrait of

PLATE 171
William Hogarth
The Graham Children, 1742
63¾ x 71¼ ins. (162 x 181cm)
(National Gallery, London)

Lord Ashburnham at some point between 1710 and 1716, while in 1712 Charles Jervas received 20 guineas for his three-quarter-length of Lord Irwin, which still hangs at Temple Newsam. In 1715 Kneller charged 60 guineas for a full-length, a price not surpassed until 1730 when Richardson could command 70 guineas for the same. A few years later Amigoni was asking 60 guineas for a full-length although his compatriot Casali apparently failed to get £50 in 1741. Hudson meanwhile seems to have charged from 12 guineas for a bust to 48 guineas for a full-length in the 1740s only to be eclipsed by the meteoric rise of his former pupil Reynolds, particularly after the latter moved

PLATE 172
William Hogarth
*James Caulfield, 1st Earl
of Charlemont, c.1759*
23½ x 19½ ins.
(59.5 x 49.5cm)
(Smith College Museum
of Art, Northampton,
Massachusetts)

to his Leicester Fields studio in 1761 when he upped his charges to 100 guineas for a full-length. No wonder the most successful portrait painters in the first half of the century, Kneller and Hudson, could afford country estates at Twickenham.

After the Coram portrait, Hogarth's most ambitious work was the charming portrait of the Graham Children, which is signed and dated 1742 (Plate 171 and Colour Plate 2). Rather unusually, given the grand scale of this picture, a sort of conversation piece on a monumental scale, the sitters were the children of Daniel Graham, the apothecary of the Chelsea Hospital and not the offspring of an aristocratic grandee.

Hogarth had a particular gift for portraying children. From the early 'Gerard Anne Hamilton in his Cradle' of 1732 he had shown great sensitivity to the particularities of youth. 'Children in infancy have movements in the muscles of their faces peculiar to their age, as an uninformed and unmeaning stare, an open mouth, and simple grin', he wrote in the *Analysis of Beauty*. How well these words apply to the Graham Children in which Hogarth distinguishes with such subtlety between the ages and personalities of the children. The picture is an allegory of the transience of childhood. The clock on the left is surmounted by a scythe-bearing Cupid, while the right hand side of the composition is dominated by the sinister presence of the cat who terrorises the goldfinch in the cage which the boy thinks is the pleasurable response to the music box he works.

By the mid-1740s Hogarth more or less seems to have withdrawn from portrait painting. His renewed interest in narrative painting is manifested in the 'Marriage-à-la-Mode' pictures although a few portrait commissions reflect this change of direction. 'Captain Lord George Graham in his Cabin' (Colour Plate 32) was probably commissioned to celebrate Graham's successful action off Ostend in June 1745. Despite the awkward disjuncture of the figures, the narrative element is once more pronounced, as in the early conversation pieces. Graham is seen smoking in his cabin before dinner. His chaplain and clerk and the dogs (one of which wears his wig) are caught singing to the music of the fife and drum played by the black servant, whilst the steward bringing in the roast duck spills gravy down the chaplain's back. Hogarth has effectively reverted to the comic narrative of old.

Hogarth flirted briefly once more with conventional portrait painting during the last years of his career. Easily the most ambitious work of this period is the portrait of his friend David Garrick and his wife of 1757 in the Royal Collection, but others, like the mysteriously unfinished portrait of his friend Lord Charlemont of c.1759, show his powers undiminished (Plate 172). By that date Ramsay was at the peak of his powers and Reynolds and Gainsborough were on the brink of greatness. On 5 November 1759 the Society of Artists was formed from the St. Martin's Lane Academy artists. Hogarth had lost control of that body and was by then a lonely and isolated figure.

BRIAN ALLEN
The Paul Mellon Centre for Studies in British Art

PLATE 173
Thomas Gainsborough
James Quinn, c.1761
90 x 59ins. (231 x 150cm)
(National Gallery of Ireland, Dublin)

Chapter 3
The Golden Age
1760-1790

1760 was an auspicious year for the arts in Great Britain. On 1 January Horace Walpole began his *Anecdotes of Painting in England* — the first history of British art. On 21 April the first public exhibition of work by contemporary British artists was held at the Society of Arts in the Strand. In May Thomas Gainsborough (1727-88), having arrived in Bath the previous year, took the lease on a handsome property belonging to the Duke of Kingston near the Abbey churchyard. Here he set up his household and studio and began his career as a fashionable society portrait painter. Several months later, Joshua Reynolds (1723-92), who had an abiding awareness of the importance of his public image, purchased an imposing residence on the west side of Leicester Fields, setting up not only a studio but also his own picture gallery. And in October, as if to confirm the dawning of a new age, the twenty-two year old George III — the 'Patriot King' — ascended the throne on a wave of public confidence.

The years 1760 to 1790 have often been seen as the golden age of portraiture in Britain, not least because it was during this period that Thomas Gainsborough and Joshua Reynolds produced among their finest works. It was also a period of transition for the portrait, as artists, conscious of the ever-increasing popularity of the genre, sought new ways to enrich its formal vocabulary and to redefine its status within the traditional hierarchy of subject matter. And yet, although portraiture was elevated as an art form during the later eighteenth century, its basis continued to be, inevitably, a business transaction between artist and sitter. The establishment and maintenance of a steady market was the surest foundation for artistic development, as one can gauge from the practice of Thomas Gainsborough on his move from Ipswich to Bath in the autumn of 1759.

Gainsborough's only serious rival in Bath was William Hoare (1707-92), who had carried out a portrait business there since 1739. Trained in Rome, Hoare had cultivated a careful, polished and somewhat earnest portrait style, employing bright, metallic colours reminiscent of Jonathan Richardson Sr. and the Italian artist Andrea Soldi (c.1703-71), who had worked in London during the 1730s and 1740s. Hoare's portrait of the Pitt Family, exhibited at

PLATE 174
Thomas Gainsborough
*'The Artist's Daughters
chasing a Butterfly', c.1757*
44¾ x 42½ ins.
(113.5 x 108cm)
(National Gallery,
London)

the Society of Artists in 1761 (Colour Plate 33), highlights the rather formal and archaic elements of the artist's style around the time of Gainsborough's arrival in Bath. The two artists seem, however, to have coexisted quite amicably, managing to divide existing patronage between them. Gainsborough's portrait business took off rapidly in Bath and, although mercurial in his personal likes (he despised arrogance or affectation), he quickly built up a solid network of patrons in the south-west among the prosperous merchants and professional classes as well as the actors and musicians in whose company he felt most at ease. Among the latter who featured as clients of Gainsborough at this time were James Quinn, the Linleys, the viol player Carl Friedrich Abel, William Jackson (later to become Gainsborough's biographer) and, of course, David Garrick, whom he met in 1766. Gainsborough's social and professional circles were always closely related. His doctor, Ralph Schomberg (who not only tended Gainsborough but also looked after his daughter, Margaret, during periodic bouts of mental

PLATE 175
Thomas Gainsborough
The Byam Family, 1764
98 x 94ins.
(249 x 239cm)
(Marlborough College,
Wiltshire)

illness), was also an amateur playwright and friend of both the artist and David Garrick, while Robert Craggs (later Earl Nugent), a prominent patron of Gainsborough, was at the same time Member of Parliament for Bristol, amateur poet and friend of Oliver Goldsmith. Gainsborough's portrait of Quinn (Plate 173), which he exhibited at the Society of Arts in 1761 and the Society of Artists in 1763, at once demonstrates the artist's facility to defuse the pomp and pretentiousness of formal portraiture by the introduction of casual yet elegant attitudes.

Gainsborough, although he sold the bulk of his portrait commissions, also used them as a form of currency in their own right, painting portraits for his doctors, Rice Charleton (Holburne of Menstrie Museum, Bath) and Schomberg, in exchange for their services. Gainsborough's circle of influence even extended as far as Walter Wiltshire, a wealthy local carrier who transported his works to London in exchange for pictures; Gainsborough presented him, somewhat appropriately, with a version of his 'Harvest Waggon' (Barber Institute, Birmingham). A measure of Gainsborough's rapid advancement in Bath was his move in 1763 to Lansdown Lodge, and thence in 1767 to 17 The Circus, where he converted two spacious interlocking first floor rooms into a studio.

As Gainsborough's social circle widened during the 1760s so his technique showed a marked increase in confidence. Already by the late 1750s his style was becoming looser, although the evidence for this is largely restricted to private studies — notably the 'Artist's Daughters chasing a Butterfly', of around 1757 (Plate 174), where, free from the constraints imposed by commissioned portraiture, Gainsborough indulged his passion for movement via broad, spontaneous brushstrokes. Just how difficult it was to reconcile such an approach to the kind of format demanded in official portraiture can be seen by a comparison with the Dehany Family (Colour Plate 34), painted by Gainsborough soon after his arrival in Bath, where only the silk draperies of the woman's dress give full range to the artist's increasingly vigorous brushwork. Even so, the handling of the flesh tones, which had previously been characterised by the painstaking application of a network of staccato-like strokes, now gave way to a more summary approach, while the general configuration of the subjects on the canvas — the three figures drawn together in an ellipse — demonstrate Gainsborough's more thoughtful attitude towards the problems of group composition.

Gainsborough, although his attention to portraiture was at times more sporadic than other professional portraitists, was possessed of a very sound technique which enabled him to work rapidly. Canvases were primed, usually with a thin layer of light grey, and brushes were carefully chosen — coarse hog's hair for general effects, fine camel hair for detailed work. Although he sometimes made preliminary compositional drawings, he usually worked up the design straight on to the canvas in a mauve pigment, the entire figure being sketched out on the canvas before he began any detailed work on the faces. From at least the 1760s we know (from the first-hand evidence of fellow artist Ozias Humphrey) that Gainsborough worked in a subdued light, allowing very little daylight into the studio while blocking in the masses, and only gradually letting in more light as he worked towards the highlights. Allied to the consolidation of his technique during the 1760s was an increasingly generalised treatment of landscape in portraiture. While in earlier portraits of the 1740s and 1750s, most notably that of Mr. and Mrs. Andrews, of c.1750 (National Gallery, London), Gainsborough had consciously allowed himself room to explore landscape painting within portraiture (pushing his sitters to one side of the picture), it now became, perforce, a subsidiary feature in his work. It was perhaps in order to compensate for this comparative lack of attention to landscape that Gainsborough's imagination was turned more fully to the issue of figurative invention. And whereas he had previously been happy to rely on the standard repertoire of traditional portrait poses — women seated primly with hands clasped, and men with hands thrust into waistcoats, legs crossed or tricorn hats tucked tightly under arms — he now became fascinated by the

PLATE 176 (left)
Thomas Gainsborough
*Isabella, Viscountess
Molyneux, 1769*
92 x 60ins.
(233.5 x 152.5cm)
(Walker Art Gallery,
Liverpool)

PLATE 177 (above)
Joshua Reynolds
Laurence Sterne, 1761
50 x 39½ ins.
(127 x 100.5cm)
(National Portrait
Gallery, London)

manner in which the incorporation of unorthodox gestures, attitudes and even expressions, could enliven otherwise formula compositions. Thus, for example, in the group portrait of Mr. and Mrs. George Byam and their eldest daughter, Selina, of 1764 (Plate 175), while the two adults admire the scenery, Gainsborough centres the quizzical gaze of the child on the viewer, at once deflating the stateliness of the image and countering the general movement of the figures towards the left of the picture plane.

In October 1760 Gainsborough produced his first full-length female portrait — Miss Ann Ford (Cincinnati Art Museum, Ohio). In the luxuriant draperies, and self-confident elegance of the figure, he was heavily influenced by Van Dyck's portrait of 'Lady Digby as Prudence' (a copy is at Windsor Castle). Indeed it was the example of Van Dyck, far more than anything he had learnt from contemporaries, that enhanced and sophisticated Gainsborough's art in the 1760s, and the opportunities for studying Van Dyck, which residence in Bath afforded to Gainsborough, must be counted as one of the most significant consequences of his time there. From Bath Gainsborough was able to travel to Paul Methuen's collection of Van Dycks at Corsham Court and to see the Earl of Pembroke's pictures at Wilton House. Moreoever, he not only had the chance to study these works but also to make copies of them. One feature which distinguishes Gainsborough from the majority of his peers was his relish for

PLATE 178
Joshua Reynolds
*'Garrick between Tragedy
and Comedy', 1762*
58¼ x 72ins.
(148 x 183cm)
(Private collection)

painting drapery and his inquisitiveness as to the potential of paint to recreate
the textures of silks, satin and lace. The clear indication of the fruits of this
labour was the series of female full-lengths which he produced from the
mid-1760s onwards — portraits such as Mary, Countess Howe of c.1763-64
(Kenwood House, London), Maria, Lady Eardley of 1766 and most startling
of all, Isabella, Viscountess Molyneux, later Countess Sefton of 1769 (Plate
176) where the bravura handling of the draperies threatens to overwhelm the
sitter.

Although he did not live in London, Gainsborough made frequent visits to
the capital for business and pleasure (while there in 1763 he contracted a
particularly debilitating bout of venereal disease), and from 1761 onwards he
showed work at the Society of Artists' annual exhibition (that year most artists
had abandoned the Society of Arts exhibition, which had been established the
previous year, in favour of the newly-formed Society). By the mid-1760s
Gainsborough was regarded as the principal rival to Joshua Reynolds. This,
it should be remembered, was a considerable achievement considering both
Gainsborough's geographical location and the fact that he worked — unlike

most of all his major competitors — alone (he did not formally engage the services of his nephew Gainsborough Dupont until 1772). Gainsborough's world in the 1760s centred in and around Bath, was in every sense far more hermetic than Reynolds's London-based practice, and yet a comparison between the two artists at this period is inevitable. First, however, it is necessary to examine the nature of Reynolds's own approach to portraiture during the 1760s.

Reynolds had emerged as a significant figure on the London art scene following his return from Italy in 1752. During the next few years, in addition to his artistic endeavours, he forged friendships and engineered the acquaintance of patrons who were to become the mainstay of his future social success. His pre-eminence as a portrait painter by 1760 emerges forcibly in the portrait of Laurence Sterne which he showed at the Society of Arts in 1761 (Plate 177). Painted in spring 1760, Laurence Sterne epitomises the strengths of Reynolds's art by this date: namely his knack of selecting suitable subject matter (Sterne was currently enjoying immense popularity as the author of the recently published *Life and Opinions of Tristram Shandy*); his familiarity with the Old Master tradition (in this instance the chiaroscuro of Rembrandt); and, via the sitter's secretive half-smile and gesture of the finger to his forehead, his ability to select the salient characteristic of his subject — in this case Sterne's wickedly clever wit. Publicity, whether for himself or his associates, was always central to Reynolds's aims. No clearer sign of his desire to use the public exhibition as a forum to expound his own theories on portraiture can be found in arguably Reynolds's greatest portrait, 'Garrick between Tragedy and Comedy', exhibited, at the age of forty-one, in 1762 at the Society of Arts (Plate 178). The appeal of this work, as in the majority of Reynolds's 'public' portraits, lies in its multiplicity of meanings. Ostensibly the picture adverts to the versatility of David Garrick as an actor through his ability to play both comic and tragic roles (although it suggests via his attitude that his natural inclination is towards comedy). On another level it reveals Reynolds's familiarity with classical precedents — the predicament of the actor echoing Hercules's choice between vice and virtue (a subject common not only in western art but also central to the discussion in one of the most important English texts on aesthetics, Lord Shaftesbury's *Characteristicks*). On a third level the portrait demonstrates Reynolds's awareness of the choice which tradition offered artists — personified on the one hand by the soft-focused sensuality of Comedy, where form is modulated primarily by colour, and on the other by the disciplined didacticism of Tragedy, whose figure is subject to the strictures of line. Painted shortly after Reynolds began to exhibit extensively in public, this portrait of Garrick stands as a symbol of the abiding choice which Reynolds knew lay open to him: either to paint according to his private instincts — as Gainsborough did — or to attempt to broaden the range of his art by the assimilation of a wide range of styles and influences.

Grand though his aspirations were, Reynolds, like any other portrait

PLATE 179
Joshua Reynolds
*Lord Rockingham and
Edmund Burke (unfinished),
1767*
57½ x 62½ ins.
(145.5 x 159cm)
(Fitzwilliam Museum,
Cambridge)

painter, was subject to the vagaries of the market. On the whole portrait sittings — and this is confirmed by the evidence of Reynolds's own sitter books — followed the 'season', that is the social calendar of fashionable clientele, which ran from October to June (the summer and early autumn was invariably the time chosen by Reynolds to make sojourns into the countryside or, later in his career, to experiment with subject pictures). Reynolds's sitter books, which survive with few exceptions from 1755 to 1790, give a more or less continuous record of the artist's day-to-day practice, as well as informing us of his busy social life. Viewed as a whole, they indicate a prodigious energy and unwavering self-discipline. Reynolds began work each day (Sundays often included) at nine and worked, invariably without a break, until his dinner hour at four in the afternoon. His studio in Leicester Fields was an octagonal-shaped room lit by one small window some nine feet from the floor. Hence, as in Gainsborough's studio, little natural light was afforded to the painter. Sitters had on average five or six one-hour sessions, although a dozen or more sittings were not uncommon. Clients were seldom painted beyond the confines of the studio (an exception being the family of the Duke of Marlborough whom Reynolds visited in the summer of 1777, probably in connection with their group portrait shown at the Royal Academy in 1778). In general Reynolds followed the practice common to Lely, Kneller, and his own master, Thomas Hudson, of painting directly from the sitter's face only. Hands were invariably painted from studio assistants or household servants, while attitudes were sketched in with the aid of prints in the artist's collection. In direct contrast to Gainsborough, the dress and various accoutrements of the sitter were of little direct concern to Reynolds. The result is that, especially during the 1760s when Reynolds employed extensive assistance, in certain full-length or group portraits there is a clear disjunction between the carefully delineated objects of the studio assistant and the loosely worked surface of the master. Moreover, as his unfinished portrait of Lord Rockingham and Edmund Burke of 1767 shows (Plate 179), accessories such as inkstands (this prop recurs in numerous portraits of this time) and turkey rugs were often added between sittings in rooms adjacent to the main studio — Reynolds being quite chary about allowing assistants to enter his own studio.

Several aspects of Reynolds's work in the 1760s distinguish it from the artist's practice during the previous decade. Most obvious, at least in female portraiture, was Reynolds's conspicuous preference for classical drapery. Whereas during the 1750s Reynolds had been content to portray women either in contemporary costume, masquerade attire, or in the ermine and velvet which accorded with their aristocratic title, he afforded himself far greater licence in the 1760s, either paring down dresses to their most abstract form or substituting them altogether with what he felt were timeless draperies — as in his portrayal of 'Lady Sarah Bunbury sacrificing to the Graces' (Plate 180), which was shown at the Society of Arts in 1765. This shift, so to speak, was in reality only a by-product of a more fundamental modification of Reynolds's outlook. In the 1760s Reynolds became increasingly fascinated in the ways in which portraiture could be used to convey information about a sitter's personality as well as his or her physical appearance. As this narrative element became more prominent in his work, he turned increasingly to Italian, and specifically Bolognese, classicism in his large public portraits, taking on board the monumental forms, purer colours and rhetorical gestures which are associated with that School. Smaller, and more intimate works, however, continued to convey the tenebrous forms engendered by a study of Rembrandt. On the whole it was not Reynolds's style but his *lack* of style which characterised his work at this time as sitters danced, flirted, embroidered, sacrificed to pagan deities, or merely meditated, in the manner of Guido Reni, Titian, Van Dyck or even Michelangelo.

One problem which continues to trouble admirers of Reynolds's portraiture is the identification of the various hands who contributed to his works. In truth, too little is still known about the day-to-day activities of those who worked in and around Reynolds's studio. Unlike its French equivalent, the *atelier,* a place in his studio guaranteed no pedagogical privileges. Pupils, assistants, and even drapery painters, had limited access to Reynolds's own studio and, as we know from the colourful accounts of James Northcote (who was resident as a pupil in Reynolds's home between 1771 and 1776), they often worked in cramped and unsatisfactory conditions. A large number of artists passed through Reynolds's studio, including, in the 1760s, Hugh Barron (1747-91) who, along with William Doughty (1757-82, in the studio in the mid-1770s), produced work most resembling that of his master. Another name associated with Reynolds's studio in the 1760s was Peter Toms (fl.1748-77), who had worked as his principal drapery painter since the mid-1750s before graduating to the studio of Francis Cotes around 1764. Finally there is Giuseppe Marchi (1735-1808), the young Italian whom Reynolds had befriended and brought back to England in 1752, and who remained with him (apart from a short stint in Wales in the late 1760s) until his death. For nearly forty years Marchi was the backroom-boy in Reynolds's studio, producing versions of popular pictures, painting draperies and even, after Reynolds's death, remedying the damage inflicted by his flawed technique.

By the 1760s Reynolds and Gainsborough both demonstrated a continual willingness to experiment — Gainsborough fitfully and instinctively, Reynolds regularly and dispassionately. And while Gainsborough looked back to tradition for particular pictorial effects, Reynolds, with characteristic ambition, sought to recapture the essence of entire philosophic systems. Those artists whom Gainsborough emulated — Van Dyck, Rubens, and later Watteau — were those with whom he had a natural sympathy, while although the artists whom Reynolds held up as paradigms were also ones he admired, they were, on the whole, those whom tradition had taught him to respect. Received wisdom which meant little to Gainsborough was the touchstone of Reynolds's art, and whereas Gainsborough painted largely to please himself Reynolds's main aim was to please others.

Aside from Reynolds and Gainsborough there are two other artists whose work achieved a new sense of maturity during the 1760s. They are the Scotsman Allan Ramsay and the London-born artist, Francis Cotes. Although the bulk of Ramsay's achievement was discussed in the previous chapter it is necessary to say something of his work in the 1760s, for it was during the years following his return from his second Italian sojourn in 1757 that Ramsay produced some of his finest work. On the accession of George III, Ramsay, through the machinations of his fellow-Scot the Earl of Bute, secured important royal patronage as well as the title of painter-in-ordinary to the King — a double-edged honour which, although it guaranteed prestige and financial security, also imposed a limit on the artist's freedom. Nonetheless, over the

PLATE 180
Joshua Reynolds
'Lady Sarah Bunbury sacrificing to the Graces', 1765
95½ x 60ins. (242 x 151.5cm)
(Art Institute of Chicago)

PLATE 181 (above)
Allan Ramsay
*Mrs. Dundas of Arniston,
1768*
29¼ x 24¼ ins.
(74.5 x 61.5cm)
(Sotheby's sale
12.7.1989, 44)

PLATE 182 (right)
Francis Cotes
*Lt.-Col. Alexander
Campbell, 1763*
50 x 40ins.
(127 x 101.5cm)
(Cawdor Castle)

next few years, Ramsay produced a superb series of female portraits including those of Martha, Countess of Elgin of 1762 (Earl of Elgin and Kincardine) and of Mrs. Dundas of Arniston (Plate 181). In these works, where the light is suffused softly over the sitter's face, Ramsay managed to combine a sensitivity for his subject with an aura of controlled reticence which, although it finds no equal in British portraiture at the time, is highly reminiscent of European counterparts such as Jean-Marc Nattier (1685-1766) and Alexandre Roslin (1718-93). Unlike Gainsborough or Reynolds — but like the above mentioned artists — Ramsay valued careful draughtsmanship in the preparation of his works and often produced preliminary drawings for portrait commissions. As a man as well as a painter, Ramsay was a far less public figure than Reynolds and compared to the often frank and full-blooded portrayals of femininity seen in the latter's work, Ramsay's women, withdrawn and contemplative, seem almost too insubstantial in an increasingly ebullient age. Ramsay's last signed works date from 1769. He continued to paint into the early 1770s although an injury to his right arm, sustained while carrying out a fire-drill in his Edinburgh home in 1773, all but curtailed his portrait practice. Although Ramsay gradually faded from view during the late 1760s it was he, rather than Reynolds, who provided the principal stimulus to one other major talent in portraiture at the time, Francis Cotes.

Francis Cotes died in 1770 aged only forty-five and as no biographer emerged then to record his achievement, he has remained an elusive figure. Indeed, as has been observed, Cotes's name was until quite recently a convenient label to pin to any decent Georgian portrait for which an author could not otherwise be found. Born in 1726, the elder brother of the miniaturist Samuel Cotes, Francis Cotes was apprenticed in the 1740s to George Knapton (1698-1778). It was, however, as a pastellist rather than an oil painter that he first earned a living, basing his style on continental artists, notably Rosalba Carriera (1675-1757), Maurice Quentin de La Tour (1704-89) and, particularly, Jean-Etienne Liotard (1702-89), whose work was important in shaping Cotes's 'realistic' approach to portraiture. Pastel was a medium prized on the Continent, and subsequently in England (Liotard worked in this country between 1753 and 1755), for its ability to provide a softer, more personal, record of the sitter. And Cotes's training in pastels, although it strictly belongs to an earlier period, is significant in forming an understanding of the prominence of pale pinks and blues in his oil portraits — especially during the early 1760s.

It was not until the late 1750s that Cotes emerged fully as a professional portrait painter in oils. Although there are indications by the early 1760s that he had looked closely at Reynolds, his work at this time still retained a marked independence — not to say idiosyncrasy, as, for example, in his portrait of Lieutenant-Colonel Alexander Campbell of 1763 (Plate 182). Despite the stark setting there is no attempt to portray Campbell as a man of valour. Indeed his quizzical gaze and the rather jaunty angle of the halberd which cuts diagonally across the picture plane lend an unexpectedly whimsical air to the work.

By 1763 Cotes had established himself in a spacious house in Cavendish Square (later occupied by Romney) which, like Reynolds at Leicester Fields, he remodelled to accommodate his expanding portrait business. He now was able to charge 80 guineas for a full-length portrait (less than Reynolds but more than Gainsborough). By this time, too, he had largely abandoned his decorative treatment of the sitter in favour of a more substantial and solid type of representation, the transition being amply evident in his 1764 portrait of Master Barwell (Colour Plate 35). As the discernible influence of Ramsay waned that of Reynolds grew. Oil painting rather than pastels now proved more lucrative and prestigious. By 1765 Cotes had risen to become a Director of the Incorporated Society of Artists, while by 1766 he was receiving, in preference to Reynolds, the patronage of George III. When Cotes turned to Reynolds for inspiration during this period it was generally in his full-length female portraits that he emulated the artist's use of the 'great style'. The parity between his own style and that of Reynolds in this department was intensified in the later 1760s when Cotes employed Peter Toms, Reynolds's drapery painter of ten years; Toms's hand (as a comparison with Reynolds's Lady Sarah Bunbury reveals) being evident, for example, in Cotes's portrait of a 'Lady as Terpsichore' (Plate 183). Although Toms, whose key role in the production of portraiture is reflected by his inclusion in the list of founder members of the Royal Academy, was successful while in the service of Reynolds and Cotes, he declined after the latter's death, taking his own life in 1777.

COLOUR PLATE 33
William Hoare
The Pitt Family, 1761
55 x 46½ins. (140 x 118cm)
This portrait by Gainsborough's only serious rival in Bath
highlights the rather formal and archaic elements of the artist's
style around the time of Gainsborough's arrival in Bath
(Private collection)

COLOUR PLATE 34
Thomas Gainsborough
The Dehany Family, c.1761-62
93 x 58ins. (236 x 147cm)
In comparison with his more personal studies,
with their broad, spontaneous brushstrokes,
Gainsborough's early commissioned portraits
are characterised by a tighter and more formal
approach
(Sotheby's sale 16.11.1988, 59)

COLOUR PLATE 35
Francis Cotes
Master Barwell, 1764
35 x 27¼ins. (89 x 69cm)
A transitional portrait — the artist has abandoned his decorative rococo treatment of
the sitter in favour of a more solid type of representation
(Sotheby's sale 18.11.1987)

PLATE 183 (above)
Francis Cotes
'Lady as Terpsichore',
c.1765
50 x 39½ins.
(127 x 100cm)
(Sotheby's sale
12.3.1986, 53)

PLATE 184 (right)
Robert Edge Pine
Mrs. Catherine Macaulay,
c.1770
50 x 40½ins.
(127 x 103cm)
(Christie's sale
22.11.1985, 121)

Before leaving portraitists who worked on the scale of life, a number of lesser but distinctive talents, each of whom achieved prominence in the 1760s, must be mentioned. The first of these is Robert Edge Pine (c.1730-88). Born in London, Pine had been working as a professional portraitist from the late 1740s, although his known works date from the early 1760s. Pine's portrait style is very competent although thoroughly idiosyncratic, his most interesting works unusually stemming from the least promising subjects — such as his unintentionally amusing portrayal of Mrs. Catherine Macaulay (Plate 184) where the po-faced subject leans wearily on five of the eight volumes of her monumental *History of England.* Pine was in many ways a frustrated history painter, his concern for narrative emerging through his interest in peopling his portraits with interested onlookers, as in his theatrical pieces or in his most celebrated portrait of the Duke of Northumberland laying the foundation stone of Middlesex Hospital (Middlesex Hospital, London), exhibited at the Society of Artists in 1761.

Another secondary, although pleasing, talent to emerge during this time was Tilly Kettle (1734/5-86). If Cotes cannot be correctly viewed as a follower of Reynolds, Kettle certainly can. Nonetheless, although he could successfully ape Reynolds, his most appealing work, as in his portrait of Colonel the Hon. Hugh Somerville (Colour Plate 36), reveals how his uncomplicated approach to composition and colour could combine to form a characteristically forthright and unpretentious image. A third noteworthy portraitist was Nathaniel Dance

(1735-1811). Although a pupil of Francis Hayman during the late 1740s it was in Rome, where Dance lived between 1754 and 1765, that he acquired his proficiency as a portrait painter. Indeed his work from that period is of some interest as it manages to combine the rather homely atmosphere of Hayman's cosy conversation pieces with the sleek and polished veneer of Batoni. On his return to England in 1766 Dance, on the strength of his Italian experience, quickly acquired a network of prominent patrons. Characteristic of his mature work is his portrait of Elizabeth, Lady Cooper with her four children (Colour Plate 37) where a polished 'Roman' finish is underpinned by typically solid draughtsmanship to give a highly competent if slightly stiff portrait. While on the subject of Nathaniel Dance it is worth mentioning Angelica Kauffmann (1741-1807) who had been close to Dance in Rome and who had returned with him to England. Although Kauffmann's later portraiture tends towards saccharine sweetness, as the influence of her decorative work intervened, for a brief period in the 1760s she demonstrated a highly developed and individual talent, as can be seen in her 1767 portrait of Joshua Reynolds (Plate 185). Here, in what is in every sense among her happiest achievements, Kauffmann somewhat improbably manages to convey the image of the future President of the Royal Academy as a moonstruck dilettante.

Finally, in this survey of some of the lesser lights of the 1760s portraiture, room must be found for the often overlooked, but highly creditable, Mason Chamberlin (1727-87). Although an exact contemporary of Gainsborough, Chamberlin often seems like a survival from an earlier age, his snug portraits of city burghers and their wives exhibiting the homely virtues to be found in the work of his master Francis Hayman. Although no stranger to the aristocracy, the best of Chamberlin is to be found in his numerous and very varied portrayals of the merchant and professional classes, such as his portrait of Mr. Crank (Colour Plate 38), where his no-nonsense approach to colour and composition produced one of the most agreeable and quietly confident images to be found during the period.

So far I have looked chiefly at portraits on the scale of life, not least because this format represents both the mainstream and, ultimately, the way forward in British portraiture during the second half of the eighteenth century. Nonetheless, it is important to look also at a quite different kind of portrait, namely the conversation piece which, as was seen in the previous chapter, provided the mainstay for so many artists earlier in the century. One artist who showed an interest in exploring the potential of the conversation piece was, as has been noted, Nathaniel Dance. His portrayals of Grand Tourists such as James Grant, Mr. Mytton, the Hon. Thomas Robinson and Mr. Wynn (Plate 186) demonstrate the strengths and weaknesses of the genre: on the one hand it was a compact and convenient record (Dance painted from versions — one for each sitter), on the other, it had a tendency to drift into staginess as sitters competed to affect an air of casual formality. Although Dance abandoned the conversation piece on his return to England, there were others who continued

COLOUR PLATE 36
Tilly Kettle
Col. the Hon. Hugh Somerville, before 1770
48½ x 35ins. (123.5 x 89cm)
Kettle's most appealing work shows an uncomplicated approach to composition and colour which combine to form a characteristically unpretentious image
(Sotheby's sale 13.7.1988, 49)

COLOUR PLATE 37
Nathaniel Dance
Elizabeth, Lady Cooper with her four children, c.1769
60½ x 50ins. (153 x 127cm)
A mature work in which solid draughtsmanship gives a highly competent if slightly
stiff portrait
(Private collection)

PLATE 185
Angelica Kauffmann
Joshua Reynolds, 1767
49 x 39ins. (124.5 x 99cm)
(National Trust: Saltram)

PLATE 186
Nathaniel Dance
James Grant, Mr. Mytton, the Hon. Thomas Robinson and
Mr. Wynn, c.1760
38⅝ x 43¾ins. (98 x 124cm)
(Yale Center for British Art: Paul Mellon Collection)

PLATE 187
Johan Zoffany
*'Mrs. Abington in . . . The
Way to Keep Him', 1768*
39½ x 49½ ins.
(100.5 x 125.5cm)
(National Trust:
Petworth Place)

to exploit its potential, among whom John Hamilton Mortimer, George
Stubbs, Francis Wheatley and most notably Johan Zoffany (1733-1810) are the
most important names.

In the same way that Reynolds may be said to have provided the benchmark
for large-scale portraiture during the 1760s so Zoffany — although his work
was by no means confined to this genre (see, for example, the stunning portrait
of his second wife, Mary Thomas, in the Ashmolean Museum, Oxford) —
may be said to have set new standards of excellence for the conversation piece.
Unlike the majority of English painters who aspired to paint history but were
confined through circumstances to paint portraiture, Zoffany began his career
in Germany as a decorative history painter. It was probably through his
experiences in Rome during the 1750s that he became aware of the career
opportunities in London, where he arrived in the autumn of 1760. After a
short spell as a stage painter his talent was spotted by David Garrick who took
him under his wing. It is not surprising, therefore, that during this decade
most of Zoffany's work was associated closely with the theatre, either group
portraits of Garrick and his circle or meticulously worked records of theatrical
productions, as in his portrayal of Reynolds's capricious favourite 'Mrs.
Abington in Arthur Murphy's *The Way to Keep Him*' of 1768 (Plate 187).
Already by 1764 Zoffany had attracted the patronage of the crown, producing
a series of informal royal tableaux — works which, as intimate records of the

COLOUR PLATE 38
Mason Chamberlin
Mr. Crank, c.1760
27¼ x 35¼ ins. (69.5 x 89.5cm)
Although an exact contemporary of Gainsborough, Chamberlin often seems like a
survivor from an earlier age with his snug portraits of city burghers and their wives
(Sotheby's sale 12.7.1989, 42)

COLOUR PLATE 39
Joshua Reynolds
Mrs. Elisha Mathew, 1777
93 x 57½ ins. (236 x 146cm)
Keen to emulate his fellow artists, especially those who posed the greatest threat, Reynolds carried out this portrait in the manner of Gainsborough with sumptuous silk draperies and expansive landscape
(Sotheby's sale 16.11.1988, 61)

COLOUR PLATE 40
George Romney
Anne Verelst, c.1771-72
92½ x 56¾ ins. (235 x 144cm)
Romney's work is here distinguished by its concern with 'finish' and its reserved statuesque quality
(With Colnaghi 1986)

unofficial aspect of the monarchy, find no equivalent until Landseer's royal portraits of the following century. Viewed as a whole, Zoffany's conversation pieces, typified by a work such as John, 14th Earl of Willoughby de Broke and his family (Plate 188), form the most detailed visual record of the domestic and social activities of the English upper classes in the eighteenth century. And yet their value as 'documents' often obscures Zoffany's other qualities such as his sure-footed approach to group composition and his gift for characterisation which at its best — as in 'The Tribuna of the Uffizi' (Plate 189) — displays a wit and invention surpassed only during the eighteenth century by Hogarth. Although Zoffany did not die until 1810, his direct influence on fellow artists was at its greatest in the years leading up to 1772, at which date he left England for a six year peregrination of the courts of Europe. He returned only briefly to England between 1779 and 1783 when he left for India, where he spent the remainder of the 1780s.

Francis Wheatley (1747-1810) was, in many ways, fortunate to attain maturity as an artist in 1772, at the exact same time Zoffany departed for Italy (ostensibly to paint the 'Tribuna' for Queen Charlotte). Wheatley's rise to a position of some eminence as a painter of conversation pieces demonstrates just how important it was for aspiring portrait painters to identify and fill gaps in the existing market. Wheatley's early conversation pieces demonstrate, in addition to an obvious debt to Zoffany, the benefits of the close working relationship he formed between 1771 and 1773 with John Hamilton Mortimer (with whom he carried out decorative work at Brocket Hall, Hertfordshire). Indeed, Wheatley's works of the early 1770s, such as his theatrical portrait of

PLATE 189
Johan Zoffany
'The Tribuna of the Uffizi'
(detail), 1772-c.78
48½ x 61ins.
(123.5 x 155cm)
(Royal Collection)

the 'Duel Scene from *Twelfth Night'* (Manchester City Art Galleries) of 1772, with its crisply delineated if rather wooden figures picked out against a wooden backdrop, owe more to Mortimer — at least stylistically — than Zoffany. As the 1770s went by Wheatley's art gained an air of increased sophistication, although in works such as the agreeable group portrait of the Oliver and Ward Families of 1778 (Plate 190) his new-found strengths are nonetheless undermined to a degree by his slightly uncomfortable handling of figurative composition — in this instance made manifest by the paradoxical lack of communication between the various participants of the conversation piece. Pleasing though Wheatley's works in this genre are, he produced little that Zoffany could not better. Although it has to be said that in a work such as his group in Clumber Park (Plate 191) he reveals an innate sympathy for the relationship between his sitters and their native landscape seldom seen in the work of his German counterpart.

Before leaving the conversation piece a word or two needs to be said about the relative contributions of Mortimer and Stubbs. John Hamilton Mortimer

COLOUR PLATE 41
Ozias Humphrey
'Ladies Waldegrave', 1780
89¾ x 57ins. (228.5 x 145cm)
Splendidly quixotic, the sisters stride purposefully across the heavens like a pair of predatory vamps; a contemporary review, however, referred to them as being 'exceedingly graceful'
(Sotheby's sale 18.11.1987, 50)

COLOUR PLATE 42
Thomas Gainsborough
Mrs. Martha Drummond, c.1779
49½ x 39½ ins. (126 x 100cm)
In this exquisite portrait Gainsborough has used his
skill in manipulating pigment to emphasise the more
ephemeral qualities of movement and passing shadows
(Sotheby's sale 16.11.1988, 57)

COLOUR PLATE 43
Thomas Gainsborough
The artist's wife, Margaret Gainsborough, c.1777
28 x 23½ ins. (71 x 59.5cm)
The late 1770s portrayals of his wife and daughters are
some of Gainsborough's most appealing works
(Sotheby's sale 5.7.1984, 274)

was, in terms of draughtsmanship, the most precocious talent to surface in the
British art world in the early 1760s. Having been in receipt of a sporadic
training under Hudson and Robert Edge Pine, Mortimer's abiding ambition
was to paint history. Like most artists, however, the bulk of his output
consisted — at least in the 1760s — of portraiture. Mortimer never visited Italy
and it is perhaps partly as a result of his lack of exposure to continental
influences that his figures, clustered around garden ornaments — as in his
portrait of the Witts Family of c.1769 (Plate 192) — or stationed across sparse
interiors, retain, in contrast to Zoffany, a rather earthy feel (although it has
to be said, by way of qualification, that as a colourist Mortimer was frequently
pedestrian). Earthiness is a quality also to be found in the small scale group
portraits of George Stubbs (1724-1806). Born in Liverpool, Stubbs moved to
London around 1759, although his pictorial inspiration remained firmly rooted

PLATE 190
Francis Wheatley
The Oliver and Ward Families, 1778
48 x 63ins. (122 x 159cm)
(Sotheby's sale 26.3.1975, 50)

PLATE 191
Francis Wheatley
*Henry Fiennes Pelham-
Clinton, 2nd Duke of
Newcastle, Col. Litchfield
and keepers in Clumber
Park, 1788*
61½ x 82½ ins. (156 x
208cm)
(Trustees of the 7th
Duke of Newcastle,
deceased)

PLATE 192
John Hamilton Mortimer
The Witts Family, c.1769
27 x 35½ins.
(68.5 x 90cm)
(Private collection)

in the English countryside. In his most characteristic portraits, such as his portrait of a 'Gentleman with a Chestnut Hunter' (Plate 193), Stubbs, through his use of muted yet warm colour, close tonal harmonies and immaculate sense of proportion, provided amongst the most satisfying images of this kind to be found in British portraiture.

The 1760s and early 1770s were marked by a diversity of styles and subject matter. The next twenty years, however, witnessed the emergence of one man — Sir Joshua Reynolds — as the dominant figure in British portraiture. As the period from 1769 to 1790 saw Reynolds's position change from that of *primus inter pares* to the self-proclaimed moderator of the indigenous artistic community, it is of some importance to examine the changes which his own work underwent during this period. In 1767 Reynolds chose for the first time not to exhibit at the annual exhibition of the Society of Artists. His reasons were explained by Edmund Burke to his protégé, James Barry, in the following manner: 'Reynolds, though he has I think, some better portraits than he ever before painted, does not think mere heads sufficient and having no piece of fancy sends in nothing this time'. By the late 1760s Reynolds considered that a distinction could be drawn between what he termed the 'cold painter of portraits' and the artist in whose portraits an element of 'fancy' or imagination was evident. Over the next twenty years Reynolds's concentration on introducing a variety of imaginative devices into his portraits — in order that they might transcend the limits of their own genre — was the single most important aspect of his outlook as a portrait painter. The capturing of likeness which was, as he himself admitted, the most sought after by the sitter, was in

PLATE 193
George Stubbs
*'Gentleman with a Chestnut
Hunter', 1768*
24 x 28ins. (61 x 71cm)
(Sotheby's sale
14.3.1990, 130)

Reynolds's eyes of secondary importance. He boasted to his pupil James
Northcote that he could teach any boy who came to his studio how to paint a
'likeness' in six months. Indeed, from the foundation of the Royal Academy
in 1769 until his death in 1792 Reynolds's portraits were consistently praised
less for the likeness which they bore to the sitter than for the way in which the
artist brought out qualities which the sitter possessed or aspired towards.

In 1769 — the first year in which an annual exhibition was held at the Royal
Academy of Arts — Reynolds showed a picture entitled 'Hope Nursing Love'
(Plate 194). The painting was unusual in several ways. First, the artist, despite
the recognisability of the sitter (a young actress named Miss Morris), chose to
exhibit it as a subject picture. Secondly, although it was the portrait of an
actress (there are several versions), Reynolds, rather than seeking to record a
specific stage performance as was the norm, concentrated on the general
characteristics of his subject — in this case the tenderness of Miss Morris (who
was at the time making an ill-starred début as the eponymous heroine of
Shakespeare's *Romeo and Juliet*). Finally, Reynolds addressed the intellect of his
audience as well as its senses, as he 'elevated' the image via a reference to a
well known pictorial precedent (namely Michaelangelo's 'Leda' whose attitude
is closely shadowed by Miss Morris's pose). Thus through this picture
Reynolds raised a whole series of ambiguities about the very nature of
portraiture.

Reynolds's own intellectual stature was, of course, strengthened during the

PLATE 194
Joshua Reynolds
'Hope Nursing Love', 1769
50 x 39ins. (139.5 x 112cm)
(Private collection)

PLATE 195
Joshua Reynolds
Lady Cockburn and her children, 1774
55 x 44ins. (139.5 x 112cm)
(National Gallery, London)

215

1770s by the *Discourses* which he delivered annually — and later bienially — at the Royal Academy. And although history painting was the focal point of the *Discourses,* portraiture was by no means overlooked. In his fifth *Discourse* of 1772, for example, Reynolds reiterated his ideas on likeness noting how 'it is very difficult to ennoble the character but at the expense of likeness, which is what is most generally required by such as sit to the painter'. Although portraiture by its very nature was concerned with individuals, Reynolds could not resist the desire to categorise his subjects: 'the very peculiarities', as he noted in his eleventh *Discourse,* 'may be reduced to classes and general descriptions, and there are therefore large ideas to be found even in this contracted subject'. Reynolds's propensity for generalisation found expression in all aspects of his art during the 1770s; his dispensation with contemporary clothing in female sitters in favour of more timeless classical draperies; his impatience with detail; his broadly applied brushstrokes; his bold use of colour; and most contentiously, his tendency to feed his imagination on the compositional devices of others. All these features emerge in a work such as the portrait of Lady Cockburn and her three eldest children of 1774 (Plate 195), which gives us a much clearer idea of Reynolds's natural affinity with the colourists of the Venetian school. It was as a result of seeing this picture, and works such as 'The Montgomery Sisters adorning a Term of Hymen' (Tate Gallery), that the *London Chronicle* was moved to pronounce on 10 May 1774 that 'while some Artists paint only to this age and this nation, he paints to all ages and all nations'.

As the 1770s went on, one of the most striking characteristics of Reynolds's portraiture was the manner in which the artist combined elements of formal grandeur with more spontaneous and light-hearted touches, as in the beautifully understated three-quarter-length portrait of Richard Crofts (Plate 196), or the playful full-length of Mrs. Lloyd of 1776, where the slender and berobed subject is shown mischievously carving her initials on a tree trunk. On the whole Reynolds was much happier in these single figure compositions than in more complex group compositions such as the two pictures of the Dilettanti Society of 1777-79 (Society of Dilettanti) where the problems of producing a multi-figured work in which each sitter required equal prominence resulted in a somewhat stilted and cramped composition. Nonetheless, it must be said that in the group portrait of the family of the 4th Duke of Marlborough of the same period (Plate 197), Reynolds, by reflecting the hierarchy of the family structure in the configuration of his composition (the level of formality being varied according to the age and sex of each sitter), proved that large, complex, compositions were not entirely beyond his capabilities. Indeed, in this group portrait Reynolds successfully managed to combine the seemingly incompatible strands of British portraiture, namely the spontaneous humour found in Hogarth's Graham Children (Colour Plate 2) with the grandeur reminiscent of Van Dyck's Pembroke Family (Wilton House).

Although the concern here is primarily with Reynolds's own work as a

PLATE 196
Joshua Reynolds
Richard Crofts, 1775
52 x 46ins.
(132 x 117cm)
(Sotheby's sale
16.11.1988, 69)

portrait painter, his approach to this genre cannot be considered without at least mentioning the role played in his art by the reproductive print. Since the late 1750s Reynolds had used the print as a means of advertising his work, and he was in the habit of loaning portraits to mezzotinters (such as James McArdell, Edward Fisher and James Watson) almost certainly free of charge. The mezzotint, with its rich velvety texture and generalising effect, was particularly conducive to the bold patterns and broad tonal range to be found in Reynolds's portraits. The very fact that Reynolds's portraits could be interpreted as types rather than merely as portrayals of specific individuals, meant that they could serve a wider market than might have otherwise been the case. Indeed there was a growing paradox during the 1770s and 1780s, in that just as Reynolds had borrowed motifs from Old Masters in order to elevate his portraits, so figures were taken from his own works — especially

PLATE 197
Joshua Reynolds
The Marlborough Family,
1778
125 x 114ins.
(317.5 x 289.5cm)
(Red Drawing Room:
Blenheim Palace)

of children — and placed in entirely new contexts by engravers of popular prints. Thus, for example, Reynolds's portrait of Lady Melbourne and her son, exhibited at the Royal Academy in 1773, was engraved by Dickinson with the title 'Maternal Affection', while Master Hare (Louvre) of 1788 emerged in print form two years later as 'Infancy'.

Reynolds, although we are often inclined to see him as setting the pace for his rivals and influencing their style, was also known to emulate his fellow artists — especially those who posed the greatest threat to his own practice. It explains why, for example, his portrait of Jane Fleming, Countess of Harrington of c.1777-78 (Plate 198), with its air of cool and polished grandeur, bears an uncanny resemblance to the kind of neo-classical concoction being produced at that time by George Romney, or why his portrait of Mrs. Elisha Mathew (shown at the Academy in 1777), with its sumptuous silk draperies and expansive landscape background (Colour Plate 39), is an unmistakable exercise in the manner of Thomas Gainsborough. Although by the late 1770s Reynolds was willing to countenance contemporary dress in his female full-

PLATE 198
Joshua Reynolds
Jane Fleming, Countess of Harrington, c.1778-79
93 x 57ins.
(236 x 145cm)
(Henry E. Huntington
Library and Art
Gallery, San Marino,
California)

PLATE 199 (above)
Joshua Reynolds
'Thais', 1781
90¼ x 57ins.
(229 x 145cm)
(National Trust:
Waddesdon Manor)

PLATE 200 (right)
Joshua Reynolds
'Mrs. Siddons as the Tragic Muse', 1784
93 x 56ins.
(236 x 142cm)
(Henry E. Huntington Library and Art Gallery, San Marino, California)

length portraits (fortunately this had never posed a problem in his grand portraits of male counterparts — some sort of uniform usually being to hand), he nonetheless continued in his most ambitious projects to follow the dictates of his own imagination. In 'Thais', for example, exhibited at the Royal Academy in 1781 (Plate 199), which was — quite literally — a thinly veiled portrayal of a well-known prostitute called Emily Pott, Reynolds deliberately cloaked the sitter in loose flowing robes in order to underline the classical allusion, implicit in the picture's title, to the mistress of Alexander the Great. (Although Reynolds could get away with it here, the display of quite so much leg would have been shocking in conventional society portraiture.) Similarly, in Reynolds's greatest portrait of the 1780s, 'Mrs. Siddons as the Tragic Muse' (Plate 200) of 1784, the artist clothed the sitter in voluminous folds of dark brown drapery in order that any remembrance of Mrs. Siddon's off-stage persona might be erased and that the elision of fact and fantasy could be made more palpable.

PLATE 201
Joshua Reynolds
*The Prince of Wales (later
George IV), 1784*
94 x 105ins.
(239 x 266cm)
(Private collection)

In 1784 Reynolds was, on the death of Allan Ramsay, made painter-in-ordinary to the King. It was not an honour which he ostensibly coveted (the salary was £50 per annum, less, Reynolds remarked, than George III's rat catcher earned). For the most part Reynolds's royal commissions were dispatched with little ceremony, being treated as routine exercises for assistants. He did, however, produce at least one royal portrait of considerable merit — that of the Prince of Wales exhibited at the Royal Academy in 1784 (Plate 201), in which the future George IV is depicted improbably reining-in his grey charger on the field of battle. Of his late works Reynolds's various portrayals of martial valour were among his best works. Among the finest of these is his 1789 depiction of the ageing naval hero, Admiral Rodney (Plate 202) who, while his physical frailty is not disguised, retains an air of authority, his angular profile silhouetted against a lowering sky. Despite the power invested in a number of Reynolds's late portraits there is, nevertheless, during the last decade of the artist's working life a far less dogmatic air about much of his portraiture. To an extent this can be accounted for by Reynolds's increased interest in the art of northern Europe — particularly his 'discovery' of Rubens in visits to the Low Countries in 1781 and again, briefly, in 1784. From this time, especially with regard to the way in which the artist handled paint, Reynolds allowed himself a far greater degree of spontaneity than he had

PLATE 202
Joshua Reynolds
Admiral Rodney, 1788-89
93 x 57ins. (236 x 145cm)
(Royal Collection)

222

PLATE 203 (left)
Joshua Reynolds
Penelope Boothby, 1788
28½ x 24ins. (72.5 x 61cm)
(Private collection: on loan to the
Ashmolean Museum, Oxford)

PLATE 204 (above)
Detail of Reynolds's portrait of Penelope
Boothby showing the weave of the canvas
through the thinly impasted face

hitherto, particularly in his child portraits of the late 1780s. Here, as in the
remarkably candid Penelope Boothby of 1788 (Plate 203), Reynolds manages
at once to be genuinely affecting and yet completely devoid of sentimentality.
This picture is, unlike so many of Reynolds's earlier works, a complete
technical success, having been executed rapidly and for the most part thinly
impasted (the weave of the canvas remains clearly visible through the sitter's
face, Plate 204).

Before leaving Reynolds something more needs to be said about his flawed
technique, not least because it is this aspect of his art which makes his paintings
at times so instantly recognisable. One claim made by his apologists, which we
find today most difficult to accept, is Reynolds's talent as a colourist since so
many of his pictures having been ravaged by the passage of time. His problems
actually started as early as the 1750s, the faces in a number of portraits from
that period now often exhibiting a chalky, washed-out look due to his habitual
use of fugitive red pigments, carmine and lake, in the flesh tones, rather than
vermilion, as was the standard practice. His use too at that time of orpiment,
an unstable yellow pigment, resulted not only in the dulling of the light areas
but also in a whole series of laboured jokes in the press about Reynolds coming

PLATE 205 (above)
William Doughty
Portrait of a lady, called
'Mrs. Gore', c.1780
30 x 24¾ins.
(76 x 63cm)
(Sotheby's sale
20.11.1985, 53)

PLATE 206 (right)
James Northcote
Henry Fuseli, 1778
30 x 24¾ins.
(76 x 63cm)
(National Portrait
Gallery, London)

off with 'flying colours'. During the 1760s more serious flaws emerged as Reynolds's technique became increasingly adventurous (he was not above scraping down the odd Old Master in order to discover how it was painted). In imitation of Venetian artists, Reynolds painted on unprimed canvas, at times employing incompatible mixtures of oils and varnishes, waxes, gums and beaten egg white, materials which, if used correctly, might have enriched his works but which all too often only hastened their decline. Finally, from the early 1770s, Reynolds worked increasingly with asphaltum, a brown, tarry pigment which, although it could lend a golden glow to a painting, was also capable of caking and coagulating to give the appearance of cold gravy, as one can easily see in the background of his portrait of Lord Heathfield of 1788 (National Gallery, London).

Reynolds's influence on his peers during the 1770s and 1780s was extensive. Nevertheless the full impact of his style was only felt in the period following his death, as one can see, for example, in the art of Beechey and Thomas Lawrence. Although these artists belong to the following chapter there are a number of other painters who emulated Reynolds during his lifetime and who should be commented upon briefly. Those artists closest to Reynolds in style were, as one might expect, those who worked in his studio. Among these the most prominent are James Northcote, Hugh Barron and William Doughty. Of these artists, Barron, who worked in Reynolds's studio from 1764-66, was potentially the most gifted painter, although, despite early promise, he seems to have preferred to pursue his interests as a musician. William Doughty, following an 'apprenticeship' to Reynolds between 1775 and 1778, practised as a portrait painter for a while in London and Ireland during the late 1770s, his so-called Mrs. Gore (Plate 205) showing just how close he could approach Reynolds's own style. Nonetheless — and this demonstrates how talent alone was insufficient grounds for building a portrait practice in eighteenth-century England — Doughty failed to establish himself independently and died on his way to India aged only twenty-five. It was only Northcote, of all Reynolds's pupils, who managed to carve out something approaching a successful career, even though today his fame, such as it is, rests on his being Reynolds's fly-on-the-wall biographer rather than on the ambitious but vapid history paintings on which he prided himself. Northcote was at times capable of producing a strong image and was at his best in bust-length studies of male sitters, such as his series of the Yonge family of 1776, or his striking portrait of Henry Fuseli (Plate 206).

Of greater interest than any of Reynolds's pupils are two artists — John Opie and John Hoppner — who, although they served no apprenticeship with Reynolds, were influenced heavily by him during the 1780s. Although the bulk of their work will be discussed in the following chapter, they deserve at least a mention here, as in both cases it is fair to say that some of their best work derives from the 1780s. John Hoppner (1758-1810) began exhibiting at the Royal Academy in 1780, at which time the overriding contemporary influence on his art was Reynolds — whose Whig patrons he also courted assiduously. At his best Hoppner was a vibrant and daring colourist, as in, for example, his portrait of Mrs. Sophia Burrell (Plate 207); at worst, he exhibits a slapdash carelessness which only caricatures Reynolds's bravura style. John Opie (1761-1807), although not exposed to fashionable London society as the 'Cornish Wonder' by his self-styled mentor, John Wolcot, until 1781, had been working as an artist since the mid-1770s. Opie was at his creative best during the 1780s when he combined a sensitivity towards characterisation reminiscent of Reynolds with his innate earthiness and a keenly developed understanding of chiaroscuro, as in the portrait of John Wolcot (Plate 208). At this time Opie's painterliness, allied to his direct manner, are reminiscent of his Scottish contemporary Sir Henry Raeburn (1756-1823) although, unlike the latter, whose often blunt portrait manner worked well for his northern sitters, Opie was increasingly restricted by the strictures of his fashionable London clientele for whom flattery was a desideratum. Far more accommodating in this area, aside from Reynolds (who preferred to flatter his audience's intelligence), was the Cumbrian-born painter George Romney.

Romney (1734-1802) arrived in London in 1762. Born in the small lakeland town of Kendal, Romney's early working life had been spent in the train of the itinerant and still underestimated artist Christopher Steele (1733-67). From Steele he picked up a precise oil technique and Steele's influence is to be found in Romney's works of the 1760s, as in his portrait of George Morewood (Plate 209) which, in its neat, prosy style is reminiscent also of Nathaniel Dance. By

PLATE 208
John Opie
John Wolcot, c.1780
19½ x 15½ ins. (49.5 x 39.5cm)
(National Portrait Gallery, London)

PLATE 207
John Hoppner
Mrs. Sophia Burrell,
c.1782
35 x 26¾ ins.
(89 x 68cm)
(Private collection)

the mid-1760s, Romney was not only technically a very sound painter but also one who showed considerable individuality and invention, as one can see in the portrait of his brothers, Peter and James Romney, shown at the Free Society of Artists in 1766, where portraiture and genre painting are brought thoughtfully together (Plate 210). And yet even before his visit to Italy between 1773 and 1775, Romney's work is distinguished from Reynolds's by its far greater concern with 'finish' and its reserved, statuesque quality. Although Reynolds and Romney remained distinctive as artists (the influence of Reynolds, if anything, was only detrimental to Romney's style), Reynolds resented Romney's presence in the capital for several reasons. First, Romney, quite independently from Reynolds, thoroughly understood how to unite elements of high art to portraiture, not only by way of reference to classical statuary or the Old Masters, but also by a keen awareness of how the principles of neo-classicism could be applied to contemporary portraiture. Secondly, Romney had nothing to do with the Royal Academy, neither exhibiting his work there nor aspiring towards membership. And while this could be viewed as an advantage for Reynolds in that it reduced the competition, it also undermined his stance by demonstrating that the Academy was quite

irrelevant to the needs of a successful British artist. Thirdly, and most ignominiously for Reynolds, Romney poached his sitters. In 1776 Romney, moved into Cotes's old house in Cavendish Square (Reynolds, who could not bear to refer to him by name referred to him simply as 'the man in Cavendish Square'). Just how Romney's style had developed since his return from Italy can be seen by a comparison between his portrait of Anne Verelst of c.1771-72 (Colour Plate 40) and the magnificent portrait of the children of the Earl of Gower of c.1776-77 (Plate 211) in which the artist's capacity to create crisply contoured forms, reminiscent of bas-relief sculpture, are softened by his ability to convey movement through and across a pictorial space.

Romney's art reached a peak of sophistication during the late 1770s, although it was not until 1781 that he met the sitter whose name is most consistently associated with him — Emma Hart, later wife of Sir William Hamilton and lover of Horatio Nelson. Romney's pictures of Emma, although numerous, cannot be counted among his best work, although in portraits such as 'Lady Hamilton at Prayer' (English Heritage: Kenwood House), where the quasi-erotic languor of sainted womanhood emerges forcibly, one gains some impression of the mesmeric effect this sitter had on her male contemporaries. Romney's ambitious portrayals of Emma during the 1780s (for example Plate

PLATE 211
George Romney
*The children of the Earl of
Gower, 1776-77*
80 x 91¼ ins.
(203 x 232cm).
(Abbot Hall Art Gallery,
Kendal)

212) do, however, form an instructive comparison with the muses Reynolds painted for the west window of New College Chapel, and a work such as Ozias Humphrey's splendid and quixotic 'Ladies Waldegrave' (Colour Plate 41) of 1780 where the two sisters stride purposefully across the heaven like a pair of predatory vamps. (Their mother strongly disapproved of their being shown with bare feet.)

Besides Reynolds and Romney (who, in the 1780s, plagued by various neuroses, increasingly retreated into the world of his own imagination), two other important artists — Benjamin West (1738-1820) and James Barry (1741-1806) — evinced an interest in historical portraiture. Although Benjamin West's reputation rests chiefly on his work as a history painter, he was an accomplished if uneven portraitist. Among his most attractive portraits are those of his wife and young family, such as that of Mrs. West with Raphael

PLATE 212 (left)
George Romney
Emma Hart, 1786
59 x 47¾ins.
(150 x 121.5cm)
(Private collection)

PLATE 213 (above)
Benjamin West
*Mrs. West with Raphael
West, before 1770*
30 x 25ins.
(76 x 63.5cm)
(Collection of the
Marquis of Lothian)

West (Plate 213) which shows a dependence (although it is by no means a servile imitation) on Raphael's Madonna della Sedia. West's public historical portraits are less satisfying, and whereas Reynolds could carry off allegorical allusions through sheer bravado, West's efforts in this direction, such as the marvellously dotty marriage portrait of Mr. and Mrs. John Custance of 1778 (Plate 214) verge on the ridiculous. West, despite his ambitious exercises in high art, lacked imagination and consequently his best works as a portraitist are those which demand the least artifice. His single male portraits, particularly his quiet but dramatic portrayals of military figures, for example Sir John Griffin Griffin of 1772 (Plate 215) demonstrate where his true talent lay. If West lacked imagination, James Barry was possessed of a surfeit of riches in this area. Barry was the artist in whom Reynolds, around 1770, had placed his greatest confidence, and yet who, by the end of the decade, had become his arch-enemy. To Barry historical portraiture, such as Reynolds practised, seemed degenerate, for rather than raising the portrait to the level of history it merely caricatured high art by introducing it into the boudoir. And yet, despite his vaunted contempt for portraiture, Barry could, when moved, produce works of the highest calibre. Witness, for example, the portraits of his mentor Edmund Burke and his relations of the late 1760s and early 1770s, such as Burke's brother-in-law John Nugent (Plate 216) where his use of dramatic lighting and inventive pose reveal a lack of patience with the strictures imposed by the conventions of society portraiture. For Barry the portrait was a window

PLATE 214
Benjamin West
*Mr. and Mrs. John
Custance, 1778*
60⁵/₁₆ x 84⅝ ins.
(153 x 215cm)
(Nelson-Atkins Museum
of Art, Kansas City,
Missouri)

to the soul, and this, not surprisingly, is seen most tellingly in his own self-portraits (Plate 217). Unlike Reynolds's self-portraits, where the artist seems confident in his powers and in his place in society, Barry's perception of himself, as revealed here, is combative and threatening. The artist is hemmed in by icons of the past, wishing to respond yet frustrated, both by the scale of his task and by his personal entrapment in a mundane, modern world.

Barry, in his heroic disenchantment with the limitations of portraiture, was in a minority as most artists welcomed the increased kudos enjoyed by the genre during the latter part of the eighteenth century. A sharp contrast can be drawn, for example, between Barry and the equally inventive, but far more flexible, Joseph Wright (1734-97). Wright, who was some seven years older than Barry, has a claim to be among the most genuinely creative — and most consistently underestimated — painters to emerge in the second half of the eighteenth century.

In terms of his personal friendships Joseph Wright's closest ally was probably John Hamilton Mortimer, with whom he was on intimate terms until the untimely death of the latter in 1778. And yet in terms of his career a closer parallel exists between Wright and his exact contemporary, George Romney.

PLATE 215 (above left)
Benjamin West
Sir John Griffin Griffin, c.1772
67 x 51ins. (170 x 129.5cm)
(English Heritage: Audley End)

PLATE 216 (above)
James Barry
John Nugent, c.1771-72
30 x 25ins. (76 x 63.5cm)
(Private collection)

PLATE 217
James Barry
Self-portrait as Timanthes, c.1780
30 x 25ins. (76 x 63cm)
(National Gallery of Ireland, Dublin)

PLATE 218
Joseph Wright
Mrs. William Pigot, 1760
49 x 39ins.
(124.5 x 99cm)
(Private collection)

Like Romney and Mortimer, Wright practised outside the sphere of the Royal
Academy. His early years also resemble Romney's, as he made his living as
an itinerant provincial portrait painter. Unlike Romney, however, Wright did
not gravitate towards London, developing his style instead entirely beyond the
confines of the metropolis — the only major portraitist of his generation
besides Gainsborough to do so. Wright's only sojourns in London were
between 1751 and 1753 and again in 1756-57 when, like Mortimer (and
Reynolds before him), he served some sort of intermittent apprenticeship with
Hudson. It is Hudson's hard edged style which predominates in Wright's
works of the early 1760s, where smooth skinned women pose rather stiffly in
silk masquerade costumes, as for example in his portrait of Mrs. William Pigot
(Plate 218). Such works, however, give little idea of the true potential of

PLATE 219
Joseph Wright
*Peter Burdett and his first
wife Hannah, 1765*
57 x 80½ ins.
(145 x 205cm)
(National Gallery,
Prague)

Wright, whose talent exploded like a bombshell in the mid-1760s, most notably in a remarkable series of virtuosi performances such as 'The Orrery' (Derby Museum and Art Gallery) of 1766 and 'The Experiment with an Airpump' (National Gallery, London) of 1768, works which count as amongst the most mesmeric images in British art. Although these pictures cannot be classed strictly as portraits (even though several sitters in both works are identifiable as friends of the artist) a contrast can be made between them and more conventional group portraiture. Here the artist, taking as his influence the Dutch and Flemish followers of Carravaggio, supplanted the externally imposed social niceties by a more empathetic spirit of enquiry, as the subjects, rather than being passive participants, absorb themselves in an activity quite independent of, and on an equal status to, the artist. Indeed it is Wright's unwillingness to accept ready-made formulae which lend a disconcerting vitality to his portraits, as in his breathtaking double portrayal of Peter Burdett and his first wife Hannah, of 1765 (Plate 219). Even in seemingly conventional subject matter, such as his portrayal of Miss Bentley holding a rabbit (Plate 220), Wright produced sensitive images which transcended the norm. Between 1773 and 1775 Wright visited Italy (he was there at the same time as Romney), returning, after a brief and disappointing spell in Bath, to his native Derby in

233

PLATE 220
Joseph Wright
Miss Bentley holding a rabbit, c.1778
51 x 39½ins. (129.5 x 100cm)
(Christie's New York sale 15.1.1988, 144)

PLATE 221
Joseph Wright
Mr. and Mrs. Thomas Gisbourne, 1786
73 x 60ins. (185.5 x 152.5cm)
(Yale Center for British Art: Paul Mellon
Collection)

1777. Although by this time his range of interests was broad, and encompassed history, fancy pictures and industrial landscape, commissioned portraiture remained an important aspect of his practice. Indeed his most radical and innovative portraits can be dated to the late 1780s such as the double portrait of Mr. and Mrs. Thomas Gisbourne of 1786 (Plate 221).

Wright, partly because he is so difficult to classify and partly because of his being cast unfairly in the role of a provincial painter, remains underestimated as a portrait painter. Another who continues to suffer from under-exposure is the American-born artist John Singleton Copley. Copley (1738-1815) was of the same generation as Wright and, in his capacity for pictorial inventiveness and for exploring the possibilities of genres, he comes closer to him than any other artist of the period. Copley, although he is commonly viewed as an artist of a later period, had been seen in England as early as 1766, when he had exhibited annually, from his base in Boston, at the Society of Artists. Following his emigration from America in 1774, Copley, after a brief but formative tour of Europe, settled in London. From 1776 onwards — although his previous work gives no clue — he revealed in his exhibited pictures a considerable talent for organising quite complex figure groupings, an ability which stemmed from his practice (surprisingly unusual at the time in England) of working out his designs on squared-up sheets of paper which were then transferred to larger

PLATE 222
John Singleton Copley
The Sitwell Family, 1786
61½ x 71ins.
(156 x 180.5cm)
(Private collection)

canvases. His skill in this direction, allied to a fluent and polished technique, resulted in his rapid advancement. His society portraits, sparkling and innovative though they can be, as in the idiosyncratic Sitwell Family of 1786 (Plate 222), do not represent the high point of Copley's *oeuvre;* this place is reserved for his most original contribution to portraiture — the 'documentary' portrait, works such as the monumental 'Siege of Gibraltar' (Guildhall Art Gallery, London), which took a contemporary event and couched it in the language of high art. In this respect, too, his more straightforward works such as the portrait of Hugh Montgomerie, later 12th Earl of Eglinton (Plate 223) form the most successful realisation of Reynolds's aspirations for portraiture on a truly heroic scale.

Wright, Copley and other major talents mentioned, who emerged in the 1770s and 1780s, were of considerable significance not only in their own right but in the way in which they provided an alternative to the tradition-tied stance

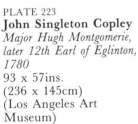

PLATE 223
John Singleton Copley
*Major Hugh Montgomerie,
later 12th Earl of Eglinton,
1780*
93 x 57ins.
(236 x 145cm)
(Los Angeles Art
Museum)

PLATE 224
Thomas Gainsborough
Jonathan Buttall — 'The Blue Boy', c.1770
70 x 48ins. (178 x 122cm)
(Henry E. Huntington Library and Art Gallery, San
Marino, California)

of Reynolds and his followers. And yet to redefine the boundaries of portraiture by dramatisation of its subjects in the course of their own activities was, of course, only one means of exploring its potential. Another alternative, and that taken by Thomas Gainsborough, was to accept given patterns of portraiture, whilst transforming them by continually addressing, in an empirical manner, a series of formal issues. It is therefore, at this point that I should like to conclude, with an assessment of the stylistic development of Thomas Gainsborough during the period 1770 to 1788.

In 1768 Gainsborough had been invited to become a founder member of the Royal Academy. It was an honour which he accepted with a marked lack of enthusiasm. His absence from Zoffany's 'Academicians' (although Zoffany did make a preparatory oil sketch of his head) is symptomatic of his abiding indifference towards the broader aims of that organisation. (In 1772 he had noted with characteristic irony how his Royal Academy Diploma 'sign'd with the King's own hand' was 'most beautifully framed & hung in my Painting-Room, *behind the door'.*) From the outset Gainsborough was sceptical of

PLATE 225
Thomas Gainsborough
*Elizabeth and Mary Linley,
1772*
78⅜ x 60¼ ins.
(199 x 153cm)
(Dulwich Picture
Gallery, London)

Reynolds's high-flown ambitions for portraiture, as he told Lord Dartmouth in a letter of April 1771: 'I shall', he commented, 'remain an ignorant fellow to the end of my days, because I never could have the patience to read Poetical impossibilities, the very food of a Painter; especially if he intends to be KNIGHTED in this land of Roast Beef, so well do serious people love froth'. Gainsborough's professed ideas on portraiture were in every sense the antithesis of Reynolds's own beliefs. For whereas Reynolds, at least up to the late 1770s, preferred not to dress his female sitters in contemporary costume, Gainsborough delighted to dwell on the texture of costly fabrics, and while

PLATE 226 (above)
Thomas Beach
Julie Keasberry, 1782
62 x 55ins.
(158 x 140cm)
(Sotheby's sale
12.3.1980, 138)

PLATE 227 (right)
Thomas Gainsborough
*Penelope, Viscountess
Ligonier, 1770*
94½ x 62ins.
(240 x 158cm)
(Henry E. Huntington
Library and Art
Gallery, San Marino,
California)

Reynolds employed the services of a ménage of pupils and assistants, Gainsborough, with the exception of his nephew Gainsborough Dupont (1754-97), disdained any help in painting draperies. Indeed it was an aspect of portrait painting which he professed to enjoy more than actual face painting. Finally, although Reynolds held 'mere likeness' in low esteem, Gainsborough considered it as the 'principal beauty and intention of a Portrait'.

In 1772 Gainsborough, in a letter to a client whose portrait he was late in delivering, noted as his excuse that he was 'obliged to cobble up something for the Exhibition or else (so far from being knighted) I should have been expel'd [from] the Society...' Rather than allowing us to imagine that Gainsborough was unconcerned about showing at the Academy, this note reveals just how keen he was (especially via its sly dig at Reynolds's knighthood) to compete in public. Already in 1770 Gainsborough had exhibited what is, justifiably, among his best known works, his uncommissioned portrait of Jonathan Buttall — better known as 'The Blue Boy' (Plate 224). This work, which signalled a more thoughtful approach to the question of colour in portraiture (it was unusual to produce a portrait which deliberately omitted any 'warm' colours), also signified the artist's deepening fascination for the art of Van Dyck. A second development of the early 1770s was the heightened mood of

PLATE 228 (left)
Thomas Gainsborough
Sophia Charlotte, Lady Sheffield, 1785
89½ x 58¾ ins.
(227.5 x 149cm)
(National Trust: Waddesdon Manor)

PLATE 229 (above)
Thomas Gainsborough
Carl Friedrich Abel, 1777
88 x 58ins.
(223.5 x 147.5cm)
(Henry E. Huntington Library and Art Gallery, San Marino, California)

romanticism, as is evident in his double portrait of 1772 of the Linley sisters (Plate 225), where looser handling is used both to bring out the ethereal qualities of his sitters and to unite them more fully to their landscape setting.

In 1774 Gainsborough moved his household and studio to London — leaving Bath to Reynolds's erstwhile pupil Thomas Beach (1738-1806) who continued until the end of the century to make a steady living in the south-west with his frank and highly competent portrait style (Plate 226). Exactly what effect Gainsborough's move to London had on his own outlook is hard to say. Certainly, it brought him into contact with a wide cross-section of sitters and a more consistent exposure to the art of others — both contemporaries and Old Masters. Gainsborough's residence in a predominantly urban environment seems also to have intensified his poetic response towards landscape which his memory taught him to see increasingly through rose-tinted spectacles. In terms of his attitude towards portraiture, Gainsborough's close physical proximity to Reynolds evidently decided him to move deliberately in directions his main rival could not follow. Whereas, for example, Gainsborough had been willing in a portrait such as that of Penelope, Viscountess Ligonier, of 1770 (Plate 227), to produce a solid monumental image of womanhood, the type of which Reynolds was so fond, he now used his skill in manipulating pigment to

PLATE 230
Thomas Gainsborough
*Henry Frederick, Duke of
Cumberland with his wife,
formerly Mrs. Horton,
attended by Lady Elizabeth
Luttrell, c.1783-85*
64½ x 49ins.
(164 x 124.5cm)
(Royal Collection:
Windsor Castle)

emphasise the more ephemeral qualities of movement and passing shadows, as in his exquisite portrayal of Mrs. Martha Drummond of c.1779, where paint is applied with an almost gossamer-like touch (Colour Plate 42). During the late 1770s and into the mid-1780s Gainsborough continued to produce numbers of female full-length portraits, such as that of Sophia Charlotte, Lady Sheffield of 1785 (Plate 228), which for sheer opulence were unequalled since Lely's Windsor Beauties of the previous century. In praising Gainsborough's skill in this area, his developing compositional gifts ought not to be forgotten. His portrait of Carl Friedrich Abel (Plate 229), for example, exhibited at the

Royal Academy in 1777, demonstrates his high degree of expertise in pictorial composition, as the sitter's movement towards the left is accentuated by the sharply angled viola da gamba, while stability is provided at the bottom left by the white head of the dog, the whole forming a solid triangle.

Despite Gainsborough's right to be regarded as at least Reynolds's equal by 1780, contemporary critical opinion on the whole held Reynolds in higher esteem, principally because of the obvious intellectual aspirations of his work (although Gainsborough did find a champion by this date in the pugnacious editor of the *Morning Herald,* Henry Bate). Nonetheless by 1783 the public was deprived of the opportunity of comparing the relative merits of the two artists because that year Gainsborough washed his hands of the Academy for good, refusing to exhibit his works there due to the insensitive manner in which he felt the Hanging Committee arranged them on the walls. From then on Gainsborough showed his work at his own home, Schomberg House on Pall Mall. Rather like Ramsay before him, Gainsborough did not particularly need to show his works in public, especially as from 1776 he had enjoyed the patronage of prominent members of the aristocracy, including the royal family. For them he produced some of his most inventive work, such as his portrait of the Duke and Duchess of Cumberland, c.1783-85 (Plate 230), who are pictured promenading, with the Duchess's sister, through Windsor Great Park, the artist achieving what he had so often striven to accomplish — a nigh perfect equilibrium between the sitters and their sylvan setting. Next to these pictures Gainsborough's most appealing achievements — although for different reasons — are his portrayals of the late 1770s of his daughters and his wife, Margaret (Colour Plate 43), in whose features Gainsborough captures, despite her disapproving gaze, a poignant sadness.

Gainsborough died in August 1788, and although Reynolds continued to paint for another year or so before he was prevented by blindness, it was the death of Gainsborough who had attracted no followers nor established any school, that brought down the curtain on the 'Golden Age' of British portrait painting. It was also in 1788 that Thomas Lawrence — the artist who was to dominate British portraiture over the next forty years — showed his first oil portrait at the Royal Academy.

MARTIN POSTLE
Institute of European Studies, London

PLATE 231
Joshua Reynolds
Mrs. Billington, 1786-89
94⅜ x 58¼ ins.
(239.5 x 148cm)
(Beaverbrook Art
Gallery, Fredericton,
New Brunswick)

242

Chapter 4

The Romantics
1790-1830

In 1790 Joshua Reynolds exhibited at the Royal Academy, among other pictures, a portrait of the singer Mrs. Billington (Plate 231), executed in his grandest style. Mrs. Billington stands on a cloud in the guise of St. Cecilia, the patron saint of music, singing and surrounded by music-making angels. She is graceful but static as she is presented to the world as a mythic being. Considering her reputation as a singer, she may well have been to some people; indeed in some circles, she is still considered to be Britain's best singer.

The exhibition also contained competent portraits by most of the other portrait painters of the day, all from the next generation of artists. Reynolds's closest rival at the time was the young Londoner John Hoppner (1758-1810). Gainsborough had died two years earlier and the intended successor to Reynolds, the American Gilbert Stuart (1755-1828) had been forced in 1787 to flee England rather quickly to escape creditors. George Romney (1734-1802) never exhibited at the Royal Academy, and in any case his portraits of the 1780s and 1790s never quite matched up to his magnificent work of the 1760s and 1770s. William Beechey (1753-1839) was still undiscovered, and the sensation of the 1782 Exhibition, the 'Cornish Wonder' John Opie (1761-1807), was paying less attention to his portraiture after the deserved success of his history painting. James Northcote (1746-1831) also attempted both history painting and portraits and while he made much of his period as a resident assistant to Reynolds, his clientele was not as distinguished as his mentor's and in any case he did not exhibit in 1790.

The 1790 exhibition was, however, one of the most momentous of the period. Near the portrait of Mrs. Billington by Reynolds hung two portraits by a practically unknown but promising artist, Thomas Lawrence (1769-1830). He had exhibited pastels since 1787 and the previous year had shown two full-length oil portraits, of Viscount and Viscountess Cremorne (Plates 248 and 249), which were strong but unexceptional (except in hindsight). However, in 1790, the twenty-two year old Lawrence exhibited two portraits that stunned everyone who saw them: a portrait of the actress Elizabeth Farren (Colour Plate 44), the mistress (and later Countess) of the Earl of Derby, and a portrait of Queen Charlotte (Plate 232). The dazzling

PLATE 232
Thomas Lawrence
Queen Charlotte, 1790
94¼ x 58ins.
(239.5 x 147.5cm)
(National Gallery,
London)

display of paint, the spontaneity and the exquisite characterisations in both portraits was such that Lawrence was catapulted to the top ranks of portraitists. This upheaval led to the nomination of the previously ignored Lawrence to become an Associate of the Royal Academy that December. It was said that the King was behind the nomination and while the Academy was 'Royal' by title and charter, its members were fiercely independent and resented outside intrusion. Therefore Lawrence's inevitable election was postponed a year until December 1791. Reynolds anointed the young artist at the 1790 exhibition by saying to him, within earshot of someone who recorded it for posterity, 'In you sir, the world will expect to see what I have failed to achieve'. The remark became a prototypical passing of the torch; Reynolds, who was practically blind, never exhibited again and died early in 1792.

John Hoppner, who, like everyone else, had been unprepared for the quality of Lawrence's two most significant entries to the exhibition, had shown only three bust-length portraits in 1790; the two that are known today (Plates 250 and 251) are exquisite characterisations and displays of colour, but would have been completely overshadowed by Lawrence's two full-lengths, not to mention Beechey's contribution of seven titled sitters. Hoppner countered the following year with a display of portraits that showed off the entire range of his talents: portraits of all sizes and social standing of sitter. For followers of the English art world, who liked nothing more than a well-publicised professional rivalry, life must have begun to look up after the death of Gainsborough and three years of petty speculation as to Reynolds's successor.

Lawrence's emergence was merely the most startling manifestation of a change taking place in English portraiture. At the time of Reynolds's death, a whole generation of artists had come to maturity nursed on the milk of his *Discourses* and trained at the Royal Academy schools. These artists were tested in order to enter the schools, had a regimen of drawing after antique casts before graduating on to the life school where they drew from nude models, and had constant contact with Academicians, some of whom were annually elected Visitors to the schools to aid students in their practice. The Royal Academy schools were a well thought out distillation of traditional European academic training and the textbook, the *Discourses,* was being etched in stone as these students studied.

The first of the next generation of artists to emerge was James Northcote, who, like Reynolds, came from Devon. Northcote was an assistant to Reynolds before spending three years in Rome where he earned membership in several foreign academies of art and an invitation to submit a self-portrait to the celebrated collection in the Uffizi Gallery, Florence. He settled in London in 1781 and immediately began producing portraits in the vein of Reynolds — almost exclusively bust-length and half-length (50 x 40 inch) portraits. These portraits earned him subsistence money while he pursued the more noble calling of history painting, at which he laboured all his life. His early works before 1790, while much like those of Reynolds, also display an affinity to other

PLATE 233
James Northcote
Mrs. Alexander
Macconachie, 1789
30 x 25ins. (76 x 63.5cm)
(Art Institute of
Chicago)

contemporary portraitists, like Hoppner. Northcote's portrait of Mrs. Alexander Macconachie (Plate 233) shares Reynoldsian conventions with many other portraits of the period, but emulates Hoppner's fashionable use of a creamy black paint, which Hoppner himself acquired from a study of Zoffany's single-figure subjects, and from Romney. Indeed, Northcote seemed to react often to contemporary taste, or to what he thought was contemporary taste. His portrait of 'Mrs. Wells as Hebe' (Plate 234), was exhibited in 1806, a year after Hoppner had exhibited a full-length portrait of Mrs. Jerningham in the same guise. Hoppner's portrait had been painted six years earlier. There is, however, evidence that portraits of this allegorical type were often painted at the insistence of the sitters.

PLATE 234 (above left)
James Northcote
'Mrs. Wells as Hebe', 1805
50 x 40ins. (127.5 x 101.5cm)
(Art Gallery of Ontario, Toronto)

PLATE 235 (left)
James Northcote
Napoleon, 1801
107 x 94ins. (272 x 239cm)
(Sotheby's sale 16.11.83, 82)

PLATE 236 (above)
James Northcote
Self-portrait, 1807
35 x 29½ins. (89 x 75cm)
(Heim Gallery, London)

Northcote's early self-portraits reveal a self-confident painter with a certain gracelessness of gesture. Northcote painted self-portraits all his life and, as with his commissioned portraits, their quality was in direct proportion to their simplicity. His full-length portrait of Napoleon (Plate 235) of 1801, not taken from the life, is exceedingly awkward, but his more straightforward self-portrait from 1807 (Plate 236) is a dignified image with rich colours and a pleasing pose in profile. Throughout his career his portraits had a hard-edgeness to them that leaves little to the imagination. The portrait of his brother with a hawk (Plate 237) from 1809, and the portrait of 'John Ruskin at age three' (Plate 238) of 1819 are typical.

Northcote's competition after his return from Italy, and for the first two-thirds of his career, was a fabricated noble savage, the 'Cornish Wonder' John Opie. Opie had been taught drawing by Dr. John Wolcot, perhaps better known by his pseudonym Peter Pindar, who had gained him entry to various Cornish collections and explained to him the rudiments of painting. As noted in the previous chapter, Wolcot brought Opie to London in 1781 where he exhibited a portrait at the Society of Artists exhibition. This entry was noted spuriously in the catalogue as 'an Instance of Genius, not having ever seen a picture'. His paintings the next year at the Royal Academy exhibition confirmed his standing as a most promising artist, whatever the extent of his training. He is said to have impressed even Reynolds, who allegedly remarked that Opie was 'like Caravaggio and Velazquez in one'. Opie's chiaroscuresque, realistic and rustic portraits in the manner of Rembrandt were instantly popular.

After a few years in the capital the novelty of Opie's rustic abilities wore thin since he had yet to master the graces of society portraiture. However, a sincere appetite for learning caused him to overcome his handicaps. He broke with Wolcot in 1783 and was painting distinguished portraits of some refinement by the middle of the decade, such as the four portraits of the Duke of Argyll's children (Colour Plate 45). Opie concentrated on history paintings after his spectacular successes in that category in 1786, and at that point and for the rest of his career, his portraits returned to the simple portrayals of sitters, usually spotlit against a dark background. Opie's second wife was a popular writer, who instigated a renewed interest in the artist's portrait career late in his life; however, his work did not change substantially. Opie's significance remains as a creator of history paintings and subject pictures.

The generation of Lawrence and Hoppner has often been categorised as 'Romantic', and evidence of true English romantic portraiture occurs as early as 1785. That year saw the exhibition of a portrait which is a touchstone of the change away from the classicism of Reynolds, to something more emotional, and more spontaneous-looking (if not truly spontaneous) and, in certain cases, meaningful. In addition, some artists began to bend the rules of portraiture as set down by Reynolds, while still adhering to most of the tenets of the *Discourses*.

PLATE 237 (left)
James Northcote
*'The Artist's Brother
holding a Falcon', 1809*
50 x 39½ ins.
(127 x 110cm)
(Arthur Ackermann &
Son Ltd., London)

PLATE 238 (above)
James Northcote
*'John Ruskin at age three',
1819*
49¾ x 39¾ ins.
(126.5 x 101cm)
(National Portrait
Gallery, London)

The portrait that signalled a diversion from past traditions was by the American John Singleton Copley and is of the three youngest daughters of George III, Princesses Sophia, Mary and Amelia (Plate 239). It has usually been considered simply a rococo conversation piece, but its size and scale force one to consider it differently. Moreover, that this picture is by the same artist who, nine years earlier, painted 'Watson and the Shark', which was itself a prototype for romantic works such as Gericault's 'Raft of the Medusa', is equally significant. The spontaneity of the picture — capturing the children conducting themselves in a manner, as Ellis Waterhouse has pointed out, that is not uncommon to children but is certainly more lively than most British parents would have liked to have perpetuated in a portrait — gives it its focus. The jungle of a background and surroundings encourage a romantic interpretation of the portrait, especially when one compares it with contemporary works by Reynolds, such as the portrait of the Duchess of Devonshire and her daughter (Chatsworth), whose spontaneity is absolutely premeditated, the poses deriving from at least two possible sources.

Copley's triple portrait was much commented upon when it was exhibited at the Academy and was almost unanimously panned by critics. The most famous review was, coincidentally, by Hoppner, who was later exposed as the anonymous critic for the *Morning Post.* Despite having three individual portraits of the same sitters in the exhibition, for Copley's picture Hoppner merely agreed with the prevalent opinions of the day. He wrote: 'What delightful

PLATE 239
John Singleton Copley
The Princesses Sophia, Mary and Amelia, 1785
104½ x 73¼ ins. (265.5 x 186cm)
(Royal Collection: Windsor Castle)

PLATE 240 (left)
Gilbert Stuart
William Grant, 1782
96⅜ x 58⅛ ins.
(245.5 x 147.5cm)
(National Gallery of Art,
Washington)

PLATE 241 (above)
Gilbert Stuart
*Henrietta Elizabeth
Frederica Vane, 1783*
65⅞ x 38⅜ ins.
(167 x 98cm)
(Smith College Museum
of Art, Northampton,
Massachusetts)

disorder! Why, you have plucked up harmony by the roots, and planted confusion in its stead! Princesses, parrots, dogs, grapes, flowers, leaves, are each striving for pre-eminence, and opposing, with hostile force, all attempts of our wearied eye to find repose'. Copley's portrait is exceedingly charming to twentieth century eyes, but one cannot deny that the royal sitters are only equal parts of a large-scale composite arrangement.

In 1785 neither Copley nor Hoppner was considered to be amongst the first rank of portrait painters. Copley was still thought of as a historical painter, and Hoppner stood behind the recognised heir to Reynolds and Gainsborough: Gilbert Stuart, another American. Stuart had arrived in London in 1775, trained with his compatriot Benjamin West, and established himself as an independent artist in 1782 after exhibiting his portrait of William Grant of Congalton skating on the Serpentine (Plate 240). Stuart's portraits are remarkably confident images painted with the compositional facility of West, the painterly fluency of Gainsborough and Romney, and with a freedom of effort that occasionally causes a passage to appear merely primed or blocked

PLATE 242
Gilbert Stuart
Hugh, 2nd Duke of Northumberland, c.1785
28 x 22¾ins. (71 x 58cm)
(Syon House, Middlesex)

PLATE 243
Gilbert Stuart
Lady Elizabeth Percy, Earl Percy, Lady Julia Percy and Lady Agnes Percy, 1787
71½ x 94ins. (181.5 x 239cm)
(Syon House, Middlesex)

in. A friend heard West observe 'that [Stuart] *nails* the face to the canvas by which he meant...that the resemblance of the person was perfect'; others testified to Stuart's abilities at capturing a likeness as well. Several artists sat to him — Reynolds, West, Copley, and the engraver William Woolett to name a few who were part of a series commissioned by John Boydell — while others happily praised his work.

The portrait of Grant skating struck everyone by its grace and movement. A portrait such as that of Henrietta Elizabeth Frederica Vane (Plate 241) illustrates Stuart's talent more readily. The treatment of the white of the girl's dress is layered and applied in the manner that West had used in portraits of the late 1770s; the sash around her waist and bow at her collar are painted in a rich creaminess that was being used to equal effectiveness by Hoppner, but which derived from Romney and the single-figure subjects of Zoffany. The background is made up of fleeting strokes to form a tree, some overhanging branches, some distant foliage, and a basket of flowers. The tree and overhanging branches, the most obvious supplementary parts of the portrait, appear to be only sketched in with a dry brush, a characteristic acquired from Gainsborough, and which is equally evident in the portrait of Grant skating. By 1785 Stuart had begun painting for the 2nd Duke of Northumberland (Plate 242), whose bust-length oval portrait against a cloudy void illustrates the artist's free brush to great effect. Dressed in a red uniform jacket that is painted in broad strokes along with the blocky whites of the stock, the decoration on the sash, the gold of the epaulettes and the powder on Northumberland's hair are applied in a delicate manner of busy staccato dabs. The technique is not so evident in the portrait of Northumberland's four children (Plate 243) painted in 1787. Here, in a larger portrait, the broad strokes dominate, but delicate touches are evident on the rim of the middle two children's caps. By April 1787 *The World* had labelled Stuart 'the Vandyck of the Time'. But by August Stuart had been forced to flee to Ireland to escape his creditors and his importance to English portraiture ended abruptly. Hoppner found himself, despite the reputations of Northcote and Opie and their status as Academicians, the most significant young portraitist working and the professional heir of Reynolds, Gainsborough and Romney.

During the second half of the 1780s Hoppner produced several notable portraits, of which the most important surviving work is the portrait of the boxer Richard Humphries, known as the 'Gentleman Boxer', more for his social aspirations than his conduct in the ring. This portrait (Plate 244) was painted for Humphries's manager, and for all practical purposes it should be discussed in the same context as a Stubbs portrait of a duke's racehorse. By its size and date it is a unique portrait; the boxer has taken up his stance in an open field (where most fights took place), and from contemporary accounts the portrait is indeed an accurate representation of Humphries's stance. Never before had a boxer been portrayed and rarely, if ever, was anyone portrayed in such undress. His semi-nudity and his depiction in such an expanse of

PLATE 244
John Hoppner
Richard Humphries, late 1780s
55¾ x 44¼ ins. (141.5 x 102.5cm)
(Metropolitan Museum of Art, New York)

windswept landscape prefigures the notion of man against nature, a strong image of continental romanticism. Here Humphries is depicted as able to conquer both man *and* nature. The picture was engraved and its dissemination throughout Europe made it a forerunner of better known images of boxers by more mainstream romantic artists, such as Gericault.

While 1790 was the year of Lawrence's ceremonious arrival on the London art scene, an astute observer might have noticed things stirring by 1789. Not only was this the first year that Lawrence produced a full-length portrait, but it also saw the emergence of William Beechey. Furthermore, 1789 also saw the most visible use of what became almost a stylistic touchstone of works by this generation of artists, which was an attempt at giving a flashy shine to the painted fabric simply by their fluency of paint handling.

PLATE 245 (left)
John Hoppner
Mrs. Sophia Fielding, 1787
31½ x 25½ ins. (80 x 65cm)
(Kimbell Art Museum, Fort Worth, Texas)

PLATE 246 (below left)
John Hoppner
Miss Charlotte Walsingham, later Lady Fitzgerald,
c.1787
48½ x 39ins. (123 x 99cm)
(Nelson-Atkins Museum of Art, Kansas City,
Missouri)

PLATE 247 (below)
William Beechey
John Douglas, Bishop of Carlisle, 1789
55 x 44ins. (139.5 x 112cm)
(Lambeth Palace, London)

It is interesting to note that in the generally accepted eighteenth and early nineteenth century European artistic capitals the leading artists were those for whom drawing (or *disegno* to use Academic parlance) was a prime consideration — for instance David in Paris, and the German Anton Raphael Mengs and his followers in Rome. However, it is in the so-called artistic backwaters, London and Madrid, where one sees the first flowering of the 'painterly' style or *colore,* a style most important to mainstream French romantic artists. While all European artists aspired to go to Rome — and many artists like Reynolds and Goya to name two from the hinterlands, actually did travel there — it was the art of Venice and Bologna, namely that of Titian, Veronese, and Correggio, diffused by various sources (Tiepolo for Goya, Rubens for Reynolds late in his career) that inspired these forerunners, as they did Delacroix and Gericault a generation later. The ability of all these artists to apply paint brilliantly to canvas in a way that arouses emotions and opens eyes to their talent is common to them all — Lawrence and Delacroix alike. It is this ability that was being sought out in the late 1780s, and reached its popularity in 1789 in England.

It seems Hoppner was the first to experiment with this painterly device of sharp flashy application and by his experiments it seems that he generated much work by other artists in this direction. Evidence of the use of this brilliantly applied paint can be detected in works by Hoppner as early as 1787, as in the portrait of Mrs. Sophia Fielding (Plate 245). Hoppner's portrait from c.1787 of Miss Charlotte Walsingham (Plate 246) is likewise accented with swatches of bright white on the drapery.

Hoppner was not alone in seeking out a sharper, flashier style of painting. Beechey, who was simply painting small whole-lengths in 1787 and only beginning to paint larger pictures in 1788, painted in 1789 a portrait of John Douglas, Bishop of Carlisle (Plate 247), in which he captured the flashy technique with great fluency. Lawrence, who only exhibited pastels up to 1789, in his first exhibited full-length portrait that year gave a taste of what he would achieve in 1790; his portrait of Viscountess Cremorne (Plate 248) offers a dazzling display of bright staccato whites. The contemporary full-length portrait of her husband (Plate 249), however, is much more subdued.

For reasons that are not clear, Hoppner ceased to use the sharp, flashy painting style on his pictures, and Beechey never quite mastered it. Beechey's portraits of 1790 are almost fully mature; he had found a style he liked and that was liked by his patrons, and it hardly varies throughout his very successful career. Hoppner decided to concentrate on a more craftsmanlike handling of paint and his work betrays more and more the fluid effort and enjoyment of paint, its qualities and viscosity, and the effects it could produce. One possible reason why Hoppner stopped using such a flashy style was that he saw others using it and did not want to be associated with the styles of artists whom he thought inferior — Hoppner was very opinionated as to his own abilities in relation to his colleagues. That he had indeed stopped using the sharp, flashy application of paint was clear from the 1790 Exhibition, when Lawrence perfected that style of work in his paintings of Miss Farren and Queen Charlotte, and Hoppner's very fine portraits exhibited that year, in a completely different mind, were utterly overshadowed.

It is difficult to make a true comparison of Hoppner's and Lawrence's best pictures in the landmark 1790 Exhibition; Lawrence's are clean and hanging in prominent galleries in London and New York while Hoppner's are both overpainted in the face of the sitter, and are not as easily accessible. One is in the Taft Museum, Cincinnati (Plate 251) while the other (Plate 250) has been on public view only once in the last fifty years when it was sold in 1985. However, the four pictures display two opposing manifestations of romantic English portraiture which were to become the most influential beacons of portrait style over the next two generations.

Lawrence's portrait of Miss Farren (Colour Plate 44), especially in comparison with Reynolds's portrait of Mrs. Billington (Plate 231), is staggering in its vivacity. Mrs. Billington is apotheosised and grandly mannered. Miss Farren on the other hand is the definition of spontaneity. She has been caught walking in a park, she looks up; she is natural and unacademic. The paint is laid on sharply, especially the white, and while Reynolds's portrait of Mrs. Billington is also thickly painted, that paint has the texture of cream. Miss Farren's paint is reminiscent of light on satin. All the way down the wrap are abstract shapes of white to simulate the sheen; the blue ribbon of the muff and the white clouds are handled in the same way, while the fur, hair and landscape are soft contrasts to the sharp, crisp handling of the paint. The colours are clear and pure, echoing the draughtsmanship. Studying these two portraits, it is difficult to believe that Miss Farren is nine years older than Mrs. Billington.

The portrait of Queen Charlotte by Lawrence (Plate 232) was doubly impressive to critics, the reason being that it was not often that a twenty year old unknown artist was granted sittings with the monarch's wife. Late eighteenth century critics were impressed with the complete freshness of the canvas; the staccato brushwork of the fabric was used to draw the eye. Lawrence received the commission through the introduction of Lady Cremorne, whose portrait he had exhibited the previous year, and he worked at the portrait of the Queen with great effort. X-radiographs show that Lawrence changed the expression of the mouth, and it is recorded that while painting the portrait he suggested to the Queen that she talk in order to look more animated. The Queen thought him 'rather presuming', but the portrait was so pleasing and recognisable that it brought Lawrence prestige, professional respect and, eventually, the position of portrait painter in ordinary to the King when Reynolds became blind. Reynolds's remark about what the world would expect to see from Lawrence caused the world to expect it right away and Lawrence, who had raised his prices substantially by 1793, had to struggle to continue in this spectacular fashion.

PLATE 248 (above)
Thomas Lawrence
Viscountess Cremorne, 1789
95 x 57ins.
(241.5 x 145cm)
(Tate Gallery, London)

PLATE 249 (right)
Thomas Lawrence
Viscount Cremorne, 1789
95 x 57ins.
(241.5 x 145cm)
(Richard Feigen Gallery,
New York)

Hoppner on the other hand, before the 1790 Exhibition, was secure in his steady rise as Reynolds's apparent successor. Since his abandonment of the sharp, flashy style of painting before the 1790 Exhibition his portraits more frequently became smaller, more introspective works, and were consequently completely different to those which Lawrence produced. Hoppner's two identified exhibits of 1790 are the portraits of the Horneck sisters, Mary Gwyn (Plate 250) and Catherine Bunbury (Plate 251). Both were well known members of the London intelligentsia and both had been celebrated by Oliver Goldsmith: Mary Horneck as the 'Jessamy Bride' and Catherine as 'Little Comedy'. Reynolds painted them several years earlier; for Hoppner, no better combination of intellect and beauty could be found in terms of decorative portrait potential. Hoppner's two portraits are superb examples of his style at the beginning of the 1790s. One portrait is set in a landscape, the figure still and the colours bright and balanced; the other has an atmospheric background, the figure is more animated and the colours are muted. Both sitters are dressed in stylish clothes, they are energetically and originally executed, and while both have been subsequently overpainted by a later hand

PLATE 250
John Hoppner
Mary Horneck Gwyn, 1790,
29¼ x 24ins. (75 x 61cm)
(Sotheby's New York sale
25.4.85, 81)

(the engravings after the paintings, which, almost as a rule, are more flattering to the sitter, depict women who were not handsome), each still clearly displays why Hoppner was so highly regarded.

Hoppner has taken as a model a type of picture perfected by Reynolds — the bust-length portrait in a landscape — and refined it still further. Mrs. Gwyn is more remote from us than any similar portrait by Reynolds; she is lost in thought and because of this detachment the viewer is able to be more intimate in his inspection of the image. Her body is composed as a triangle, thereby adding solidity to the picture. The costume is painted with gusto: the whites are a great mass of strokes, culminating on the surface with a combination of contoured brushmarks and abstract, seemingly irrelevant squiggles. It is over the landscape, however, in which Hoppner's brushwork

PLATE 251 (left)
John Hoppner
Catherine Horneck Bunbury, c.1790
30 x 25ins. (76 x 64cm)
(Taft Museum, Cincinnati)

PLATE 252 (below left)
Thomas Lawrence
John, Lord Mountstuart, mid-1790s
94 x 58ins. (239 x 147.5cm)
(Private collection)

PLATE 253 (below)
Thomas Lawrence
'Kemble as Rolla', 1800
132 x 88ins. (335.5 x 223.5cm)
(Kansas City Art Institute: on loan to the Nelson-Atkins
Museum of Art, Kansas City, Missouri)

is at its most torrid. The trees in the distance are a scumbled bunch of greens, browns and yellows with a dark brown snake to indicate a trunk. The leaves of the tree behind Mrs. Gwyn's head, however, have been formed by the appearance of a wind-blown downpour of paint, in its abstraction far beyond anything Gainsborough or Romney dared put on canvas and more spattered than any work of Reynolds. The thick darkness created by brushstrokes behind the head emerges to the end of the branches where pigment overlaps the sky in a flurry of paint that might just as well have been slapped on with Hoppner's fingertips. Apart from a few slops of deep blue, the sky itself is made up of thick applications of white, so thick that in two places the paint has not merely dripped, but run over a blue streak. The portrait of Mrs. Gwyn is Hoppner's first great mature work, and although only a bust-length portrait, it demonstrates great sophistication.

The portrait of Catherine Bunbury is an altogether different picture. As befitting Goldsmith's 'Little Comedy', Mrs. Bunbury is more animated. The head is set at an attractive angle, which enlivens the composition. She stands in profile to the waist, head to the viewer, in front of a cloudy, stormy sky. The colours are muted and the only bright spots are the blue of her cap ribbon and sash and the black of her shawl. The brushwork is what one notices most about the painting. The background is entirely scumbled paint, primarily shades of grey, with some white and tending towards black at the bottom. As with the portrait of Mrs. Gwyn, the impression of texture and solidity is achieved completely at the expense of draughtsmanship, unlike the work of Lawrence in 1790.

As with everyone else, Hoppner was unprepared for Lawrence's success at the 1790 Exhibition; no one could have foreseen that such a young unknown artist would make such an impression. Hoppner appears, therefore, to have made up his mind to show off all his powers over the next two years to impress the public where he hoped the future of English portraiture really lay. In 1791 and 1792 he exhibited six full-length portraits of the royal family, and another smaller portrait of a well-known royal mistress.

Most of the royal portraits by Hoppner dazzle merely by their subject; they are grand, straightforward portraits. But one stands out in particular, and it is Hoppner's answer to Lawrence's Miss Farren: his portrait of the Duchess of York (Colour Plate 46). Though it has little of the spontaneity of Miss Farren, if a full-length grand portrait can be intimate, this one surely is. The picture was meant to be seen from a distance, but that does not detract from the delicacy of execution in the Duchess's face, or the vitality of Hoppner's brush elsewhere on the canvas.

The portrait of the Duchess is one of the few elaborate full-length portraits by Hoppner in which he excelled in terms of graceful composition. Taking Reynolds as his starting point, Hoppner has demythicised the archetypal grand manner portrait, for instance Reynolds's 'Lady Sarah Bunbury sacrificing to the Graces' (Plate 180), and has portrayed the Duchess in an unoriginal but

COLOUR PLATE 44
Thomas Lawrence
Miss Farren, 1790
94 x 47½ ins. (239 x 146cm)
Lawrence's spontaneity is well seen in the sharp application of paint, especially the white, while the fur, hair and landscape are soft contrasts to the crisp handling of the paint
(Metropolitan Museum of Art, New York)

COLOUR PLATE 45
John Opie
The 6th Duke of Argyll as a boy, mid-1780s
50 x 40ins. (127 x 101.5cm)
One of four portraits of the Duke of Argyll's children, the painting illustrates Opie's
early ability to master the graces of society portraiture
(Private collection)

completely believable setting — she is simply posing for her portrait, her ladies-in-waiting are arranging her gown, and it is all not only natural, but graceful and captivating. The Duchess, who was prettier than most royals of the period, has been painted with a remarkable, delicately structured face, the shadows sharing that delicacy which might only be expected in a bust-length or a cabinet picture.

The gown is given the texture of satin by miles of hatching and built-up paint. Hoppner's lines are broken — completely unlike the shocking brightness of Lawrence's Miss Farren — but the appearance of texture is equally successful, though executed in a more subdued manner. The paint on the sitter's right arm, deep in shadow, is a mass of abstract strokes and colours while the blue drapery on the vase and balustrade is highlighted with a dribbled line of curves, looping and squiggling. The Pomeranian dog, symbolic — or perhaps a portrait — of one of the Duchess's several pets (at least twenty were recorded) is a ball of white sfumato, with individual strokes and an occasional white blob, which recalls the treatment of the Duchess's own powdered hair.

These details of execution are lost from a distance; the only explanation for them is that Hoppner simply enjoyed what he was doing. This portrait of the Duchess of York is one of Hoppner's masterpieces; never did he paint a more sympathetic and happy image in a full-length portrait of woman.

The 1790s were almost exclusively the possession of Lawrence and Hoppner. Much ink has been spilled concerning the great rivalry between the two, but in reality it simply did not exist. Lawrence was still maturing as an artist, and as a person. He began to overextend himself, taking on more portraits than he could finish, and leased a studio in a fashionable part of London, for which he could not pay. Before long he was deep in debt.

For all of Lawrence's crown connections, indeed because of them perhaps, Hoppner was still the first painter of the day. Hoppner's sitters during the early 1790s were primarily the political opposition, the cream of the English social and cultural aristocracy. Lawrence was a young painter for an old régime: indeed, many of his portraits — and some of his best ones of this period — are of older ladies. To add to Lawrence's problems, William Beechey was receiving crown commissions in the early 1790s as well.

While his smaller works were most consistently well received, it was Lawrence's grandest works that gave him the most trouble, paradoxically, considering that the two works that made his reputation were full-lengths. These paintings had a tendency to suffer from a curious elongation of the figure that never left Lawrence's work in this size. It can also be seen in Lawrence's masterpiece of the middle years of the 1790s, the portrait of John, Lord Mountstuart (Plate 252), but in this case it is used to great effect.

Because of the characterisation of the sitter in this picture, Mountstuart has been called the Byronic hero of English portraiture. He is placed in a stormy Spanish landscape (the Escorial is at the back left) and is shown wearing Spanish costume. The stormy sky, brilliant brushwork seen in the sitter's waistcoat, and his contrapposto stance on what seems to be a cliff edge give this portrait a romanticism that equals what one expects of an artist such as Delacroix. However, it has an underlying classical structure that gives it significant historical grounding. It has been shown that the figure is based on Michelangelo's David, and it is this combination of classical preparation and intuitive painterly execution that gives Lawrence his romantic sensibilities. Oddly, while Lawrence was obviously capable of such masterpieces, he never painted such a romantic image again, possibly because of the unfavourable reviews the picture received. He was very sensitive to the barbs of critics and colleagues and was certainly stung by comments that 'the whole [of the portrait] wants brilliancy'.

The theatricality of Lawrence's portraits reflects the artist's interest in the theatre. His reputation declining, he turned to painting outsized canvases to restore his past acclaim. They only succeeded in irritating his colleagues and numbing the public. Most of these paintings took the form of portraits of the actor John Philip Kemble, the brother of the celebrated Mrs. Siddons, in character. The most famous example is 'Kemble as Hamlet' (Tate Gallery); perhaps the more typical of the group is the portrait of 'Kemble as Rolla' (Plate 253). These pictures are extremely dramatic, an effect not unenhanced by a discoloured varnish on many of them. Heads and hands are spotlit, and Kemble is seen from the viewpoint of the spectator at his feet looking up, as if seated in the front row of the stalls in a theatre observing the actor standing at the front of the stage. The backgrounds are marvellously atmospheric with smoke, clouds, and occasionally some rising moons. The pictures broke completely new ground as theatrical portraits, away from the conversation piece small group portraits of the generation of Garrick by Johan Zoffany. Lawrence's large portraits can be seen as the portrait offshoot of grand history paintings that the artist was trying to produce at this time, paintings such as his fifteen foot tall effort titled 'Satan summoning his Legions' (Royal Academy).

Lawrence's insistence on painting these unremunerative subject pictures and large portraits were one cause of his decline; another was his disastrous love life. He was in love with the two Siddons daughters, Sally and Maria; they both kept him on the string, and then they both died, which slightly altered his concentration. Lawrence's financial condition continued in a miserable state and he was put under the thumb of a financial manager. A colleague of Lawrence saw the artist's father, who, on his deathbed, told him 'what Fortune had presented to his son, he was kicking before him as fast as he could'.

Another problem for Lawrence concerned the rise of William Beechey. Beechey's short-lived interest in the application of sharp, flashy paint in the late 1780s is evident in a few of his portraits, in particular that of Bishop Douglas of Carlisle (Plate 247). Like Hoppner, he seems to have abandoned the style, perhaps after seeing what Lawrence could do with it. However, Beechey was able to paint solid, sympathetic portraits, with a degree of

COLOUR PLATE 46
John Hoppner
The Duchess of York, 1790
107 x 83ins. (272 x 210cm)
Although intended to be seen from a distance, this does not detract from the delicacy
of execution in the Duchess's face, or the vitality of Hoppner's brushwork elsewhere
on the canvas
(Private collection)

COLOUR PLATE 47
William Beechey
Miss Jane Reade, 1813
84 x 51ins.
(213.5 x 129.5cm)
There is much
movement in Beechey's
works, but it rarely
appears spontaneous
(Spencer Museum of
Art, University of
Kansas)

movement, that pleased many. His early large portraits, for instance that of
Mr. Oddie's children (Plate 254), and his smaller ones, such as the portrait of
John Granville (Plate 255, long wrongly attributed to Hoppner), are typical of
those he painted around 1790, when his clientele included nobility for the first
time. These portraits are bright, with a slightly sentimental quality that has
traditionally appealed to the middle rungs of moneyed English society.

Critical praise and titled sitters came to Beechey in 1790, but his clientele
remained almost exclusively the clergy, the military and the bourgeoisie —
'merchants and sea captains' as John Opie put it to Farington. When in 1797
Beechey exhibited six portraits of the royal family, his career soared. His
success with these images caused him to become the favourite painter of the
King and Queen, who were not known for their adventuresome taste in art.
Beechey was indeed patronised by merchants and sea captains, and the
portraits of Admiral Sir John Thomas Duckworth, Bt. (Plate 256) and Mark
Pringle (Plate 257, also long wrongly attributed to Hoppner) are typical of
Beechey's work throughout his career. Taken stylistically, they could have
been painted at any time during the last forty years of his life.

Beechey's *oeuvre* does include a more inventive aspect, involving primarily

PLATE 255 (left)
William Beechey
John Granville, c.1790-95
30 x 24¾ins. (76 x 63cm)
(Detroit Institute of Arts)

PLATE 256 (above)
William Beechey
*Admiral Sir John Thomas
Duckworth, Bt., 1810*
55½ x 44½ins.
(141 x 113cm)
(Christie's sale 21.9.87,
216)

portraits of women and children. His portrait of Lady Beechey and her baby (Plate 258) falls into the Reynoldsian tradition of mothers and infants with an added degree of sweetness. However, it was in larger-scale portraiture that Beechey used his inventive powers to full effect, and used them best during the years around the turn of the century. The portrait of 'Mrs. Montague and her Sister decorating a Bust of Handel' (Plate 259) derives either from the portrait by Reynolds of 'Lady Tavistock decorating a Bust of Flora' (Woburn Abbey), or his portrait of the Montgomery sisters (Tate Gallery). Beechey seems to have fallen prey to the same urge that captured Copley in 1785 in his portrait of the three daughters of the King. The flora and flying drapery of the Montague portrait give it a neo-romantic feeling, rather than proto-romantic. Beechey's portrait of Mrs. Raymond Symonds and family (Plate 260) is another rosy-cheeked vortex of muslin with just a touch of movement to give the picture a focus away from its unflamboyant execution. The figure of the boy is cribbed from a Hoppner portrait of the children of the Duke of Dorset, and while Reynolds was castigated for borrowing poses, Beechey was so popular with his sea captains and merchants that any complaint of plagiarism on his part was unheard of. In a portrait of a Mrs Scottowe (Plate 261), Beechey gave his sitter an open sketchbook revealing a landscape drawing, but upside-down to the viewer. Mrs. Scottowe looks up from this book, no pencil of her own in sight, while seated out of doors and wearing a formless white costume. Her gesture of turning some pages of the sketchbook is artless, despite its attempt at depicting a graceful gesture, and this portrait typifies Beechey's

COLOUR PLATE 48
Henry Raeburn
Lord Newton, c.1806
50 x 40ins. (127 x 101.5cm)
Raeburn's powers of psychological penetration were often rendered by strong
shadows and dark backgrounds
(Dalmeny House)

COLOUR PLATE 49
John Hoppner
Sir George Beaumont, c.1803
30½ x 25¼ins. (77.5 x 64cm)
The finest of his bust-length portraits, Hoppner has
exposed his friend with searching scrutiny and
psychological depth
(National Gallery, London)

COLOUR PLATE 50
Thomas Lawrence
The Baring Group, 1807
61 x 89ins. (155 x 226cm)
Lawrence has attempted to capture a particular
moment, and in the pose of the deaf Sir Francis
Baring has pulled it off handsomely
(Baring Brothers & Co. Ltd., London)

PLATE 257 (above)
William Beechey
Mark Pringle, c.1800
30 x 25ins.
(76.5 x 63.5cm)
(Art Institute of
Chicago)

PLATE 258 (right)
William Beechey
Lady Beechey and her baby,
c.1793
29½ x 24½ins.
(75 x 62cm)
(Detroit Institute of
Arts)

preoccupation with a conscious attempt at 'invention', a desire to infuse his portraits with some sort of novelty that distracts the eye from the lethargy of his brushwork. There is much movement in Beechey's works, but it rarely appears spontaneous. He produced competent pictures in the manner of Reynolds and in a style that pleased those who thought him worth patronising. A portrait of Miss Jane Reade (Colour Plate 47) takes a chestnut of a subject in English portraiture — a woman with a harp — and does nothing to it but use it once again to portray yet another English rose. The Reade family was one of several who would have only Beechey paint their portraits; Sir John Reade, Miss Reade's brother, commissioned two portraits of himself by Beechey, and another of their mother, as well as this one.

All the London portraitists had to compete for their Scottish patrons with Henry Raeburn, who worked in Edinburgh. Raeburn's reputation was well known and sophisticated travellers visited his studio to see just how good he was. Farington recorded his own visit in 1801, noting that some of his portraits had 'an uncommonly true appearance of nature', and believed, wrongly, that Raeburn had used a camera obscura. Raeburn is known for his searching and almost spooky portraits in strong, deep colours, that at times are as psychologically compelling as any produced at any time, and at others are so cursorily treated that one wonders if he might have run out of paint (an inconsistency likewise noted by Farington). Raeburn has been compared to Velazquez since Wilkie visited Spain in 1828, shortly after Raeburn's death,

PLATE 259 (left)
William Beechey
*'Mrs. Montague and her
Sister decorating a Bust of
Handel', 1802*
95 x 57ins.
(241.5 x 145cm)
(Private collection)

PLATE 260 (above)
William Beechey
*Mrs. Raymond Symonds
and her family, 1803*
95 x 57ins.
(241.5 x 145cm)
(Private collection)

and it was Wilkie who noted a great characteristic of the master's style, his 'square touch'.

Raeburn was born outside Edinburgh in 1756 and was an orphan by the time he was nine when he was listed as a scholar at George Heriot's Hospital in Edinburgh; there he gained a classical education. He was apprenticed to the goldsmith James Gilliland in 1772 and for twelve years until his departure for Italy in 1784, his artistic development is sketchy, although he was still with Gilliland in 1778, a year past the normal length of an apprenticeship.

Raeburn certainly had contact with Reynolds on the way to Italy and it is likely that other London artists had a chance to see Raeburn's work on his return in the summer of 1786. He had already developed the 'square touch', surely gained from the study of the few paintings of Velazquez in Rome, and his powers of composition were reinforced by the study of Raphael and Michelangelo as Reynolds would have suggested. An early work after his return from Rome, the portrait of Mrs. Ferguson of Raith and her two children (datable to about 1787 by costume), displays an ambitious Reynoldsian effort but with Raeburn's distinctive directness that has been called 'the portraiture of common sense'.

273

COLOUR PLATE 51
Thomas Lawrence
The Prince Regent (later George IV), 1815
106¾ x 79¾ ins. (271 x 171.5cm)
One of several portraits by Lawrence of the Prince Regent, it served to establish
him as one of the foremost portrait painters of the day
(Sotheby's sale 16.11.88, 73)

COLOUR PLATE 52
Thomas Lawrence
The Calmady Children, 1824
30⅞ x 30⅛ ins. (78.5 x 76.5cm)
Painted with Lawrence's usual brilliance, with bright whites, clear colours and
evocative landscape, this is his best known portrait of children and one which has
been celebrated for its happy evocation of childhood exuberance
(Metropolitan Museum of Art, New York)

PLATE 261 (above)
William Beechey
Mrs. Scottowe, 1802
50 x 40ins.
(127 x 101.5cm)
(Private collection)

PLATE 262 (right)
Henry Raeburn
Mrs. James Gregory,
c.1798
50 x 40ins.
(127 x 101.5cm)
(National Trust for
Scotland: Fyvie Castle)

Raeburn came into his own in the 1790s when he painted a number of leading Scottish intellectuals in a manner that has been demonstrated to have derived from the philosophy of Thomas Reid, whom Raeburn painted, and who advocated an empirical naturalism while emphasising the role of intuition in the powers of perception. The use of this intuition by the portrait painter is manifested in the same sort of treatment used by Hoppner: a completely painterly style of representation, where colour and form are rendered by strokes and blocks of paint as seen in the portrait of Isabella McLeod, Mrs. James Gregory (Plate 262) of c.1798. The 'square touch' is noticed particularly in her collar and belt, while the treatment of the face is created in a more subtle, modulated fashion. Raeburn's first exhibited work in London, the portrait of Sir John and Lady Clerk of Penicuik of 1792 (Plate 263), was remarkable for its effect of light and the detached representation of its sitters, while Hoppner and Lawrence were battling on flashier grounds.

In his treatment of male sitters Raeburn's powers of psychological penetration were often rendered by strong shadows and dark backgrounds as in the portrait of Lord Newton of c.1806 (Colour Plate 48) or John Clerk, Lord Eldin (Plate 264) of 1820. The painter was able to capture the same sort of expression of noble thought or intensity of purpose in his sitters whether they looked directly at the viewer or gazed away.

It is in Raeburn's portraits of children that one questions his motives. Works such as the Elphinstone Children (Plate 265) or the Drummond Children (Metropolitan Museum of Art, New York), have a curious orange autumnal

PLATE 263
Henry Raeburn
*Sir John and Lady Clerk of
Penicuik, 1792*
57 x 81ins.
(145 x 206cm)
(National Gallery of
Ireland, Dublin)

aura to them that is completely unlike the cheerful autumnal feeling one sees in Beechey, Hoppner or Lawrence. At the same time the blocky technique of Raeburn, when used on the whites of a young child's garments, presents the children almost as ethereal beings amidst a forest. Portraits such as 'The Leslie Boy' (Plate 266) call out for further research as to their exact meaning.

Raeburn was elected R.A. in 1815, and was knighted and appointed King's Limner in Scotland in 1822. His reputation was substantial and his influence continues to be strong even to the present in traditional portraitists such as George J.D. Bruce. His work personifies the idea of Scottish common sense in the way Copley's American portraits captured the straightforward Yankee.

Hoppner regained his status as the primary portrait painter in England in the late 1790s until his premature death in 1810. He vocally considered himself the premier portraitist in Britain and, by the end of the 1790s, no one seriously questioned him. However, unlike Beechey or Lawrence, he never enjoyed painting grand portraits, preferring instead to capture a good likeness that spoke of the personality of the sitter. When he was forced to paint a full-length or some other portrait larger than a Kit Kat he often either failed miserably or produced works full of awkward gesture; he rarely succeeded as he did with

PLATE 264 (above)
Henry Raeburn
John Clerk, Lord Eldin, 1820
50¼ x 40ins. (128 x 101.5cm)
(Scottish National Portrait Gallery, Edinburgh)

PLATE 265 (above right)
Henry Raeburn
The Elphinstone Children, c.1812
78 x 60½ins. (198 x 153.5cm)
(Cincinnati Art Museum)

PLATE 266 (right)
Henry Raeburn
'The Leslie Boy', c.1795
30¼ x 25ins. (77 x 63.5cm)
(Cincinnati Art Museum)

278

the portrait of the Duchess of York (Colour Plate 46). On the other hand, some of Hoppner's large portraits are ground-breaking in their meaning and new use of old motifs. Hoppner was well versed in the history of his art and was exceedingly well educated, having been raised in the Palace and become part of the Chapel Royal choir (his mother worked in some unknown capacity for the Crown). He was aware of what had come before him in terms of portraiture, of what was considered acceptable. Hoppner had a gift for bending the rules of portraiture that Reynolds had dictated by example, and more literally, in terms of art in general, in his *Discourses*.

The successful examples of Hoppner's larger portraits are all interesting for different reasons; 1797 saw one of the most fascinating. Hoppner's portrait of Richard Brinsley Sheridan's second wife and their young son (Plate 267) has always been considered a rather pretty, sub-Reynoldsian portrait; however, it makes a distinct statement about English art, and English society. Discounting certain details, as Hoppner himself no doubt would have done (such as the lack of an expected flank on one donkey), the portrait is the earliest full-length portrait painted as a genre scene. Mrs. Sheridan is portrayed as a rustic farmwife fetching water with her son upon her back. The motif of a child on the back of another figure derives from Reynolds and his much more elegant portrait of Mrs. Payne Gallwey and her son, who is dressed as for court (Taft Museum, Cincinnati). This portrait in turn is based on the antique 'Faun and a Kid', now in the Prado. The Royal Academy had acquired a cast of this sculpture by 1781 and Hoppner would certainly have been aware of its arrival as well as its significance. By making the portrait a full-length, as opposed to Reynolds's smaller use of the pose, Hoppner here has reversed the idea behind Reynolds's ideal portraits, such as that of Lady Sarah Bunbury. Here the figure has been made distinctly 'un-ideal' — it is distinctly rustic; and no one had done that before in a full-length portrait.

Hoppner's picture owes much to Gainsborough, and his portrait of Mrs. Sheridan greatly resembles Gainsborough's 'Cottage Girl with Dog and Pitcher' in the Beit Collection. Indeed, in costume she looks as if she has just walked out of one of Gainsborough's 'cottage door' pictures. This romanticising rustication can be seen in the context of a sentimental, almost Rousseauian return to nature and, being an English picture, there was about as much gravity to it as there was when Marie Antoinette played milkmaid in the grounds of Versailles. The portrait has a very homely, maternal feeling about it, which might have attracted Hoppner's friend Sheridan — the first Mrs. Sheridan having died five years earlier. Few, if any, English portraits up to this time present their sitter in such rustic costume. The costume was always meant to be appropriate to the setting in portraits of this period: in country scenes, for instance, a riding habit or hunting clothes. Mrs. Sheridan, while by no means in rags as is Gainsborough's 'Cottage Girl', is in earthy-toned clothing (and rather up-to-date in cut, with her empire waist) while her son wears a tattered hat. They are dressed as the homogenised poor. Whereas in

PLATE 267
John Hoppner
Mrs. Sheridan and her son, 1797
99¾ x 59ins. (238 x 150cm)
(Metropolitan Museum of Art, New York)

PLATE 268
John Hoppner
*Emily St. Clare as a Bacchante,
1806*
94½ x 59ins. (240 x 150cm)
(Nelson-Atkins Musuem of
Art, Kansas City, Missouri)

Reynolds's day a 'country' portrait might mean being surrounded by sheep, Hoppner's portrait portrays Mrs. Sheridan as a working woman, a rustic, hauling her baby on her back as she fetches water. John Barrell has recently pointed to the prevalence of peculiarly 'English' rustic-rural scenes in the genre painting of the period as one patriotic result of the Napoleonic wars then taking place. Similarly, the rustic Mrs. Sheridan may also be seen as an image of industry leading to a happy life, spelled out only too clearly by the eighteenth century poet James Thomson in *The Seasons*. As Barrell argues, 'the poetry makes it unambiguously clear that in England the means of life may be amply secured, but only by those who work for them: there is no room in "Happy Britannia" — the phrase is James Thomson's — for the indolent of whatever station in life'. Hoppner's portraiture, as exemplified by the portrait of Mrs. Sheridan, is among the first in England to have a deeper social meaning other than the suggestion made by the classical pose; and Hoppner was equally turning that convention on its ear. The painter was choosing classical poses purely for their formal interest; by his death in 1810 that idea had completely caught on with England's portraitists. Lawrence would later become an expert at using 'inappropriate' poses for his portraits.

In 1803 Hoppner's health failed and in the meantime the Royal Academy was in political turmoil. With both his professional and personal life seemingly crumbling around him, Hoppner began choosing his sitters with more discretion. Whereas in the 1780s and 1790s, he painted many female sitters, in the last five years of his exhibiting life, only a quarter of his portraits are of ladies. A letter survives in which he states that he will paint no more children and while he was unsuccessful at keeping that promise, he increasingly insisted on painting smaller, bust-length portraits the closer he came to the end of his life. Exceptions occur, naturally, as in the portrait of Emily St. Clare (Plate 268), the mistress of Sir John Leicester, but even in this arguably successful full-length portrait Hoppner has enjoyed himself. Letters survive to prove that Hoppner tried to paint the girl in a more simple attitude, but was frustrated by Leicester, who was at that time the most important patron of contemporary British art. So Hoppner, in a brilliant paradox, chose an antique pose, that in its original meaning would never have been chosen for a portrait (but, in fact had been used several times by Romney and others in a very innocent guise) and indeed used it in its original meaning. The pose derives from figures of maenads or bacchantes, the lascivious followers of Bacchus, and perhaps the only true application of the pose would be in the portrait of a mistress of a man who seemed to have a weakness for young girls. Indeed, in 1810 Leicester pensioned off this mistress of an indeterminately young age to marry a sixteen year old.

Hoppner's preferred portrait size was the bust-length. Around 1790, the date of the portrait of Mrs. Gwyn, Hoppner developed a method of rendering a face based on Venetian prototypes, with a sfumatic application of paint and richness of colour unobtainable by his colleagues, who considered him the best colourist since Reynolds. Indication of Hoppner's debt to Venetian renaissance portraiture comes from a portrait from about 1792 of his closest friend, the writer and editor William Gifford (Plate 269), which plainly derives from the portrait by Titian of a man, which was then, as now, in the Royal Collection. Each man has his finger in a book, his face punctuated by the light tones of his shirt or waistcoat. The Venetian style was used by Hoppner for all types of sitters, for instance in a 1796 portrait of the Duke of Clarence (Plate 270), and for women, as seen in a compelling portrait of Benjamin Franklin's daughter, Sarah Bache, a friend of Hoppner's American wife. Hoppner later

added the Reynoldsian convention of a crimson curtain to the background of his portraits. Used equally for the average peer, as in a portrait, possibly of the Marquis of Buckingham (Plate 271), or for sitters of more intimate acquaintance, the device added a richness of colour to the images, which are all completely subdued in tone, almost taking the palette to a minimum of primary colours.

Of these bust-length portraits, none is finer than the one of Hoppner's friend, the patron and collector Sir George Beaumont (Colour Plate 49). The restricted pose and colours, combined with the luscious richness in what colour there is (accented by Beaumont's gaze away from the viewer and the luminous red curtain) expose the sitter with searching scrutiny and psychological depth. The paint is handled with great flair in the white neckwear and the hair, the whites painted with stabs and twists of a loaded brush, the hair built up with browns and topped with wisps of thin grey paint. The execution of the face is similarly layered and structured.

While the bust-length format was preferred by Hoppner, he was able to enlarge it in some cases if the sitter did not insist upon a grand pose. The portrait of William Pitt (Plate 272) was considered a brilliant likeness and was so popular that Hoppner may have painted a few versions himself before turning the copy work over to assistants. Hoppner began the portrait, as he often did for important commissions, with a sketch from the life in which the head and the face are modelled with bold straight brushmarks, the loose handling evidence of Hoppner's spontaneity (Plate 273). The body is simply

PLATE 271 (above)
John Hoppner
Portrait of a man, possibly the Marquis of Buckingham,
c.1803
30 x 25ins. (76 x 63.5cm)
(Private collection)

PLATE 272 (above right)
John Hoppner
William Pitt the Younger, 1805
56¾ x 43½ins. (144 x 110.5cm)
(Collection of Viscount Cowdray)

PLATE 273 (right)
John Hoppner
Sketch for the portrait of William Pitt the Younger, 1804
23½ x 18ins. (59.5 x 45.5cm)
(Stowe School)

blocked in with an outline of Pitt's shoulders and lapels, and coloured only by the primed canvas.

The painting is well composed, an unflamboyant representation of an unflamboyant man. Hoppner selectively emphasised the sober black and grey tones he was using more frequently at this time. Although dull tones predominate, the picture has a remarkable brightness. The curtain and robes are painted in rich golds, as is the patch of light on the column, and Pitt's hair, which in his forty-sixth year was almost white, has again been painted, as in the Beaumont portrait, and in most other works of this type, with wisps of paint from a dry brush. Quite short, almost translucent brushstrokes of greyish-white paint have been layered to give the impression of a head of hair.

There is some indication of Hoppner's old spontaneity in these late bust-length portraits, the type of spontaneity seen in the landscape background of the 1790 portrait of Mrs. Gwyn (Plate 250), but none so much as in his few late portraits of ladies. He made his name when young by painting Whig beauties from the court of the Prince of Wales in a style reminiscent of Reynolds, but his portraits of the same circle late in his life are rendered in a very personal manner. In a portrait of Mrs. Augustus Phipps (Plate 274) of c.1805, the background has become exceedingly atmospheric and stormy, the clouds and light merely suggested by the wild attacking of the brush; the sitter's face has been structured and built up in a similar technique to that of Beaumont and Pitt. In what is probably a very late work, a portrait traditionally supposed to be of the Prince of Wales's former mistress Mrs.

PLATE 276
Thomas Lawrence
*Lady Elizabeth Foster, later
Duchess of Devonshire,
c.1805*
94.5 x 58ins.
(240 x 148cm)
(National Gallery of
Ireland, Dublin)

286

Fitzherbert (Plate 275), the background is vaguely recognisable as a landscape, but is executed, along with the sitter's clothing and hair, with a splattering that resembles nothing so much as a New York School drip painting.

Hoppner was idiosyncratic as an artist and as a person; in temperament he resembled his one-time friend J.M.W. Turner, who himself learned much from Hoppner's brush technique. Hoppner, like Gainsborough, seems to have been somewhat a victim of fashion, which, much to the detriment of his posthumous reputation, changed shortly after his death. Like Gainsborough, he endured a nominal rival; Hoppner's was Thomas Lawrence, who was able to erase lingering memories of Hoppner's portraiture by his brilliant full maturity. To paraphrase Ellis Waterhouse: happily, death carried Hoppner away in time for the heroes of Waterloo to be painted by Lawrence.

Lawrence emerged from his unfortunate personal life about 1805, when he exhibited a portrait of Lady Elizabeth Foster (Plate 276). Lady Elizabeth is portrayed as a Sibyl, standing above Tivoli in the background at the right, and the vortex of light at the back, the rich colours and the classically derived pose represent Lawrence's best qualities of his later years, and those qualities he would follow faithfully the rest of his career. He was on a rigid financial rein by his bankers and he seems to have recovered from the deaths of his lady friends. The years 1806 and 1807 saw the exhibition of two of his finest pictures. The round portrait of Mrs. Maguire and her son (Plate 277) was exhibited in 1806 with the title 'A Fancy Group', because the sitters were the mistress and son of the Marquis of Abercorn. Lawrence has taken the sitters and made them into a Michelangelo tondo. The boy twists like the Virgin in the Doni Tondo — the two pictures are almost the same size — his legs recalling the St. Bartholomew in the Sistine 'Last Judgement', and even with his unruly hair giving him a roguish look, he recalls Caravaggio's 'Amor Triumphant'. The interaction between the three figures — dog included — unites the group and is literally touching: the boy's little hand on the dog's big nose is a beautiful and highly effective gesture. This picture is the beginning of Lawrence's use of Hoppner's method of using traditional poses for all manner of figures. No one in Reynolds's day would have taken the pose of the Virgin and used it for the figure of what was known in social circles as a Marquis's illegitimate son. One of Lawrence's great gifts was taking these distinguished poses for use in portraits of just about anyone and combining them with a rich palette and a flashy brush, indeed few artists have ever equalled Lawrence's facility with a paint brush.

In 1807 Lawrence exhibited a triple portrait of Sir Francis Baring, John Baring, and Charles Wall (Colour Plate 50). Commissioned by Sir Francis as a pendant to a triple portrait by Reynolds of Lord Lansdowne, Lord Ashburton, and Colonel Barre of 1788-89, it was to be part of a trio of group portraits, comprising his political friends by Reynolds, his domestic connections by Benjamin West, and Lawrence's portrait of the family in business. Here, as in the Maguire tondo, Lawrence has attempted to capture a particular moment. Purely in terms of pose, it is an unsuccessful picture as the individual figures appear mannered. But what smacks of 'invention' in Beechey is pulled off handsomely by Lawrence with the utter brilliance of his brush, and by the quotation he makes in the pose of Sir Francis and the urgent reaction of his son-in-law. In a gesture of homage to Reynolds, Lawrence has given the deaf Sir Francis the pose of Reynolds's self-portrait with his hand to his ear (Tate Gallery). The colouring is clear and distinct and was compared by one critic to Veronese. The sumptuousness of the fabrics contrasts with the intricacies that Reynolds painted in the robes of the sitters in his own triple portrait.

At Hoppner's death in 1810, Lawrence wrote to a friend that the event 'leaves me without a rival'. While the strength of Beechey's work and the possibility of a move to London by Henry Raeburn caused Lawrence to delay raising his prices for another year, by 1812 he was unquestionably the most important portrait painter in Europe. His portraits from the 1810s are frequently technically flashy, yet compositionally unflamboyant images of the leading citizens of the country. The portrait of the Duke of Wellington (Plate 278) (better known for having appeared on the back of the old £5 note), dates

PLATE 278
Thomas Lawrence
*The Duke of Wellington,
c.1815*
36 x 28ins.
(91.5 x 71cm)
(Victoria and Albert
Museum, London:
Apsley House)

from about 1815 and is typical of the period. Lawrence unhesitatingly flattered his subject as no other painter of Wellington ever did, but somehow one hardly cares; Lawrence took great care to be sure the picture was an ordered whole. The black sash that Wellington wears should, by definition, be striped, and like his 'presumptuous' suggestion that Queen Charlotte should talk to animate her features, Lawrence had the equal presumption to paint out the stripes. 'Never mind,' said Wellington, 'they merely constitute me Generalissimo of the Armies of Spain'. It is interesting to compare Lawrence's portrait with both Goya's masterpiece of a portrait of Wellington in the National Gallery and Hoppner's unsuccessful full-length of the Duke at Stratfield Saye (that was at least noted for its likeness). Lawrence's sitter bears not the slightest resemblance to the man painted by Goya or Hoppner, nor to the man caricatured by contemporary political cartoonists.

Lawrence's continued fascination with Michelangelo is evident in the portrait of his friend Isabella Wolff (Plate 279), the estranged English wife of the Danish Consul in London. Completed around 1815, she takes much of her form from the Erythraean Sibyl on the Sistine ceiling, a study for which Lawrence owned. He had been intrigued by the pose for some years; the picture was begun about ten years earlier and a drawing for another portrait, of Mrs. George Stratton, reveals a similar positioning. Significantly, Lawrence never copied poses exactly but used just enough to enable the viewer to understand the origin. Lawrence may also have had in mind Veronese's St. Helena, with her head resting on her hand. Further evidence of Lawrence's Michelangelesque infatuation is the book Mrs. Wolff examines containing drawings of the Delphic Sibyl and a nude figure in the style of Michelangelo. But however Michelangelesque the composition, the painting is purely Lawrencian. The brilliance of the sheen of Mrs. Wolff's fabric had not been equalled since Lawrence exhibited his portrait of Miss Farren (Colour Plate 44) in 1790. But where Miss Farren's cloak was painted with broken abstract flashes, Mrs. Wolff's tunic is rendered by sheets of white paint. The danger of painting large areas of white has been demonstrated by Beechey's portraits of Mrs. Scottowe (Plate 261) or Miss Jane Reade (Colour Plate 47), but in the hands of an artist such as Lawrence, the colour takes on a luminescence. It is sumptuously painted and accented by the rich crimson; the satin is equally crisp while the headband and cloak are painted with a three-dimensionality that recalls Veronese.

After Waterloo, Lawrence was commissioned by the Prince of Wales, who had by then become Prince Regent, to paint the rulers and commanders of the victorious Allied nations. Knighted and sent across Europe in 1818 and 1819, he returned with some of the most brilliant portraits of the age. The pictures hang today in the Waterloo Chamber at Windsor Castle and are paragons of confidence, both in terms of sitter and painter. The portrait of Archduke Charles of Austria (Plate 280), standing before the clearing clouds of war, is posed nonchalantly; as one critic has noted, the portrait is a perfect balance between flamboyance and restraint. The Archduke is known to have been a very short man; Lawrence's theatrical setting, on the order of his portraits of Kemble, transforms the diminutive Archduke into a statuesque warrior.

The most significant portrait of the group is undoubtedly the portrait of the Pope, Pius VII (Plate 281). It falls into a great tradition of papal portraiture, from Raphael and Velazquez, down through Lawrence's contemporaries Jacques-Louis David and Vincenzo Cammuccini. The Pope is posed seated, in the papal tradition, but not on the papal throne, rather on the chair upon which he is carried into St. Peter's during ceremonial occasions. Through the arch in the background are three of the most influential works of antique sculpture: the Apollo Belvedere, the Laocöon, and the Belvedere torso, these

PLATE 279
Thomas Lawrence
Mrs. Isabella Wolff,
c.1803-15
50½ x 40½ ins.
(128 x 102.5cm)
(Art Institute of
Chicago)

being not only the finest models for contemporary students, but returned spoils from the Napoleonic wars. The application of white on the papal robe does not rival that of Mrs. Wolff's, but in this picture red is an equally important colour as it frames the Pope's face and is part of the larger decorative trappings. It gives a great regal presence to the aged, but very much alert Pope. There are many accounts of the repartee between artist and sitter, and their mutual admiration comes through in Lawrence's work. This portrait has an intimacy that is absent in the other Waterloo pictures and particularly in the other Vatican portrait, of Pius's Secretary of State, Cardinal Consalvi (Plate 282).

Red is used to further effect in Consalvi's portrait, it being, not least, the colour of a Cardinal's robes. Lawrence has applied the paint with similar sumptuousness to that in the portraits of Pius and Mrs. Wolff. Consalvi is protected by a red curtain, matt in its resemblance to velvet, offsetting the sheen of the robes. The prime colours in this portrait — red, white and gold — are the colours of the period in England. The architect John Nash used them throughout Buckingham Palace and the effect is overwhelmingly grand. Behind Consalvi is Maderno's façade of St. Peter's, partly in shadow, as if a spiritual symbol of the Catholic church should not detract from its temporal and political leader.

Eugene Delacroix met Lawrence in London and almost undoubtedly saw the portraits of Pius VII and Consalvi while there. He was most perceptive in his appreciation of Lawrence's work and wrote a long article about the portrait of Pius in the *Revue de Paris,* in which he wrote, 'despite the facility of the style, nothing is more conscientious than Lawrence's effort'. Indeed, all of Lawrence's spontaneity was highly laboured. Lawrence wrote an eight-page letter in response, which, in another example of Lawrence's fame, was stolen before Delacroix had had a chance fully to digest it.

After his own portrait was completed, Pius asked for a portrait of the Prince Regent. It portrays the Prince in Garter robes, and is a version of a painting in Dublin, but Lawrence also painted the Prince in various costumes, including a Field Marshal's uniform (Colour Plate 51), coronation robes, and private dress. Needless to say, the portraits in Garter robes allowed Lawrence the opportunity to show off his technique, but the relative simplicity of the portrait of the Prince in private dress (Plate 283) is the most satisfying, perhaps because of the almost touching awkwardness of the sitter.

Delacroix's appreciation of Lawrence's work suggests that he was aware of Lawrence's other work apart from the paintings of Allied leaders. Lawrence's portraits of women and children are what have marked him for most of the century and a half since his death, and they are marvellously flamboyant images. As Beau Brummell forced male plumage into the closet permanently, Lawrence's portraits of male sitters began to take on a repetitive quality because of their costume. Late full-length images, such as the portrait of Lord Nugent (Plate 284), are not as visually exciting as smaller works, such as the 1822 portrait of George Canning (Plate 285) whose intense stare, delicate gesture of his left hand, moon-like bald head and crimson curtain-backdrop transform a simple bust-length portrait into an image of powerful energy. Lawrence's portraits of ladies and children enabled him to continue to paint with the flashy brush that he had enjoyed throughout his career. The great array of taffetas, particularly seen on younger ladies, were seemingly made to be represented by Lawrence's brush.

The flamboyance of Lawrence's brush late in his career can be illustrated by a work such as the portrait of the Hon. Mrs. Seymour Bathurst (Plate 286). In execution the painting is sumptuous, with flashes of white over grey and highlighted by the rich gold of her jewels. The portrait, for all its surface

PLATE 280 (above left)
Thomas Lawrence
Archduke Charles of Austria, c.1818-19
106 ¾ x 70 ¼ ins. (271 x 178.5cm)
(Royal Collection: Windsor Castle)

PLATE 281 (above)
Thomas Lawrence
Pope Pius VII, c.1818-19
106 x 70ins. (269 x 178cm)
(Royal Collection: Windsor Castle)

PLATE 282 (left)
Thomas Lawrence
Cardinal Consalvi, c.1818-19
105 ¼ x 68 ¾ ins. (267.5 x 174.5cm)
(Royal Collection: Windsor Castle)

PLATE 283
Thomas Lawrence
George IV, 1822
106½ x 70½ ins.
(270.5 x 179cm)
(Wallace Collection,
London)

pattern, bears evidence of what must have been a brush with contemporary
French portraiture. With her long neck and sloping shoulders, the anatomy of
Mrs. Bathurst speaks very loudly of Ingres, whose works Lawrence must have
seen on his second trip to Paris in 1825. A portrait of the Duchesse de Berri
(Plate 287) also reveals Lawrence's curious interest in Ingrian anatomy, as

PLATE 284 (left)
Thomas Lawrence
Lord Nugent, c.1813
94 x 58ins.
(239 x 147.5cm)
(Christie's sale 20.11.87,
99)

PLATE 285
Thomas Lawrence
George Canning, 1822
35½ x 27½ins.
(90 x 70cm)
(Leger Galleries,
London)

does another portrait of an English lady, the Countess of Belfast (Plate 288).

Lawrence's abilities to paint children matched those of Reynolds, who was another confirmed bachelor. Hoppner surely understood children better, being a father of five, but Lawrence and Reynolds covered their ignorance with great invention. The portrait of Julia Peel by Lawrence (Plate 289) is an artificial image combining the influence of Reynolds and Van Dyck and evocative of the romantic sensibilities of landscape and human beings. The little child is surrounded and enveloped by the landscape but is seemingly protected by the crimson curtain over her head.

Surely Lawrence's best known portrait of children is that of Emily and Laura Anne Calmady (Colour Plate 52). It is painted with Lawrence's usual brilliance, with bright whites, clear colours and an evocative landscape, and has been celebrated for its happy evocation of childhood exuberance. On one level the picture is a homage to Michelangelo in its tondo form and gestures from various figures in 'The Last Judgment'; further evidence of Lawrence's genius was in borrowing those poses and applying them believably to a portrait of two girls.

The Calmady children were painted in 1824, at the height of French romanticism. But the romanticism of English portraiture is defined by its roots

PLATE 286 (above)
Thomas Lawrence
The Hon. Mrs. Seymour Bathurst, 1828
56 x 44¼ins. (142 x 112.5cm)
(Dallas Museum of Art)

PLATE 287 (above right)
Thomas Lawrence
The Duchesse de Berri, 1825
36 x 28ins. (91.5 x 71cm)
(Musée National du Chateau de Versailles)

PLATE 288 (right)
Thomas Lawrence
The Countess of Belfast, c.1829
35½ x 27½ins. (90 x 70cm)
(Private collection)

in the generation before Lawrence, the generation of Reynolds and Gainsborough. English artists of the generation after Reynolds were highly intelligent, they constantly met and discussed art and artistic theory, and they were technically and visually curious. It is this generation that took the teaching and the experience of the masters like Reynolds and refined them, bringing them up to date in a world of Napoleonic turmoil.

JOHN WILSON
Curator of Painting and Sculpture
Cincinnati Art Museum

PLATE 290
George Hayter
Sketch for a portrait of Princess Victoria, 1832
18⅛ x 12ins. (46 x 30.5cm)
(Royal Collection)

Chapter 5
The Victorians
1830-1880

The portraiture of any epoch may be seen as a measure of individual and national confidence and self-esteem. Painters are commissioned or volunteer to record not just the likenesses of their contemporaries, but also to inform posterity how a generation sees itself and how it hopes to be regarded by its descendants. A society which feels insecure, politically or materially, may respond by promoting images of its own members which suggest permanence and imperviousness to threat; conversely, when a mood of intellectual and moral certainty prevails the self-image of individuals is often modest and contained. These opposing tendencies operate both on a long historical scale and contemporaneously; during the early and mid-Victorian periods an evolution of portrait styles occurred — from a tradition which depended upon grandiose formulae inherited from the seventeenth and eighteenth centuries, through to the direct and egalitarian observation of individual sitters. Even within the careers of artists who were prepared or proud to represent the age, to provide its painted memorial without cynicism or resentment, there is a wide variety of approaches, and the portraiture of the second and third quarters of the nineteenth century serves as a reminder of the unpredictability of the Victorian frame of mind.

Since the middle of the eighteenth century portraiture had been perceived as one of the signal achievements of English and Scottish art and a tradition which had been maintained with great continuity. However, the death on 7 January 1830 of Sir Thomas Lawrence, President of the Royal Academy and foremost portrait painter of the Regency, seemed to interrupt the chain of careers which stretched back to the age of Van Dyck, and left British art enfeebled and lacking leadership. A portrait style which derived from Lawrence, although seldom conducted with the verve and virtuosity which made his works so individual, was practised by the generation of artists born in the 1790s or soon after the turn of the nineteenth century and who came to prominence in the years after Lawrence's death. Martin Archer Shee succeeded Lawrence to the presidency and exhibited portraits each year at the Academy; few of these, however, are memorable works of art.

George Hayter (1792-1871) was a more original and ambitious painter than

Shee, and may be seen as representative of the artistic mood in the years before and after Queen Victoria's accession to the throne. As a young man he had travelled in Italy, and there had come to appreciate the purpose of High Art — by which term was meant historical and mythological subjects — to uplift and delight a cultivated circle of patrons. From 1818 Hayter was based in London, and found himself in demand as a portraitist, a speciality which he at first sought to combine with neo-classical figurative subjects. Gradually, however, Hayter came round to a type of painting more easily understood by the generality of English patrons: events from contemporary life which include portraits of the eminent men and women of the age; and as such he became, in his own words, the 'painter of history in his own time'. The first of these subjects 'The Trial of Queen Caroline' (National Portrait Gallery), was exhibited in 1823; later, following a further period abroad, he embarked upon a painting of the House of Commons during its first sitting after the Great Reform Bill of 1832 (Colour Plate 53). Each member appears as a recognisable portrait, made on the basis of an individual study.

In 1832 Hayter gained a commission to paint the Princess Victoria. The sketch (Plate 290) for this portrait shows with what bravura the initial idea for a composition might be blocked out. The future Queen stands in an open colonnade surrounded by the clutter of the schoolroom. In 1837 the Queen appointed him Painter of History and Portraits, saying of him that he was 'Out and out the best portrait painter in my opinion'. In 1840 it was he who provided the state portrait of the new Queen (Guildhall Art Gallery), as well as a group portrait of the coronation (Royal Collection). Despite the refusal of the Royal Academy to admit Hayter as a member (perhaps because of the irregularity of his domestic life), he was for a while the most prominent portraitist of the age. His fortunes deteriorated in the 1840s, partly as a result of the influence of the Prince Consort, who preferred Landseer and Winterhalter as painters in the service of the court.

The young Queen had fairly unsophisticated ideas about art, and made modest demands upon her portraitists. John Partridge (1790-1872) enjoyed royal patronage in the early years of the reign; his dashing portrait of Prince Albert in the uniform of the Hussars (Royal Collection) was well received (the companion piece of the Queen, also in the Royal Collection, was considered less successful), and shortly afterwards he was appointed Portrait Painter Extraordinary to H.M. the Queen and H.R.H. Prince Albert. Partridge's portrait of William Lamb, Viscount Melbourne shows what he was capable of (Colour Plate 54).

Typical of the generation of portraitists who came to prominence in the 1830s, and whose works are original enough without departing from inherited formulae of composition, was Margaret Carpenter (1793-1872), who had a successful professional career painting children (Plate 291). She worked with freedom and feeling, delighting in the pile of velvet and the gleam of well-brushed hair, and in a series of Eton Leaving Portraits expressed the epicene

beauty of youth. Charles Robert Leslie (1794-1859), like Hayter and Partridge, gained commissions to paint portraits of the Royal Family including, for example, 'The Christening of the Princess Royal' (Royal Collection). His painting of the Grosvenor Family (Colour Plate 55) is essentially a conversation piece in which meticulously studied portraits of each member of the family are welded together into a delightful scene of domestic life.

In the 1830s a taste for sweet and psychologically unchallenging paintings of young people in pleasant domestic surroundings grew up. When the Queen was drawn by Alfred Edward Chalon (1780-1860) he showed her as a doll-like creature, mindless and without expression (Scottish National Portrait Gallery), and despite this the watercolour seems to have met with approval. Many members of society were represented in this way, and the boundary between portraiture and fashion-plate was uncertain. The ultimate expression of this tendency were the *Keepsake* annuals, which were issued between 1827 and 1852, where coloured engravings after paintings of fashionable young women of the period — usually treated in a prettified and artificial way and given fanciful titles — delighted a wide public. One of the most technically adept of the many artists who supplied the *Keepsake* magazines was the Scot, Robert

Thorburn (1818-85), whose portrait of Andalusia Grant, Lady Molesworth, was engraved and published (Plate 292). However, not all artists of the 1830s were uncritical of their sitters. Frederick Cruikshank (1800-68), for example, gave a candid but affectionate portrait of a middle-aged woman, self-conscious and perhaps rather silly, seated among the emblems of her respectability (Plate 293).

If English portrait painting in the 1830s felt the loss of Lawrence, Scottish portraitists were also dependent on a native tradition, in their case that

established by Sir Henry Raeburn who had died in 1823. William Allan (1782-1850) became President of the Royal Scottish Academy in 1837 and was admired both for his subject paintings and his portraits, of which Sir Walter Scott and his youngest daughter, Anne, is an example (Plate 294). John Watson Gordon's (1788-1864) representations of Scottish literary figures — James Hogg 'The Ettrick Shepherd' (Scottish National Portrait Gallery), Professor Wilson (who wrote under the pseudonym of Christopher North), and his several portraits of Walter Scott — are expressive and characterful. Of a later period is his portrait of the Reverend Thomas Chalmers, a dour but sympathetic work of impressive physical presence (Scottish National Portrait

PLATE 295
John Watson Gordon
Christian Broun, wife of the 9th Earl of Dalhousie,
1830
50 x 40ins. (127 x 101.5cm)
(Private collection)

PLATE 296
Andrew Geddes
The daughters of George Arbuthnot of Elderslie,
1839
71½ x 94ins. (181.5 x 239cm)
(Christie's sale 22.11.85, 113)

Gallery). As a painter of women he may be judged by his elegant portrait of Christian Broun, wife of the 9th Earl of Dalhousie (Plate 295). Francis Grant wrote of Watson Gordon in 1827: 'His talents are of a very high class and his portraits, which are faithful delineations from nature, are painted in a firm manly style...Mr. Watson Gordon is at present acknowledged to be the first portrait painter in Scotland'. A near contemporary of Watson Gordon was Andrew Geddes (1783-1844) who was also best known as a portraitist. Geddes's painting of the daughters of George Arbuthnot of Elderslie (Plate 296), in which the six girls are wearing dresses of the period of Charles I, shows his conscious emulation of historical styles of portraiture. Characteristic is his standing portrait of David Wilkie, where the breadth of handling belies the small scale of the work (Scottish National Portrait Gallery).

A few years younger than Watson Gordon and Geddes were the portraitists Robert Scott Lauder (1803-69) and Daniel Macnee (1806-82). The former worked with William Allan and subsequently spent a period in Europe, studying renaissance and baroque art. After his return in the late 1830s he began work as a portraitist, and also painted religious subjects; from this period comes his delightful portrait of John Gibson Lockhart, with his wife Sophia Scott (Plate 297). Highly romantic is his portrait of the artist David Roberts, the subject dressed in the robes of an Ottoman warrior (Scottish National Portrait Gallery). Lauder had among his pupils various distinguished Scottish portraitists of the late century, including William Orchardson (1832-1910) and George Reid (1841-1913). Daniel Macnee studied at the Trustees' Academy in Edinburgh (where he was a fellow-student of Lauder) but in due course he returned to his native Glasgow where he built up an extensive portrait practice — his only rival being Graham Gilbert. Macnee painted with great facility, and was particularly respected for his charming and utterly relaxed portraits of female sitters, of which the 'Lady in Grey' (in fact a portrait of the artist's daughter, modelled on Reynolds's portrait of Nelly O'Brien) may serve as an example (Colour Plate 56). Macnee succeeded Watson Gordon as President of the R.S.A. Lauder and Macnee exhibited portraits in London as well as in Scotland, and consequently gained national reputations (international in the case of Macnee who was a prize-winner at the Paris Universal Exhibition of 1855).

A distinction may be drawn between those painters who were portraitists first and foremost and who depended upon portrait commissions for their livelihoods, and those who were principally known for other types of work but who occasionally produced portraits. David Wilkie (1785-1841) owed his wider reputation to his scenes of popular life, but he also painted portraits and in these he was perhaps less constrained than various of his portrait-specialist contemporaries. Wilkie could manage the grandest style of portraiture — his state-portrait of William IV, the King seen wearing the uniform of the Grenadier Guards, has a scale and physical presence equal to Lawrence's royal portraits (Plate 298); on the other hand, his portrait of the Duke of York, has

PLATE 297
Robert Scott Lauder
John Gibson Lockhart with his wife Sophia Scott, n.d.
30¼ x 25½ins. (77 x 65cm)
(Scottish National Portrait Gallery, Edinburgh)

PLATE 298
David Wilkie
William IV in the uniform of the Grenadier Guards, 1833
105 x 69ins. (267 x 173cm)
(Victoria and Albert Museum: Apsley House, London)

an informal air, as if the painter had caught his royal subject unaware (National Portrait Gallery). A delightful domestic scene is set in his portrait of Joseph Wilson and his grandson; the old man pauses for thought with his spectacles on his forehead, while the boy is poised with pen and paper to record his grandfather's words. The two figures are lit by the light of the fire beside which they sit (Plate 299).

William Mulready (1786-1863), who had been born in Ireland a year after Wilkie's birth in Scotland, was likewise an occasional portraitist. Two works, both paintings of people whom Mulready had known well, demonstrate his particular skill: the Countess of Dartmouth and 'Interior with a Portrait of John Sheepshanks' (Plate 300). Lady Dartmouth was exceptionally tall and Mulready seems to recall a slightly self-conscious but at the time relaxed posture. The rectilinear arrangement of the background suggests with amiable understatement the setting of a great house, from the marble volute of the chimney piece and the richly framed Claude landscape, to the wicker log basket and snoozing terrier. John Sheepshanks, a textile magnate who formed

PLATE 299 (left)
David Wilkie
Joseph Wilson and his grandson, c.1839
31 x 27ins.
(78.5 x 68.5cm)
(Christie's sale 7.7.67, 115)

PLATE 300 (above)
William Mulready
*'Interior with a Portrait of John Sheepshanks',
1832-34*
20 x 15¾ins (51 x 40cm)
(Victoria and Albert Museum, London)

a great collection of contemporary art, is perhaps more aware of the splendour of the room he occupies, and is observed commanding a servant who carries a tray and letters. In his fondness for the colour and detail of the peripheral areas Mulready anticipates the portraiture and interior painting of the middle part of the century.

Mulready's friend John Linnell (1792-1882) was a prolific portraitist in his earlier career and up until about 1846. Many of his models were friends and fellow artists, and are painted on a small scale and in informal circumstances — Mulready himself was painted by him in 1833 (National Portrait Gallery) — but Linnell also accepted commissions, and supported himself and his family by that means. His portrait of Mrs. Henry Stephen, wearing a wide brimmed hat and seated in an open landscape, is dated 1830, and in 1838 he gave a characteristically feathered and loosely defined treatment of Sir Robert Peel (then in opposition following the defeat of his first government). Here we find no trace of pomp, but rather a gentle and sensitive looking man engaging on terms of equality with the spectator (Plate 301). Later Linnell devoted himself to landscape, and portrait commissions were forwarded to his friend George Richmond. Linnell stated that of the two genres 'portraits [he] painted to live, but [he] lived to paint poetical landscape'.

As a young man in Cork, Daniel Maclise (1806-20) made portrait drawings of the eminent people he encountered; he scored a notable success with his portrait of Walter Scott (British Museum) who visited Ireland in 1825, and in

PLATE 301 (above)
John Linnell
Sir Robert Peel, 1838
17⅞ x 14⅞ ins. (45.5 x 38cm)
(National Portrait Gallery, London)

PLATE 302 (above right)
Daniel Maclise
Richard Sainthill, n.d.
18 x 14ins. (45.5 x 35.5cm), pencil
(Peter Nahum Gallery, London)

PLATE 303 (right)
Daniel Maclise
Charles Dickens, 1839
36 x 28⅛ ins. (91.5 x 71.5cm)
(Tate Gallery, London: on loan to the National
Portrait Gallery, London)

PLATE 304
Edwin Landseer
The Viscountess FitzHarris,
1834
16¾ x 21ins.
(42.5 x 53.5cm)
(Private collection)

due course Maclise found he could support himself by this means. Maclise's drawing of the Irish numismatist and antiquarian Richard Sainthill, seen standing before the Gothic tomb of his ancestor (Plate 302), shows the precise and linear style of draughtsmanship which he developed. He claimed to have drawn nearly a thousand portraits of this type in his early career. His chief ambition as an artist, however, was to paint historical subjects, and when his career was established he made fewer drawings and resisted commissions for oil portraits except in the case of friends. One of the masterpieces of early Victorian portraiture is Maclise's 'Charles Dickens' (Plate 303). The novelist is seen seated at a table on which lies a manuscript; he pauses in thought and gazes abstractedly towards the light of the window. The portrait was commissioned by Dickens's publishers and appeared as an engraved frontispiece to *Nicholas Nickleby*. The work was applauded when first seen, Thackeray writing of it: 'As a likeness [it is] perfectly amazing; a looking-glass could not render a better facsimile. Here we have the real identical man Dickens; the artist must have understood the inward Boz as well as the outward before he made this admirable representation of him'.

An occasional, and usually reluctant, portraitist was Edwin Landseer (1802-73), of whom Richard Ormond has written: 'Portraiture was not [his] natural *métier,* and he resented its demands...No sooner had Landseer established a name as a portraitist — and he was constantly in demand — than he began to tire of it'. In 1854 Landseer told the Duke of Devonshire that he

COLOUR PLATE 53
George Hayter
'The House of Commons, 1833', 1833-34
118¼ x 196ins. (300.5 x 498cm)
Hayter turned from the themes of High Art to paint a series of large-scale groups which record events in public life, and in doing so became what he called the 'painter of history in his own time'. In this work, which shows the first sitting of the House of Commons after the Great Reform Bill of 1832, each Member of Parliament appears as a recognisable portrait, painted on the basis of an individual study
(National Portrait Gallery, London)

COLOUR PLATE 54
John Partridge
William Lamb, 2nd Viscount Melbourne, 1844
50 x 40ins. (127 x 101.5cm)
Partridge was a fashionable portraitist in political and court circles in the 1840s, and for a few years was one of the young Queen Victoria's most favoured artists. His painting of Lord Melbourne is imbued with the sense of propriety expected of portraitists who operated in the public domain
(National Portrait Gallery, London)

COLOUR PLATE 55
Charles Robert Leslie
The Grosvenor Family, 1833
40 x 57ins. (127 x 101.5cm)
This representation of the domestic life of an aristocratic family is essentially a conversation piece in the tradition of Hayman and Zoffany; meticulously studied portraits are welded together into a scene which is apparently naturalistic, and yet in which much thought has been given to psychological and physical conjunction (Private collection)

thought of himself as an animal painter rather than a portraitist, and that he would undertake portraits only when 'combined with the picturesque or with a sort of Story'. Landseer's portrait of the Viscountess FitzHarris contains the elements which were to establish his popularity: a seductive if unrevealing vision of aristocratic life; a figure who is both languid and imperious; an immaculate representation of textures; and a delicious quality of cast light from the open casement (Plate 304).

In 1838 Landseer was commissioned to paint a life-size equestrian portrait of Queen Victoria, which was intended to hang with the state portraits of the British royal family. The artist was in difficulty from the start and the portrait was never finished. More successful was his 'Windsor Castle in Modern Times' in which the royal couple and their first-born, Princess Victoria, are seen surrounded by the trophies of the chase (Plate 305 and Colour Plate 8). What appears relaxed and informal resulted in fact from long meditation on how a queen and her prince-husband should present themselves in the modern age. The Queen may perhaps have despaired of receiving the picture, for she wrote in 1845: 'Landseer's Game Picture (begun in 1840!!)...is at long last hung up in our sitting room...& is...altogether very cheerful & pleasing'. The closest thing to a formal royal portrait to be undertaken by Landseer shows Victoria and Albert in costumes of the period of Edward III, and was done to commemorate a fancy-dress ball given at Buckingham Palace in 1842 (Plate 306).

Landseer failed as a royal portraitist because he believed that an artist should

PLATE 306
Edwin Landseer
*Queen Victoria and Prince
Albert in fancy dress,
1842-46*
58¼ x 44⅛ ins.
(148 x 112cm)
(Royal Collection)

use humour to give clues to a sitter's personality, but this sense of fun was not
condoned by royal protocol. Occasionally, particularly when working on a
small scale and without the pressure of a commission, Landseer brought
members of the royal household to life in his paintings — an example is his
study of Princess Victoire which combines a strain of caricature with perfect
observation (Plate 307).

If various distinguished British painters of the early Victorian period
deliberately avoided a dependence on portraiture, there were nevertheless
many willing portrait specialists. A leading figure in the art world of the mid-
century, indeed from 1866 to 1878 President of the Royal Academy, was

COLOUR PLATE 56
Daniel Macnee
'Lady in Grey', 1859
50 x 40ins. (127 x 101.5cm)
A feeling for colour and handling is best seen in Macnee's works of the late 1840s and
1850s, and particularly in the portraits which he did of friends and family. This
relaxed and charming painting shows the artist's daughter, seated in a garden with
embroidery in her lap, looking inquisitively up to the spectator
(National Gallery of Scotland, Edinburgh)

COLOUR PLATE 57
Henry Nelson O'Neil
'The Landing of H.R.H. The Princess Alexandra at Gravesend, 7th March 1863'
52 x 84ins. (132 x 213.5cm)
Victorian patriotism was indulged in records of events such as this — the arrival in this country of the bride of the Prince of Wales. Carefully observed portraits of the distinguished company are combined with an atmosphere of the utmost festivity (National Portrait Gallery, London)

COLOUR PLATE 58
Richard Dadd
Sir Alexander Morison, 1852
20 x 24ins. (51 x 61cm)
This portrait of one of the doctors who cared for the inmates of the Bethlem Hospital, to which asylum Dadd was committed after he murdered his father, conveys the quality of humane compassion one man may have for another
(Scottish National Portrait Gallery, Edinburgh)

PLATE 307 (above)
Edwin Landseer
Princess Victoire, 1839
17½ x 14ins.
(44.5 x 35.5cm)
(Royal Collection)

PLATE 308 (right)
Francis Grant
*Sketch for the equestrian
portrait of Queen Victoria,
c.1845*
39¼ x 54ins.
(99.5 x 137cm)
(Royal Collection)

Francis Grant (1803-78). In the portraits he painted of the prominent figures of the age — politicians, soldiers, sportsmen, and men and women of the *bon ton* — he introduced a grandeur and scale which had not often been seen since the passing of Lawrence. Grant may not have been an artistic pioneer, but he understood and utilised the traditions of British portraiture. Billowing draperies and stupendous columns provide the architectural setting, and figures are placed well back from the plane of the picture surface lest the spectator should learn too much about their appearance or imagine himself on terms of equality. These paintings were done to furnish country houses, as presentation portraits from loyal tenants or clansmen, or to embellish clubs and government offices, paid for by subscription of the members or by the Exchequer. They hung with works by Van Dyck, Reynolds and Gainsborough, and Grant, not in any way daunted by this, learnt how to adapt his style so his works would blend harmoniously with their neighbours.

This painter's career was tersely summarised by Queen Victoria in 1838: 'Grant, a very good-looking man, was a gentleman, married a Miss Norman, and now paints for money'. Grant spent his money on, among other things, fox-hunting and it was appropriate that he should have sought to recoup by painting hunting scenes. Works such as 'A Meet of the Fife Hounds' (Scottish National Portrait Gallery), cabinet-sized but incorporating recognisable portraits of men and animals, gained him a considerable reputation. Grant first painted the Queen in 1840; his 'Queen Victoria riding out with her Gentlemen', is an effective and bustling scene (Royal Collection). Later in the decade he embarked on an equestrian portrait of her alone and, having been

PLATE 309 (left)
Francis Grant
John Charles, 7th Earl of Seafield, with his son Ian, 1858
94 x 60ins.
(238.5 x 152.5cm)
(Christie's sale, Cullen House, 22.9.75, 523)

PLATE 310 (above)
Francis Grant
Henry Charles Fitzroy Somerset, 8th Duke of Beaufort, and his wife Georgiana, 1864
approx. 132 x 96ins.
(345 x 244cm)
(Badminton House)

warned off by Landseer who thought that Grant's first scheme was too similar to the royal portrait with which he was struggling at the time, he conceived of a painting of the Queen mounted on a rearing horse with a distant view of Windsor Castle. The sketch for this subject (Plate 308), which is dependent upon Velazquez rather than Van Dyck, shows with what verve the untrained artist handled paint and how confidently he arranged the outlines of the composition.

Gradually the Queen came to disapprove of Grant, and he in turn resented the demands and obligations of royal patronage. Even so his career prospered and many of his best works date from the 1850s and 1860s. His portrait of the 7th Earl of Seafield with his son Ian, is a splendid representation of a great Highland laird (Plate 309). The double equestrian portrait of the Duke and Duchess of Beaufort, which was exhibited at the R.A. in 1864, epitomises the sporting aristocracy — bluff and unaffected, and standing in their own vast demesne (Plate 310). Grant was concerned with image rather than personality, and never introduced any detail which was untoward or required explanation. His nearest approach to an experimental or spontaneous type of painting was in the portraits of his daughter Mary Isabella.

Portraitists found Queen Victoria increasingly hard to please. A lady-in-

COLOUR PLATE 59
Edward Burne-Jones
Maria Zambaco, 1870
30 x 21⅛ ins. (76 x 55cm)
Burne-Jones painted this portrait both as a tribute to Maria Zambaco's striking beauty
and as declaration of his love for her. Cupid, the god of love, holds back a curtain to
reveal the sitter to the spectator; a peacock feather quill has wrapped around it a love
message from the painter; and the sitter's hands rest upon the page of an illustrated
book in which is represented Burne-Jones's own painting, *Le Chant d'Amour*
(Clemens-Sels Museum, Neuss)

COLOUR PLATE 60
Anthony Frederick Augustus Sandys
Mrs. Jane Lewis, 1864
26 x 22ins. (66 x 56cm)
Sandys's technical skill allowed him to introduce a degree of realism into his paintings
and drawings unsurpassed by any of his contemporaries. This immaculate portrait of
an elderly woman, seen seated in a richly furnished interior, has a strange and eerie
quality — the woman's physiognomy and dress, and the trappings of the interior, are
observed in microscopic detail, yet the mood of the painting remains impassive and
remote
(J. Paul Getty Museum, Malibu)

PLATE 311
Franz Xaver Winterhalter
'The Reception of King Louis-Philippe at Windsor Castle', 1844
136 x 189ins.
(345 x 480cm)
(Musée National du Château de Versailles)

waiting, Eleanor Stanley, described how on one occasion in 1845 'the Queen fired a terrible broadside at English artists both as regards their works and...their prices, and their charging her particularly high...' It was fortunate that in 1842 a German artist was presented to her who was, she thought, 'an excellent man full of zeal for his art, of goodwill, obligingness and real modesty' — Franz Xaver Winterhalter (1805-73). The Prince Consort agreed, and from this time on the artist visited the court most summers and in the years 1842-71 painted more than a hundred works for the British royal family. Winterhalter was a court artist in a way that none of his English counterparts was; he devoted himself heart and soul to the royal families of Europe, and was content to have no other career as an artist. He came into his own with paintings such as 'The Reception of King Louis-Philippe at Windsor Castle' (Plate 311), understanding the exact degree of informality which might be mixed with the decorum of the occasion, and making such events appear both immediate and momentous. Equally, his state portraits combine dignity (and a close observation of the iconography of royal portraiture) with remarkable naturalism.

Winterhalter, unlike Landseer, did what he was told, and reserved his best efforts for his royal patrons. In 1843 the Queen commissioned what she called 'the *secret* picture' of herself, with shoulders bare and hair unbraided, as a

320

PLATE 312
Franz Xaver Winterhalter
Queen Victoria
25¾ x 21ins. (65.5 x 53.5cm)
(Royal Collection)

PLATE 313
**Franz Xaver
Winterhalter**
*Albert Edward, Prince of
Wales, 1846*
50⅛ x 34¾ ins.
(127.5 x 88.5cm)
(Royal Collection)

present for her husband (Plate 312). She wrote of its reception: 'The surprise was so great, and he thought it so like, and so beautifully painted. I felt so proud and happy to have found something that gave him so much pleasure'. This work of unashamed sensuality hung in Albert's dressing room. In 1846 Winterhalter painted 'The Royal Family', which is perhaps the most highly evolved of all his celebrations of royal connubial happiness and fecundity (Royal Collection). Of great character and charm is the portrait of the Prince of Wales, hands in the pockets of his sailor suit and full of jaunty fun (Plate 313).

On the occasion of Winterhalter's death Victoria wrote to one of her daughters: 'His works will in time rank with Vandyck. He painted you all from your birth. There was not another portrait painter like him in the world'. In 1847 an exhibition of Winterhalter's royal portraits was held at St. James's Palace; this was a popular success, but made little impact among artists or critics for most of whom Winterhalter was anathema. The *Athenaeum*'s critic expressed a generally held artistic prejudice: 'The Queen and Prince, though likenesses, are yet sensual and fleshy visions of those distinguished persons...[There is] such an odour of paint, and such a want of taste — as makes us frankly rejoice that it is not from the hands of an Englishman'.

A good living was to be made from painting portraits — there was always

COLOUR PLATE 61
James McNeill Whistler
*'Harmony in Grey and Green: Miss
Cicely Alexander'*, 1872-73
74¾ x 38½ ins. (190 x 98cm)
Whistler believed that a portrait
was a self-contained entity which
depended upon formal qualities
of line and colour rather than
the degree of likeness. He
attempted to convey the
personality of the sitter by stance
and silhouette rather than any
momentary expression, and for
this reason his portraiture may
be regarded as one of the classic
achievements of Victorian art
(Tate Gallery, London: on loan
to the National Gallery, London)

COLOUR PLATE 62
George Frederic Watts
Katie Lewis, 1882
56 x 31ins. (142 x 79cm)
Watts's portrait of the
daughter of the distinguished
lawyer Sir George Lewis was
almost certainly a
commissioned work. The
child, who was also painted
by Burne-Jones, is seen
seated in an undefined
interior. She has a wistful
air, and yet seems resigned
to the attentions of the
portraitist
(Private collection)

PLATE 314
Stephen Pearce
'The Arctic Council,
planning a Search for Sir
John Franklin', 1851
46¼ x 72⅛ ins.
(117.5 x 183cm)
(National Portrait
Gallery, London)

a queue of people, from the Queen and court through to hundreds of thousands of self-made men, who wished themselves or their families to be commemorated in paint. In addition to the painters of different subjects who would sometimes undertake portrait commissions there was a legion of jobbing portrait specialists who satisfied this commercial demand. Grant charged 300 guineas for full-lengths and 400 guineas for life-size equestrian portraits in the 1840s; and in 1845, according to his sitters' book, he undertook twenty-two commissions and earned about £3,500 — equivalent to a good professional salary and sufficient to allow him to live in considerable style. The dealer Colnaghi wrote to a client in Paris apropos portraitists' fees: 'Les prix que M. Winterhalter demande à Londres pour un portrait en buste est de cent guineas, un portrait jusqu'aux genoux 200 gns, en pied 300 gns. Ce sont les mêmes prix que les artistes anglais demandent'. So it seems that a price structure was well established, at least at the top of the market. Prices tended to increase as the century progressed; the fashionable portraitist Richard Buckner earned as much as £3,000 a year in the 1850s and over £6,000 in the 1860s for his sugary portraits of women and children. George Elgar Hicks found that, from a part-time portrait practice, he earned as much as £4,000 a year several years running in the 1880s. The brisk portrait trade in Victorian England attracted many foreign-born artists in search of a better living than they could make at home.

Portraiture was a genre endorsed by the Royal Academy. Large numbers of portraits were shown at the summer exhibitions, and further commissions

PLATE 315
Henry Wyndham Phillips
'The Royal Commissioners for the Exhibition of 1851',
n.d.
82½ x 141ins.
(209.5 x 358cm)
(Victoria and Albert Museum, London)

were presumably received on these occasions. A feeling of resentment grew up against academicians who monopolised space for their portrait output; a critic wrote in 1859: 'It really is quite pitiable walking through the rooms of the present Royal Academy Exhibition to look round upon the walls and watch the wholesale plunder of space by these greedy hacksters...Grant R.A. sends six portraits'. The problem was exacerbated by the works themselves often being so very large. As *Fraser's Magazine* put it in 1860: 'John Smith, Esq...in the catalogue does not make more show than any other entry, but John Smith on the wall represents at least thirty or forty square feet of space...' A tendency grew up in the middle of the century for portraits to pass under the anonymity of genre titles. *Fraser's* disapproved of 'the distinguished portrait entered under some fancy title like "The Mossrose", or "The Young Housewife", or "Looking Forward". These portraits, whose modesty is so great that they cannot bear publicity, even under the orthodox disguise of "ladies" or "gentlemen" are becoming so common'. Grant was accused of this practice, but he was worried himself by the predominance of portraits or portrait-style subjects at the summer exhibitions, explaining to the R.A. Commission of 1863 that academicians were tempted to 'give way to the importunities of people who wished their portraits to be exhibited', and suggesting that if R.A.s and A.R.A.s were restricted to four exhibits fewer portraits would be shown overall.

If Grant was the most prominent of the portrait specialists of the mid-century he was still only one among many. Among the artists regarded by Richard and Samuel Redgrave as representative of the mid-Victorian age the name of Henry William Pickersgill (1782-1875) was coupled with that of Grant, but in reality he lacked Grant's instinctive talent and sense of style. Pickersgill's forte seems to have been the representation of professional men, complete with the trophies of their trades — scientists surrounded by specimens, lawyers draped in wigs and gowns, and so on; the Redgraves wrote him off as 'a portrait painter whose works are distinguished more by their being satisfactory likenesses than for any artistic qualities they possess'. William Boxall (1800-79) painted dutiful portraits of his contemporaries — his output was considered uneven by the Redgraves — and he is perhaps best represented by the portrait of the sculptor John Gibson which he gave to the Royal Academy as his diploma piece. John Prescott Knight (1803-81), who combined a career as a portraitist with the secretaryship of the R.A., was more kindly treated by the Redgraves; portraits such as that of Sir Charles Barry (National Portrait Gallery) 'are characterised by excellent drawing, and are ably placed upon the canvas, and are good in colour and masculine in execution'.

There was a steady demand for group portraits, which frequently celebrated the spirit of enterprise and mutual reliance of professional life in the Victorian age. John Lucas (1807-74) often painted engineers and inventors; his 'Conference of Engineers at the Menai Straits prior to floating a Tube of the Britannia Bridge' commemorates the technical ingenuity which was transforming the landscape. Stephen Pearce (1819-1904) was commissioned to paint 'The Arctic Council, planning a Search for Sir John Franklin' in 1851, a group which consists of carefully studied portraits of ten gentlemen in naval uniforms, each psychologically unrelated to the next (Plate 314). Henry Wyndham Phillips (1820-88) painted 'The Royal Commissioners for the Exhibition of 1851', a work which makes it clear that the artist's principal function was documentary — to give a literal and comprehensive account of the proceedings in which each party is given approximately equal prominence in the concentric groups around the figure of Prince Albert. Anything more animated, or more pictorially experimental, would not have satisfied the Commissioners (Plate 315). Patriotic feelings were indulged in records of events in public life such as 'The Landing of H.R.H. The Princess Alexandra at Gravesend, 7th March 1863' by Henry Nelson O'Neil (1817-80), a work which seeks to convey a sense of the pressure of a festive crowd with an accurate record of the distinguished people present (Colour Plate 57).

In most British cities there operated portraitists who enjoyed local followings, and in some cases these provincial artists had distinct talent even if their works may have appeared old fashioned by metropolitan standards. Such an artist was the Liverpool-based William Daniels (1813-80), who found such patronage and opportunity for exhibiting his works in his native city that he abandoned an early attempt to extend his practice to London and only very occasionally showed at the R.A. Among those of his works which remain in Liverpool, are 'Young Girl by a Pedestal' and Master Edmund Kirby, each painted with a sombre range of colours and strong contrasts of light and shade (both Walker Art Gallery).

The Grand Manner, with its apparatus of devices calculated to command the respect of the spectator, and which owed its origin to the works of Van Dyck, represented one principal strand in Victorian portraiture and indeed survived the period. An alternative tradition, which dealt in terms of directness and intimacy, grew up in the middle years of the century, deriving in part from a long tradition of miniature painting and portrait draughtsmanship. These two extremes of scale, and the different artistic purposes of each type — on the one hand to seek to impose upon a spectator, on the other to draw closer to the sitter and to reveal as much as possible both physically and psychologically — amounted to a schism of styles. There is a political dimension to this; portraiture may be seen as a form of personal propaganda — is deliberately so used by prominent figures in any age. Conversely, a style of portraiture which is candid and which does not seek to impress may be seen as the expression of a belief in equality and the claims of the individual. Realism in art served the purpose of differentiation, of allowing one man to see, understand and sympathise with another.

At an opposite pole to the type of portraiture which sought to display the prestige of the sitter was the art of Richard Dadd (1819-86). In the late 1830s and early 1840s Dadd made drawn portraits of members of his family and of members of the circle of artists known as The Clique; these are conventional enough although often full of character. After his incarceration in Bethlem Hospital he painted two extraordinary portraits, each of doctors who cared for him: Dr. Charles Hood (Private collection) and Sir Alexander Morison (Colour Plate 58). The first of these shows a young man seated on an ornamental bench in a garden; the second is of an older man, in fact Hood's predecessor at the Bethlem Hospital, seen standing before a panorama of the Firth of Forth. The landscape setting of each portrait was painted from memory. Both men radiate concern and sympathy for their painter-patient, who suffered from a type of mania they were among the first to try to understand.

As a young man George Richmond (1809-96) joined the circle of artists known as The Ancients, who gathered around the figure of Samuel Palmer and revered William Blake. His early portraits, including that of Palmer (National Portrait Gallery), are small in scale and dependent upon those of his father Thomas Richmond, who was a professional miniaturist, and the example of John Linnell. In 1831, as Raymond Lister has written, 'the responsibilities of marriage and a family . . . made Richmond reappraise his art. He had a fine gift for portraiture; and he turned to that to the exclusion of most other work'. In the course of his long career he painted and drew a vast assembly of men and women — a list of his sitters has about 2,500 entries, and includes members of the aristocracy, clergy and literary world.

Richmond's oil portraits are in a sense less original than his drawings. His

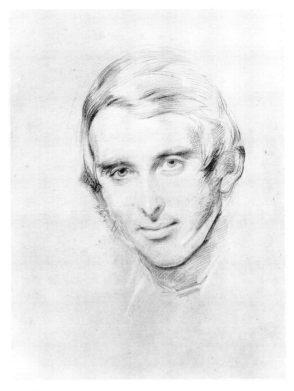

PLATE 317
George Richmond
John Ruskin, c.1843
17 x 14ins. (43 x 35.5cm), chalk
(National Portrait Gallery, London)

PLATE 316
George Richmond
William Wilberforce, 1833
17¼ x 13ins.
(44 x 33cm),
watercolour
(National Portrait
Gallery, London)

watercolour of William Wilberforce takes the spectator right into the book-strewn study of the reformer; the angle of vision is deliberately low, and one finds oneself face to face with the man who, sitting back in his chair, strains his head forward as if to catch the words of a conversation (Plate 316). Also painted in watercolour are Richmond's delightful family portraits, which are again products of the conversation piece tradition, for example 'The Four Daughters of John Bird Sumner, Archbishop of Canterbury' (Victoria and Albert Museum). Richmond's highly finished chalk drawings of his contemporaries — among many others John Ruskin (Plate 317) and Charlotte Brontë (National Portrait Gallery) were drawn by him — are works of extreme skilfulness, both for their accuracy of representation and for the sense of personality which they convey. They are built up from patterns of hatched chalk on buff-coloured paper, and usually concentrate on the head of the sitter; their realistic quality is remarkable and it comes as no surprise to find that the artist studied portrait photographs. Richmond's oil portraits are honest and informative; he neither flatters his sitters nor embarasses them with their pretensions. His portrait of Sir Henry Russell, done in 1850, shows a bare-headed man who seems to glance away from the spectator, and who is neither arrogant nor overbearing. Extremely sympathetic is the portrait of Mrs. William Fothergill Robinson, in which the old lady, who appears strong-willed

PLATE 318
George Richmond
Mrs. William Fothergill Robinson, 1870
37 x 27¾ins. (94 x 70.5cm)
(Fitzwilliam Museum, Cambridge)

PLATE 319
William Holman Hunt
'New College Cloisters,
1852', 1852
14 x 9⁵/₁₆ ins.
(35.5 x 24.5cm)
(Jesus College, Oxford)

and composed, sits with hands resting in an open book (Plate 318). Richmond's aim in portraiture was to convey a close likeness by naturalistic but, at the same time, carefully controlled means, in his words 'the truth lovingly told', a precept which places him in close relationship to the aesthetic philosophy of his younger contemporaries, the Pre-Raphaelites.

During the formative years of the Pre-Raphaelite movement, when the principle of minute observation of the forms of nature was established, relatively few portraits were painted — simply because the young artists who formed the Pre-Raphaelite Brotherhood received few portrait commissions, and in any case they preferred to get on with the literary and modern-life subjects which were their chosen *métier*. They did, however, find time to draw one another; the many pencil and chalk portraits of and by members of the P.R.B. reveal both the youthful appearance and mannerisms of the movement's protagonists, and convey something of the camaraderie and mood of mutual reliance which brought them together.

One of the first Pre-Raphaelite oil portraits is Holman Hunt's of Frederic George Stephens, done in 1846-47, in which the model is seen looking intently at the spectator as he turns in his chair (Tate Gallery). Hunt (1827-1910) was commissioned to portray the Tractarian cleric John David Jenkins in a painting entitled 'New College Cloisters, 1852' (Plate 319). In a letter to the

PLATE 320
William Holman Hunt
Henry Wentworth Monk, 1858
20 x 26ins. (51 x 66cm)
(National Gallery of Canada, Ottawa)

PLATE 322
John Everett Millais
Mrs. Coventry Patmore, 1851
7 ¾ x 8ins. (19.5 x 20.5cm)
(Fitzwilliam Museum, Cambridge)

PLATE 321
John Everett Millais
James Wyatt with his granddaughter Mary, 1849
14 x 17 ¾ ins. (35.5 x 45cm)
(Private collection: on loan to the Tate Gallery, London)

painting's owner Hunt wrote that John Ruskin had 'pronounced the portrait of the Curate to be the best he had ever seen as a specimen of painting, and as, he almost ventured to say, a likeness'. Hunt took care to give an accurate account of the fall of light from the lancets of the cloister — causing Jenkins's face to be lit from the side; equally he made symbolical reference to the High Church Anglicanism of which Jenkins was an advocate. A third portrait by Hunt which may be regarded as a product of Pre-Raphaelitism in its primary phase, that of Henry Wentworth Monk, was painted in 1858. Again he represented a visionary individual, the eccentric but prophetical Bible scholar who campaigned for a Jewish state in Palestine. The hirsute figure is tightly enclosed within the overall format, cut off at the shoulder and only just allowed space to display various emblems of his beliefs (Plate 320). Pre-Raphaelite artists felt a constant urge to draw closer to their subjects, seeking to study in minute detail the physiognomy of the sitter, thus to understand the intense emotional state of the individual.

Perhaps the first portrait to be commissioned from any member of the Pre-Raphaelite group was that by John Millais (1829-96) of the Oxford print dealer and collector of paintings James Wyatt with his granddaughter Mary, seen in the drawing room of Wyatt's house in The High and surrounded by his treasures which include a portrait of his daughter-in-law, Mary's mother, by Boxall. Great immediacy is injected into this portrait by the way in which the attention of both sitters seems to have been caught in a single moment by the artist (Plate 321). More severely iconic are his two small portraits, of Mrs. Coventry Patmore (Plate 322) and Wilkie Collins (National Portrait Gallery), in which the sitters' features are studied with intense and objective vision and without the distraction of peripheral detail.

Millais's portrait of John Ruskin, conceived and begun in the summer of 1853 while the painter and critic were staying together at Brig o'Turk in Scotland, is less concerned with the personality of the subject than with his philosophy. Ruskin stands on a rock in the bed of a Highland burn, meditating upon the processes by which the physical landscape is built up and destroyed (Plate 323). The minute representation of the natural details of the painting gave the artist much trouble, and he had to be chivvied by Ruskin before it was finished. The likeness and the stance of the figure were worked on by Millais in his studio in Gower Street during the following winter. One of the most powerful of all Pre-Raphaelite paintings, fulfilling as it does the fundamental criterion of fidelity to nature, is also a signal achievement in the history of Victorian portraiture. It is self-conscious in the way that most types of portraiture of any degree of elaboration must be — deriving from the artist's and sitter's thoughts as to how an individual may best be presented to posterity — and yet here all grandiosity and hubris are swept aside to reveal a man who stands bare-headed and bent at the knee before the elements of nature.

Several other artists in the Pre-Raphaelite circle were occasional portraitists. As a young man Dante Gabriel Rossetti (1828-82) found the techniques of oil

PLATE 323
John Everett Millais
John Ruskin, 1853-54
31 x 26¾ ins.
(78.5 x 68cm)
(Private collection)

painting difficult and he failed to achieve the degree of realism which characterised the movement in its formative stage. He was, however, a superb draughtsman; two examples serve to indicate the range and sensitivity of his portrait drawings in chalk, pencil and watercolour: one of Elizabeth Siddal, resting with her head on a pillow with her left hand raised to her face and her eyes downcast (Plate 324); another of Robert Browning, his characterful face tightly enclosed by the edges of the paper (Plate 325). Rossetti's friend George Price Boyce (1826-97) painted watercolour studies of young girls in the Pre-Raphaelite circle, which are similarly restricted in their format, and which are imbued with tender intimacy (Plate 326). John Ruskin (1819-1900) made watercolour portraits of friends, and to these he brought a characteristic expressiveness of draughtsmanship; an example is his profile of a beautiful young woman, Mrs. Kevill Davies (Plate 327).

Ford Madox Brown (1821-93) was not a member of the Pre-Raphaelite Brotherhood, but he was nevertheless dedicated to the principles of the group. Brown dispensed with all conventions of portraiture and confronted his sitters with candid accounts of themselves. One of the most extraordinary of all Pre-Raphaelite portraits is that by Brown of William Michael Rossetti (Plate 328). The critic's head and shoulders are contained within a square format and seen against the pattern of printed wallpaper. The qualities of immediacy and objectivity of the portrait are aided by the searching light of an oil or gas lamp which shines brightly on the sitter's bald head and which casts a single shadow on the glistening textures of the background. Brown's portrait of James

PLATE 328 (above)
Ford Madox Brown
William Michael Rossetti,
1856-57
6¾ x 6½ins.
(17 x 16.5cm)
(National Trust:
Wightwick Manor)

PLATE 329 (right)
Ford Madox Brown
James Leathart, 1863-64
13½ x 11ins.
(34.5 x 28cm)
(Private collection)

Leathart, who is likewise seen at close range, was the result of a commission (Plate 329). In the background may be observed the version of Brown's own painting 'Work' which Leathart owned, and to the left through an open window is seen the lead works on the bank of the Tyne at Newcastle of which he was the proprietor. It is understood from these references that the sitter was an industrialist as well as a patron of Pre-Raphaelite art. And yet, although these naturalistically treated emblems are represented in a spirit of mundane pride, the sitter remains forthright and self-confident and does not seem to shelter behind his achievements or possessions. Extraordinary for their directness of characterisation, and for their avoidance of all artifice or obscurity, are the drawn portraits which Brown made of his wife Emma (Plate 330).

Pre-Raphaelite portraits are usually small in overall size, even if occasionally, as for example in Millais's John Ruskin, a monumental quality is achieved. This was a style of painting which was, by its very nature, laborious, time-consuming and, in its pure form, seldom seen. As a constituent of the portraiture of the Victorian age the works of Hunt, Millais, Rossetti and Brown, and the few others who adopted the technique, represent a small part; but for their passionate belief that the art of portraiture, sincerely undertaken, might reveal the true individuality of the sitter, these paintings are profound and important. In its unaffected belief in the function of observation Pre-Raphaelite portraiture was paralleled by one of the popular art forms of the period — photography; a new sophistication of pictorial effect was learnt by painters from the work of photographers, just as photographers in turn

334

PLATE 330
Ford Madox Brown
Emma Madox Brown, 1867
15¼ x 14⅞ins. (39 x 37.5cm), chalk
(Philadelphia Museum of Art)

PLATE 331
Dante Gabriel Rossetti
Frederick Leyland, 1879
18 x 15½ins.
(45.5 x 30.5cm), chalk
(Delaware Art Museum,
Wilmington)

inherited or plagiarised the conventions and objectives of portrait painting. Pre-Raphaelite painters and photographers alike aimed to represent the physical presence of the sitter, in the words of Elizabeth Barrett Browning, 'the sense of nearness involved in the thing. . .the very shadow of the person lying there fixed for ever!'

The Aesthetic Movement, into which various of the precepts of Pre-Raphaelism were transmuted in the later 1860s, fostered a style of portraiture which, while remaining for the most part naturalistic, was concerned with the deliberate manipulation of mood as a means of exploring the sitter's inner soul. This was what W.M. Rossetti called the 'modern ideal' in portraiture. Furthermore, at a time when narrative subjects for paintings were discredited, certain painters found in the representation of their contemporaries an opportunity to explore in direct and non-literal terms the self-esteem and elegance of modern life. The theory of 'art for art's sake' released at least some painters from the dictates of commissions, and portraits came to be regarded as works of art in their own right rather than mere likenesses of individuals.

Among the artists who had previously been associated with Pre-Raphaelitism, D.G. Rossetti painted few portraits in his later career although the features and statuesque bearing of Jane Morris are familiar from his many paintings of sinister and predatory women. His portrait drawings, for example that of his friend and patron Frederick Leyland (Plate 331), have a granular quality and dark tonality quite different from his earlier draughtsmanship. Edward Burne-Jones (1833-98) occasionally painted portraits of women and children, but only of sitters of whom he was particularly fond, and once again

PLATE 332
Anthony Frederick Augustus Sandys
Cyril Flower, Lord Battersea, 1877
43½ x 29½ ins. (110.5 x 75cm), chalk
(Norwich Castle Museum)

PLATE 333
Walter Crane
*'Violet and Lily, Daughters
of Edmund Routledge,
Esq.', 1877*
19¼ x 27ins.
(49 x 68.5cm),
watercolour and
bodycolour
(Julian Hartnoll,
London)

a precise distinction between portraiture and a type of subjectless figurative art is hard to draw. To take a specific example, his painting of his mistress Maria Zambaco is much more than a straightforward record of her beguiling beauty, but is also a coded declaration of the artist's feelings (Colour Plate 59). Later portraits by Burne-Jones, such as his portrait of Madame des Landres (Private collection), are elegant but lacking in animation; the artist believed that 'the only expression allowable in great portraiture is the expression of character and moral quality, not of anything temporary, fleeting, [or] accidental', and as such his portraits have something of the symbolical gravity of his subject paintings.

An artist who, like Burne-Jones, was encouraged in his early career by the example and friendship of Rossetti, was Frederick Sandys (1829-1904). In the 1860s he worked both as an illustrator and portraitist, and in each sphere a precocious technical skill allowed him to introduce extraordinary degrees of realism to his works. Two half-length portraits of elderly ladies seated in richly furnished interiors, Mrs. Susanna Rose (Detroit Institute of Art) and Mrs. Jane Lewis (Colour Plate 60), demonstrate this capacity, and remind one of an earlier tradition of domestic portraiture in which the representation of furnishings was as important as the sitter's own physiognomy. Following the example of George Richmond, in about 1869 Sandys more or less gave up oil painting in favour of draughtsmanship in pencil and chalk. The immaculate, if mechanical, quality of his large-scale portrait drawings, such as Cyril Flower (Plate 332) or Charles Augustus Howell (Ashmolean Museum, Oxford), ensured his success as a fashionable portraitist.

The Grosvenor Gallery, founded in 1877, immediately became the show-

Albert Joseph Moore
William Connal, Junior, 1886
13¾ x 10½ ins. (35 x 26.5cm)
(York City Art Gallery)

Blanche Lindsay
Princess Louise, c.1878
9¾ x 6½ ins.
(25 x 16.5cm),
watercolour
(Christopher and Jenny
Newall)

place of the advanced styles of painting spawned by the Aesthetic Movement. Many portraits, often of distinguished members of society, and in a wide range of styles and on varying scales, were shown there. Edward John Poynter (1836-1919) took advantage of the first Grosvenor to exhibit a series of watercolour portraits which he had painted some years earlier: of his own wife, of Mrs. Baldwin and of Georgiana Burne-Jones (the three of whom were sisters), and of Sarah Heseltine, wife of the collector of drawings and contemporary paintings J.P. Heseltine (all in private collections). The following year Walter Crane (1845-1915) sent to the Grosvenor his double portrait of Violet and Lily Routledge (Plate 333), painted in gouache. The two girls are seen winding wool and seated on an upholstered bench; the patterns of a dado and screen provide a rectilinear background. Blanche Lindsay (1844-1912), wife of the Grosvenor's proprietor Sir Coutts Lindsay, exhibited there in 1878 a watercolour portrait of Princess Louise (Plate 334), one of Queen Victoria's daughters and herself a painter and sculptress whose works were seen at the Grosvenor. Towards the end of the decade during which the annual Grosvenor exhibitions were the most important events of the artistic

PLATE 336
**James McNeill
Whistler**
*'Arrangement in Grey and
Black: Portrait of the
Painter's Mother', 1871*
56¾ x 64ins.
(144 x 162.5cm)
(Musée d'Orsay, Paris)

season Albert Moore (1841-93) showed there one of his rare portraits, of his
patron William Connal, Junior, a work which exudes the casual mood and
urbane self-confidence of the late century (Plate 335). Much of the prejudice
and pretence which characterised the Victorian Royal Academy was overcome
at the Grosvenor, and refined and understated portraits, in all media, were
seen there to advantage.

As a painter and as a man James McNeill Whistler (1834-1903) expressed
the true spirit of Aestheticism: a devotion to the cause of beauty in art and a
contempt for the vulgar interests of the philistine. His portraits (some of which
were first seen at the Grosvenor) convey the sophistication, the grace and the
subtlety of the age. His career as a painter in London began in 1859 but it was
not until a decade or so later that he began to work regularly as a portraitist.
Whistler spent about three months of the summer of 1871 working on his
famous 'Arrangement in Grey and Black: Portrait of the Painter's Mother'
(Plate 336); it was exhibited at the R.A. in 1872, but not before a scandal had
broken over the selection committee's first decision to refuse it. One of the
most compelling images to come down from the nineteenth century, the
painting depends upon abstract qualities of line, silhouette and tone to convey
a sentiment of peacefulness and passivity. Psychologically disengaged in the

PLATE 337
James McNeill Whistler
'Arrangement in Grey and Black No 2: Portrait of Thomas Carlyle', 1872-73
67⅜ x 56½ins.
(171 x 142cm)
(Glasgow Art Gallery and Museum)

same way is Whistler's portrait of the writer and sage Thomas Carlyle: 'Arrangement in Grey and Black No. 2' (Plate 337). When Carlyle was persuaded to sit to Whistler he did not anticipate how much time would be involved — the artist worked directly on to the canvas and, when he was dissatisfied with the result, whole areas of paint were wiped out so that he might begin again. Carlyle complained that Whistler seemed concerned only to get 'the *coat* painted to ideal perfection, the face went for little'. Whistler believed that each part of the composition was as important as any other and that the portrait's impact depended as much on the stance and outline of the figure as on its physiognomic likeness. Whistler's third great portrait of the 1870s is entitled 'Harmony in Grey and Green: Miss Cicely Alexander' (Colour Plate 61). This resulted from a commission, and again took much longer than was anticipated. The child, who is wearing a dress which Whistler himself designed and about which there was much discussion and difficulty, stands against a black and grey-green wall. A spray of daisies enters the composition to the right, butterflies flutter about, and a cloak or coat is draped over a stool placed on the matted floor.

Whistler made much of his belief that paintings should be complete and self-contained in their decorative function — not requiring a familiar text to make them intelligible or, in the case of portraits, needing to be justified as images of specific men and women. As he wrote: 'Take the picture of my mother exhibited at the Royal Academy as an Arrangement in Grey and Black. Now that is what it is. To me it is interesting as a picture of my mother; but what can or ought the public to care about the identity of the portrait?' Nevertheless, Whistler could render the character of his sitters with acuteness, giving thought to gesture and posture, as well as overall complexion of colour and tone, to support his insight. In *The Red Flag* he dismissed naturalistic imitation as a means available to the true artist: 'It is for the artist to do something beyond this: in portrait painting to put on canvas something more than the face the model wears for that one day; to paint the man, in short, as well as his features. . .'

In the 1870s and 1880s Whistler painted many portraits. The majority of his subjects are seen in poses loosely derived from Velazquez or Watteau, often standing in semi-darkness or in undefined settings. His portrait of Maud Franklin, 'Arrangement in White and Black' (Plate 338), shows a pretty girl whose insouciance is perfectly expressed by the cool way in which she rests her hands on her hips; while his 'Arrangement in Black: La Dame au Brodequin Jaune — Portrait of Lady Archibald Campbell' (Philadelphia Museum of Art) represents a woman who seems to be both disdainful and flirtatious. Whistler announced on one occasion that he was going to paint 'all the fashionables', but in reality he was too wilful, and perhaps also too sharply perceptive about the characters of his potential patrons, to be considered reliable as a professional artist.

Frederic Leighton (1830-96) was a reluctant portraitist, resisting commissions and generally unwilling even to paint friends. Like Burne-Jones and unlike Whistler he was inhibited from displaying what he knew about human nature or documenting his personal friendships in works of art. As a rule, his best portraits are of people from whom he was detached by differences of age and sex. May Sartoris, who was the daughter of the artist's close friend Adelaide Sartoris, is seen tripping along and drawing her velvet skirts up from the dusty road. She engages the spectator with a soulful gaze, but remains impassive (Plate 339). From the late 1870s comes Leighton's portrait of the Countess Brownlow, seen in an open landscape, holding a bunch of red roses, and wearing flowing draperies of glacial whiteness (National Trust: Belton House). Immensely tall, and indifferent to the intrusion of the spectator's gaze, the figure stands before us like some Ionic caryatid, without emotion or

PLATE 339
Frederic Leighton
May Sartoris, c.1860
59⅞ x 35½ins. (152 x 90cm)
(Kimbell Art Museum, Fort Worth, Texas)

PLATE 338
James McNeill Whistler
'Arrangement in White and Black: Portrait of Maud Franklin', c.1876
75⅜ x 35¾ins. (191.5 x 91cm)
(Freer Gallery of Art, Washington, D.C.)

animation. In another portrait, of Sir Richard Burton (Plate 340), Leighton dispenses with the landscape background and drapery passages which he painted so well, but focuses rather on the model's menacing eyes and scarred physiognomy. This painting has the intensity of a Tintoretto portrait of a doge of Venice; all decorative qualities have been abandoned in favour of an austere analysis of the signs of character to be seen in a man's face.

Millais's later career was to a great extent given over to portraiture, and he was a prominent exhibitor at the R.A. and Grosvenor of large but often rather

PLATE 340 (left)
Frederic Leighton
Sir Richard Burton,
c.1872-75
23 ½ x 19 ½ ins.
(58.5 x 49.5cm)
(National Portrait
Gallery, London)

PLATE 341 (above)
George Frederic Watts
Alfred, Lord Tennyson,
c.1863-64
21 ⅛ x 20 ¼ ins.
(61 x 51.5cm)
(National Portrait
Gallery, London)

vacant paintings of people in public life and members of society. The facility for the handling of paint which he had previously demonstrated had deteriorated in the 1870s and 1880s into something which was both mannered and messy; and the sheer volume of portraits which he produced meant that few were original or informative although most were probably good likenesses. Perhaps the best portraits of his later career were of men rather than women, where he was encouraged towards a greater sobriety of approach; Gladstone (National Portrait Gallery), Disraeli (Plate 354) and Tennyson (Lady Lever Art Gallery) were all treated by him, as was Carlyle, a painting with which Millais had difficulties and eventually left unfinished, and of which Ruskin concluded: 'Millais may represent the pathos of a moment, not of a lifetime' (National Portrait Gallery).

Among the most distinguished of all Victorian portraitists was George Frederic Watts (1817-1904), whose highly wrought paintings of his eminent contemporaries command the spectator's respect even if they are seldom elegant or inviting. From the middle of the century onwards he combined portraiture with a type of allegorical painting, derived from his study of Titian and Michelangelo, with which he hoped to raise the standard of British art. His portraits, like his subject paintings, were undertaken with a serious purpose; from the time of the Crimean War (1854-56) he had conceived of a role for himself as the creator of a gallery of national heroes, each portrait to be instigated by the painter rather than the result of a commission. In 1861 the scheme was sufficiently far advanced for the *Athenaeum* to report: 'Mr. Watts

PLATE 342 (above)
George Frederic Watts
John Stuart Mill, 1873
26 x 21ins.
(66 x 53.5cm)
(National Portrait
Gallery, London)

PLATE 343 (right)
Edward John Poynter
Eliza Eastlake, 1864
16½ x 12½ins.
(42 x 31.5cm)
(Yale Center for British
Art: Paul Mellon Fund)

PLATE 344 (opposite)
**Valentine Cameron
Prinsep**
*Miss Mary Wyndham, later
Countess of Wemyss, c.1870*
65¼ x 30¼ins.
(165.5 x 77cm)
(Collection of the Earl of
Wemyss)

has expressed his intention to leave the nation, at his death, the valuable and interesting collection of contemporary portraits he has been for some years, and is still, forming'. In the mid-1860s various writers and poets, including Tennyson (Plate 341), Browning and Carlyle, were painted for the series — and this represented the period of Watts's greatest achievement as a portraitist. For a number of years from 1872 financial pressures caused Watts to restrict his portrait practice to those who were prepared to pay for his services, although his remarkable portrait of J.S. Mill was added to the series in 1873 (Plate 342), but after 1880 he embarked upon a new campaign of recruitment to what was by then called the Hall of Fame. Matthew Arnold and Cardinal Manning were enlisted at this time. In 1882, on the occasion of a winter exhibition at the Grosvenor Gallery which included various portraits from the Hall of Fame, the *Magazine of Art* wrote of Watts's portraiture: 'There is not one that does not testify to his unrivalled power of mental diagnosis, not one that does not stamp him as a leader amidst the intellectual forces as well as amidst the painters of his generation'. (All the Hall of Fame portraits are in the collection of the National Portrait Gallery.)

Watts sought to represent the heroic virtues of his subjects by abstract means, as he wrote, 'not by accentuating or emphasising, but rather keeping in mind those lines which are noblest'. His portraits are remarkable for their determined honesty and their avoidance of all magniloquence. These men and women (in fact all but two of the portraits are of male sitters) are seen as hesitant and uncertain, and are viewed without any of the lustre that portrait painters may sometimes confer. These are heroes among men, but their eminence is seen to be hard won and their lives clouded by struggle and disappointment. Watts occasionally undertook private commissions, painting men, women and children from different walks of life out of friendship or because he needed the income. However, even his adolescent sitters, such as Katie Lewis (Colour Plate 62), were often made to seem doleful and distracted, and acquired a gravity hardly befitting their age.

Various painters who had been born in the later 1830s or the 1840s gained considerable reputations as portraitists before the end of the period in question. E.J. Poynter has already been mentioned as the author of a series of watercolour portraits done in the 1870s, but an even earlier example of his portrait painting is that of Eliza Eastlake, seen in profile and wearing a silk dress, an image which speaks volumes about the steadfastness of character of the sitter (Plate 343). Poynter continued occasionally to paint portraits until after the end of the century. Valentine Cameron Prinsep (1838-1904) was a friend and acolyte of G.F. Watts, and his portraits are sweeter versions of those of his master. Prinsep's charming portrait of Miss Mary Wyndham was exhibited at the R.A. in 1870 (Plate 344); his portrait of fellow-artist George Heming Mason (National Portrait Gallery) is sombre but distinguished, in the mould of Watts's Hall of Fame series. William Blake Richmond (1842-1921), who was the son of George Richmond, was another who combined portraiture with a range of other subjects. His portrait of Rhoda Liddell (Plate 345) was

PLATE 345 (above)
William Blake Richmond
Rhoda Liddell, 1867
35 x 27ins. (89 x 69cm)
(Private collection)

PLATE 346 (right)
William Blake Richmond
Andrew Lang, c.1886
44 x 33½ins.
(112 x 85cm)
(Scottish National Portrait Gallery, Edinburgh)

painted in his early career, while from the 1880s comes the extraordinary and alarming portrait which Richmond painted of the Scottish illustrator Andrew Lang. The hollow-cheeked and enervate man turns away from the spectator's gaze, and is seen to slump back listlessly; his right hand, which is a mass of knotted veins, plays nervously with the leg of the chair in which he sits (Plate 346). Richmond was sought after as a portraitist, receiving commissions to paint, among many others, William Gladstone (private collection) and Alexandra, Princess of Wales. This last was beset with difficulties, and led Richmond to warn other artists to avoid being drawn into what he described as 'that most unsatisfactory branch of art — court painting'.

Another who should perhaps be mentioned in the context of High Victorian portraiture is James Tissot (1836-1902) who came to London as a refugee from the Paris Commune in 1871 and immediately secured a reputation for portraits and genre scenes in fashionable settings. His portrait of Colonel Frederick Gustavus Burnaby demonstrates how the boundary between the two spheres was confused; the way in which the sitter lounges back in the composition, arrogantly indifferent to the presence of the spectator would have struck English patrons or gallery-goers as something alien and vulgar (Plate 347). Tissot ignored, or was unaware of, the English sense of propriety in portraiture, whereby a sitter presented himself to make the best possible overall impression, and not simply to show off good looks or an elegant uniform.

PLATE 347
James Tissot
*Colonel Frederick Gustavus
Burnaby, 1870*
19½ x 23½ ins.
(49.5 x 59.5cm)
(National Portrait
Gallery, London)

Frank Holl (1845-88) wrote with disarming simplicity of his own approach to the techniques of portraiture: 'I am sure I don't know how I do it. I just look at my subject, and then try to drag him, himself, on to the canvas before me. I know nothing hardly of what colours I use, except as they represent what I see'. Holl had great painterly skill whatever his subject, but came to realise the restriction that a diet of portraiture places upon an artist. Having been regarded as a rising man at the summer exhibitions of the 1870s with a series of modern life subjects, he was disconcerted in 1878 to find his portrait of a certain Mr. Richardson the object of higher praise than his important and large-scale composition of that year, 'Newgate'. The following year he exhibited a portrait of the engraver Samuel Cousins, R.A. (Tate Gallery) which again met with critical acclaim; he was encouraged to capitalise on his success by painting more portraits and shortly afterwards, according to his biographer, was 'innundated with portrait commissions'. Holl's portrait of William Agnew (Plate 348), painted in 1883, demonstrates his capacity to give a convincing likeness by means of a technique which was both precise and painterly.

Various of Holl's fellow artists who had also attempted subjects which recorded the way of life of working people, began to spend more of their time painting portraits. During the 1880s Luke Fildes (1843-1927) turned from the scenes of modern life such as 'Applicants for Admission to a Casual Ward', upon which his reputation had been based, to portraits of elegant individuals;

PLATE 348
Frank Holl
William Agnew, M.P.,
1883
40 x 50ins.
(101.6 x 127cm)
(Thos. Agnew & Sons
Ltd. London)

the portrait of his wife which he exhibited at the R.A. in 1887 — *soignée,* but essentially characterless — served as an advertisement of his availability as a jobbing society portraitist (Plate 349). In due course he was to paint the state portraits of both Edward VII and George V (both Royal Collection). Hubert von Herkomer (1849-1914) likewise turned to portraiture, and gained great prestige from the watercolour studies he made of famous contemporaries, including John Ruskin (National Portrait Gallery) and Richard Wagner. The fluency and spontaneity of his watercolour technique is seen in his portrait of the artist Cecil Gordon Lawson (Plate 350).

Artists found portrait commissions, for which they knew they would be well paid, a temptation hard to resist, even when they had ambitions to paint imaginative subjects. Very few portrait specialists have ever succeeded in

PLATE 349
Luke Fildes
Mrs. Luke Fildes, 1887
56½ x 38¼ ins. (143.5 x 97cm)
(Walker Art Gallery, Liverpool)

continuing indefinitely to introduce a fresh and original quality to their staple product, and historically both British art and individual artists' careers have suffered from a pattern of patronage which has encouraged portraiture ahead of all other genres. G.F. Watts, who was less subject to the demands of importunate clients than most, exclaimed in frustration: 'No one can imagine the intense weariness of my existence as a portrait painter... No one knows what it costs me, and yet when I take people's cheques, I feel as if I were cheating them'. In 1888 Millais wrote a letter to Holl which fairly sums up the frustrations and tedium of professional portrait painting in the late nineteenth century: 'You have been ill, and I don't wonder at it, with the quantity of work you have done this year. Portrait-painting is *killing work* to an artist who is sensitive, and he must be so to be successful, and I well understand that you are prostrated by it. Every one must have his say, and, however good the performance may be, there is some fault to find'. And yet, despite this state of affairs, increasing numbers of artists accommodated themselves to the commercial demand for portraits and it is probably fair to say that the late Victorian middle and upper classes were more lavishly portrayed than any equivalent group in history.

Those Victorians who commissioned portraits of themselves or their families, who subscribed towards the cost of portraits of their friends or colleagues, or who simply paused to admire or criticise portraits of the eminent men and women of the age when they appeared at exhibition, believed implicitly in the usefulness and importance of the art form. Portraiture provided a stimulus to a pride in the history and achievements of the British people — the National Portrait Gallery, which was founded in 1856, was both the outcome of, and a spur to, that general interest in the faces, as well as the lives, of the heroes of earlier ages. Portraits were valued as a means of edification and education which it was the duty of governments to make available to the people; portraits of great men were, in the words of Palmerston, speaking in the House of Commons, 'an incentive to mental exertion, to noble actions, [and] to good conduct'.

However, portraiture was to the Victorians much more than just a means of instruction or form of personal propaganda. Lines from Tennyson's *Lancelot and Elaine,* which he wrote in 1858-59 to form one of the books of *Idylls of the King,* serve to define the portraitist's larger purpose:

> As when a painter, poring on a face,
> Divinely thro' all hindrance finds the man
> Behind it, and so paints him that his face,
> The shape and colour of a mind and life,
> Lives for his children, ever at its best
> And fullest.

Victorian portraits may be judged according to their differing degrees of psychological engagement between artist and sitter. Many portraitists were shy of too direct an investigation; Francis Grant concluded in his Academy *Discourse* of 1873: 'I need hardly add how absolutely essential it is that, in the department of portrait painting, truth to nature should be combined with taste and refinement. A portrait which may be a strong resemblance, and yet replete with vulgarity, is simply an abomination'. Others abandoned the proud and polemical purposes of portraiture, but instead gave affectionate and honest accounts of men and women who seem to invite our friendship. In the best Victorian portraits the spectator has the feeling that he might know and converse with the subject as if in the company of the living individual. These qualities of animation, of depth of emotion, and of spontaneity of mood combine to make certain paintings of the period so compelling, and are the factors which allow the modern spectator such rewarding insights into the state of mind of the age.

CHRISTOPHER NEWALL

PLATE 351
James Jebusa Shannon
'The Stairs', *c.1896*
75¾ x 36ins. (192 x 91.5cm)
(Cartwright Hall Art Gallery, Bradford)

352

Chapter 6
'Well-bred Contortions'
1880-1918

There is no clear distinction between Victorian and Edwardian portrait painting. Many of the venerable Victorian portraitists lived on into the new century, while others were succeeded by competent pupils who maintained and adapted their mannerisms. Many had Victorian reputations as painters of mythological or social realist subjects, and Edwardian reputations as portraitists. The great portraits of Millais, Watts, Fildes and Herkomer were produced late in their careers in an ambiance which was increasingly attuned to respond to their excellence. The cavalcade of images of politicians, industrialists, field marshals and clerics emphasised social function. Such portraits had to be reproducible. They had to work in the context of the illustrated newspaper and the framed premium plate. Photographs, now commonly available, had none of the prestige of the reproducible painted portrait. They lacked the scale and presence of painting; they were too democratic; they might be good enough for a *carte de visite,* but they possessed no authority.

Portraiture drew its authority from traditions of patrimony, hence its appeal to those *nouveaux riches* who had no background and whose portraits were commissioned because they could be paid for. While the collector of Pre-Raphaelite pictures in the 1860s might be mildly embarassed by his wealth and, as a consequence, take a keen interest in workers' education, public health and other matters of social utility, by the 1890s this type had learnt to flaunt his riches. The desire for self-projection and the display of opulence called into being an elite group of painters. Osbert Sitwell, in a celebrated utterance, observed that his clients went to a painter like Sargent because he could make them appreciate how rich they really were. The massive increase in the importance of portraiture in the period between 1880 and 1920 is closely allied to new attitudes to wealth, and the relationship between painters and patrons lies at the heart of its study.

Many contemporary writers attest to the renewed importance of portraiture. This genre provided 'one of the most profound sources of artistic inspiration' which had 'within recent years' been given 'its rightful place' according to Frank Rinder in *The Art Journal* in 1901. The recognition of this phenomenon

PLATE 352
James McNeill Whistler
George W. Vanderbilt, c.1879-1902
82⅛ x 35⅞ ins. (208.5 x 91cm)
(National Gallery of Art,
Washington, D.C.)

occurred in the context of a discussion of one of the most important young portrait painters of his generation, James Jebusa Shannon (1862-1923). At Queen Victoria's command, the young Shannon had been asked to paint one of her ladies-in-waiting. Arguably the opportunity came too early in his career, and Shannon endeavoured to avoid type-casting. Initially he could not afford to be classified exclusively as a portraitist. A contemporary described him as 'an artist first and a portrait painter afterwards'. Indeed it is the case that many patrons preferred to be portrayed by 'artists' rather than mere portrait painters. The perception of the provider was important. At times Shannon painted what were described as 'fanciful subjects' such as 'The Stairs' (Plate 351) and 'In the Springtime' (Colour Plate 63) which hover on the edges of portraiture and effectively extend its possibilities. Confidence led to the flouting of convention.

Often the leading portrait painters of the Edwardian era were artists who had effectively made their reputations in other genres. For painters such as Frank Holl, Luke Fildes, Arthur Hacker, Solomon J. Solomon, Charles Wellington Furse, Ralph Peacock, John da Costa, John Lavery, James Guthrie and many others, the essential career path was to achieve success at the Royal Academy or the Paris Salon before turning to portraiture. Norbert Franks in George Gissing's novel *Will Warburton* (1905) presents the type at his most cynical. Franks began a picture of a waif from the slums which he initially dubbed 'The Slummer'. With some 'prettifying', this was dispatched to the Royal Academy exhibition as 'A Ministering Angel' and it became a popular success, enabling the artist to pay off his debts. He readily acknowledges that the only way to ensure his new standard of living is by painting portraits. At one point in the narrative he declares:

> I've just finished a portrait — a millionaire's wife, Lady Rockett...Of course it was my Slummer that got me the job. Women have been raving about the girl's head; and it isn't bad, though I say it. I had to take a studio at a couple of day's notice — couldn't ask Lady Rockett to come and sit at that place of mine in Battersea; a shabby hole. She isn't really anything out of the way, as a pretty woman; but I've made her — well you'll see it at some exhibition this winter, if you care to. Pleased? Isn't she pleased! And her husband, the podgy old millionaire baronet, used to come every day and stare in delight.

Whilst this is obviously a caricature, and it would be wrong to attribute such duplicity to all or any of the major portraitists of the age, there is often a sense of deliberate upward mobility in the lives of painters. It was beyond the bounds of possibility for a member of the aristocracy to become a painter, but it was certainly true that the painter, those of a select elite, became socially acceptable. Nick Dormer in Henry James's *The Tragic Muse* loses his parliamentary career and a good marriage by being too interested in art. At the other end of the spectrum, an ideal dinner table for Lady Tweedsmuir

contained a painter, as well as a politician or two, a musician, and a sprinkling of women famous for their looks. Artists went out of their way to join the social mêlée — to dress correctly, to ride and to hunt . . . If they were handsome, like Shannon, it was a bonus. Memoirs and diaries attest to their social skills.

With portraiture in the Edwardian period we are therefore dealing with a set of social interactions analogous to but more complex than those of the court painters of the seventeenth century. Shannon became painter to the Rutlands, Sargent was painter to the Wertheimers, Wyndhams and Marlboroughs, and Lavery to the Churchills and Asquiths. The model for this kind of relationship was that to which Whistler aspired when he painted the portrait of the millionaire, George Vanderbilt (Plate 352). He was Velazquez and his patron was 'the modern Philip'. On occasion, when the relationship between the painter and his patron was particularly close the pictures produced form more of a visual diary than a once-and-for-all-time effigy. Sargent's pictures at Broadway and Fadbury in the late 1880s represent identifiable people, boating or sketching, outside the controlled environment of the studio. Canvases produced in 1916 by Lavery at The Wharf, Sutton Courtenay (Plate 353), illustrate incidents in the life of the Oxfords and Asquiths. During this perod, portraitists were also visual reporters.

The great Victorian portraitists, Millais, Watts, Holl and Fildes, had worked to stricter conventions. In male portraits, particularly of politicians and generals, a commanding presence was a matter of necessity. Certain military types and members of the gentry cultivated their appearance to such an extent

PLATE 354 (left)
John Everett Millais
Benjamin Disraeli, Earl of Beaconsfield, 1881
50¼ x 36½ ins.
(127.5 x 92.5cm)
(National Portrait Gallery, London)

PLATE 355 (above)
Charles Wellington Furse
'Field Marshal Earl Roberts on his Charger Vonolel', 1893-95
134 x 179ins.
(340.5 x 454.5cm)
(Tate Gallery, London)

that they looked like what their portraits might be expected to look like. This was the basis of the confusion between the artist-narrator and his rather stiff visitors in James's *The Real Thing*. The gentrified Major and Mrs. Monarch were expected to be portrait clients rather than models for pot-boiler illustrations. On a more elevated level, Disraeli, Salisbury and Chamberlain were painted in half- and three-quarter-length so that the spectator might not become too intimate with their features. At the same time, being seen in full-length was too remote for men in the public eye. A grave and serious manner was appropriate while, at the same time, their features should be sufficiently obvious as to provide the rudiments of instant visual recall. Disraeli, commissioned by W.H. Smith from Millais, was 'a piece of contemporary history' (Plate 354). His image was strictly circumscribed as the product of five one-hour 'seances'. In the event, the Earl of Beaconsfield gave only two sittings before succumbing to his final illness. At the Queen's command the picture was inserted late in the Royal Academy. *The Times* approved its 'just neglect of any ornamental accessory' and felt 'that no amount of work could have improved it'.

The idea that a portrait's success did not depend upon elaborate planning and arduous sittings was increasingly favoured by patrons. So too was the desire to break with hallowed formulae. In equestrian portraits traditional rocking-horse representations gave way to pictures such as Furse's 'Field

COLOUR PLATE 63
James Jebusa Shannon
'In the Springtime', 1896
50 x 40ins. (127 x 101.5cm)
One of Shannon's 'fanciful subjects' which hover on the edges of portraiture and
extend its possibilities
(Private collection)

COLOUR PLATE 64
John Singer Sargent
The Misses Vickers, 1886
54¼ x 72ins. (138 x 183cm)
Voted the 'Worst Picture of the Year' when it was shown at the Royal Academy, it
was considered highly risky to submit to Sargent for a picture before 1893, when his
portrait of Lady Agnew of Lochnaw was exhibited at the Royal Academy
(Sheffield City Art Galleries)

PLATE 356
John Singer Sargent
Vernon Lee, 1881
21 x 17ins. (53.5 x 43cm)
(Tate Gallery, London)

Marshal Earl Roberts on his Charger Vonolel', from which the painter deliberately removed extraneous detail (Plate 355). Brilliantly, the young artist extrapolates the wild races of India and South Africa who have been subjugated by he who sits astride the equally wild Vonolel.

The success of painters like Sargent and Bastien-Lepage lay in their ability to snatch a glimpse of the sitter. The life, which in Millais and Watts was suspended for the sake of a likeness, was somehow trapped in Sargent's portrait of Vernon Lee (Plate 356). 'Souvenirs', or tokens of friendship, such as this, were not the result of a commercial transaction. The snapshot quality came to be favoured, particularly by female sitters. One reviewer of the mid-1890s noted the growing desire for works which captured 'cette apparence qui a été nous, à une seconde de notre vie'. The painter's skill could almost be measured by the speed of execution. The general changes of attitude which had led Whistler to admit that his nocturnes were 'knocked off' in an afternoon, but were 'the experience of a life-time', got through to clients. The command of this intangible 'experience', the highly developed skills with materials, lay at the basis of the commission. Legros portrait heads, often painted as demonstration pieces, on a stage, with an audience present, were known as 'time-studies' and were strictly the product of one hour. Sitters might reconcile themselves to long feats of endurance in the studio, but they often wished the end result to look as if it represented an instant in time. Sitters, often mistakenly, made a simple connection between seeming rapidity of execution and the reputation of the artist. J.J. Cowan, an Edinburgh paper manufacturer, commissioned a full-length portrait of his wife and daughter

PLATE 357
James McNeill Whistler
'Arrangement in Grey and Green:
J.J. Cowan', c.1893-1900
37 x 19¾ins. (94 x 50cm)
(National Gallery of Scotland,
Edinburgh)

COLOUR PLATE 65
John Singer Sargent
The Marlborough Family, 1905
131 x 94ins. (332.5 x 239cm)
Invited to Blenheim Palace and shown Reynolds's great portrait of the 4th Duke of Marlborough and his family, Sargent was commissioned to paint an equally imposing canvas of the present incumbent and his offspring, in which he managed to suggest the qualities of a life lived beyond the canvas
(Blenheim Palace: Red Drawing Room)

COLOUR PLATE 66
John Lavery
'Hazel in Black and Gold', 1916
72½ x 36½ ins. (184 x 93cm)
Lavery's self-confidence is seen
in this full-length *tour de force*
(Laing Art Gallery, Newcastle
upon Tyne)

PLATE 358
James McNeill Whistler
'Arrangement in Black: Portrait of Senor Pablo de Sarasate',
1884
85¼ x 42¾ins. (216.5 x 108.5cm)
(Carnegie Museum of Art, Pittsburgh)

PLATE 359
James McNeill Whistler
'Arrangement in Black and Gold: Portrait of Comte Robert de
Montesquiou-Fezensac', 1891
82⅛ x 36⅛ins. (208.5 x 92cm)
(Frick Collection, New York)

364

from Lavery which was unveiled after ten sittings, and saw no reason why Whistler, 'a master of his art', should require longer for his own half-size portrait. After seven years and around sixty four-hour sittings, he was amazed to reflect that the portrait was still incomplete (Plate 357). Temperament, in Whistler's case, lengthened the chances of success. Hapless sitters like Cowan, impressed no doubt by the portraits of 'The Artist's Mother' and Carlyle which, by the 1890s, had been acquired by the Louvre and Glasgow Art Gallery respectively (Plates 336 and 337), were unprepared for eccentricity. One of Whistler's subjects whose portrait did arrive at a state of completion, emphasised repeatedly the efforts required of him in arduous sittings. When quizzed about how much he had to pay for what was an acknowledged masterpiece, he ruefully remarked 'one has to give him more than one is able'.

Whistler's contribution to British portraiture during the last twenty years of the century was immense. It was he who insisted that portraits were not simply the record of someone's features. They had to be sympathetic arrangements or 'harmonies' in the musical sense. People had to be made to conform to decorative and formalist principles. For this reason, Whistler preferred the full-length to the three-quarter view. Figures should stand within their own space, at a discreet distance from the spectator. He was appalled by the competition for hyper-reality in some Victorian naturalism which 'had the sole aim of making it appear as if the subject was about to spring to life... and in the midst of this unseemly struggle for prominence', Whistler declared, 'the gentle truth has but a sorry chance'. In all of this, Whistler proposed aesthetic principles deduced from Velazquez — 'the Master of Madrid himself, beside this monster success of mediocrity, would be looked upon as mild and uninteresting'. Velazquez habitually preferred single figures against monochrome backgrounds. There was, to Whistler, an agreeable formality about a court, ruled by the Inquisition, in which everyone was garbed in black. It was in this manner that Duret, Pablo de Sarasate (Plate 358) and Robert, Comte de Montesquiou (Plate 359) were represented. Low tones and 'sunken' effects became a fashion. When his prospective model addressed James's artist in *The Real Thing*, her dim smile 'had the effect of a moist sponge passed over a "sunk" piece of painting'. In Montesquiou's case, the painter felt that he was expressing the very essence of the sitter's aristocratic lineage. To do this, he appeared to be 'pumping away something of his individuality'. The portrait was therefore an exchange of life between the subject and that material which the artist deployed. Whistler encouraged this mystification by referring to his portraits as if they were the very people they represented.

The portrait's mystic power had a long heritage in European culture stretching back to the Pygmalion legend. It had been reworked for a Victorian audience in Edgar Allan Poe's tale *The Oval Portrait*. This short story contains, in an extreme form, many of the assumptions which were current at the end of the nineteenth century. The narrator, a wounded knight, seeks shelter in a remote chateau in the Apennines. Before falling asleep, he is mesmerised by

COLOUR PLATE 67
Giovanni Boldini
Consuelo, Duchess of Marlborough and her son, Lord Ivor Spencer-Churchill. 1906
87¼ x 67ins. (221.5 x 170cm)
In Boldini's slashing brushstrokes the bravura style of early twentieth century portraiture achieved its apex
(Metropolitan Museum of Art, New York)

COLOUR PLATE 68
William Orpen
'Young Ireland', 1908
35 x 25ins. (89 x 63.5cm)
As an Irish painter Orpen was swept along by the demand for a cultural identity, and
this portrait, one of the most extraordinary images of the Edwardian years, draws the
spectator into direct confrontation with a young woman whose features differ
markedly from those of the conventional Edwardian beauty
(Private collection)

PLATE 360
James Jebusa Shannon
Lady Henry Bentinck, 1898
88¼ x 52¼ ins.
(224 x 132.5cm)
(Private collection)

the portrait of a young girl. He is 'confounded, subdued and appalled' by its 'absolute *life-likeness*'. Presently, he discovers that this was the portrait of the wife of a painter of 'high renown'. Immured in the studio, the painter had become totally obsessed by his work, while his model grew pale and ill during the long sittings. Finally when the work was complete, the painter cried out 'this is indeed *life* itself!' At this moment he turned to his model and she was dead. Although he was a gothic writer of the 1840s, Poe's reputation was forged in the final quarter of the century among the decadent Anglo-Saxon followers of his French translator, Charles Baudelaire. The most obvious aspect of his story concerns the identity of the protagonists. The artist is male and beauty resides in the young women he depicts. The maintenance of male hegemony is essential to the story. Depiction is a form of control, a primitive capturing and containing. The undercurrents here run so deep in the iconography of the age, that they can scarcely be more than alluded to here. Much of the portraiture of the period is predicated upon the belief that in art a beautiful essence will be distilled and held. The central myths of *The Oval Portrait* were of deep significance to Oscar Wilde whose *The Picture of Dorian Gray* was a much subtler and more elaborate construction. Nevertheless, it too involves an exchange of life between portrait and sitter.

Such accounts emphasise the mental fight involved in the production of portraits and often characterise the artist as someone imbued with demonic powers. It was this for which sitters, looking for mere professionalism, were unprepared. Yet throughout the 1890s the wives of the new rich wanted to achieve a 'look' which expressed more than mere surface likeness. Artistic groups like the Souls required an allusion to spirituality. It was this which led George Moore and Walter Sickert to attack the school of the 'white satin duchesses'. Moore advocated that a gallery be established specifically to display them in all of their infinite variations. Shannon was the manager of the dress shop, and he was ably assisted by Solomon J. Solomon, J.H.F. Bacon, Ralph Peacock and many others. Sickert, writing in *The New Age* in 1910, commented upon the close alliance between this form of painting and fashion. Women were to be seen in this year's hat, beneath which '...the place that is filled in works of art by the obscenity called the body, is replaced by a perpendicular cascade of chiffon on which gleams the occasional gem, and always *de rigeur*, an oscillating chain. In this chain are twisted delicate fingers without nails. Their well-bred contortions suggest a soul slightly misunderstood'.

As styles wavered in the early years of the century, such heroines could appeal to a great variety of visual sources — they could look like high renaissance madonnas, like pompadour courtesans, or Pre-Raphaelite sirens. Shannon's portrait of Lady Henry Bentinck (Plate 360) was a reworking of Gainsborough's Countess Howe, while Dicksee's Lady Inverclyde (Plate 361) was unmistakably Rossettian. Although this vague symbolism generally evaporated as the Great War approached there were persistent reminders of it in the work of artists like de Laszlo and Salisbury.

COLOUR PLATE 69
William Orpen
The Vere Foster Family
78 x 78ins. (198 x 198cm)
A group portrait which reveals Orpen's dependence on precedent, the figures
modelled on Velazquez and Whistler, and the whole ensemble containing recollections
of Van Dyck and Snyders
(National Gallery of Ireland, Dublin)

COLOUR PLATE 70
Gerald Leslie Brockhurst
'Ranunculus', 1914
24 x 18½ ins. (61 x 47cm)
A unique, dream-like portrait and one which holds an important place in pre-First
World War painting
(Sheffield City Art Galleries)

PLATE 361 (above)
Frank Dicksee
Lady Inverclyde, 1910
54¼ x 43ins.
(138 x 109cm)
(Glasgow Art Gallery
and Museum)

PLATE 362 (right)
John Singer Sargent
*Lady Agnew of Lochnaw,
1892-93*
49 x 39¼ins.
(124.5 x 99.5cm)
(National Gallery of
Scotland, Edinburgh)

The central figure in this personification of the physical and mental luxury of the Edwardian *grande dame* was John Singer Sargent (1856-1925). During Whistler's absence in Paris in the 1890s, and before such painters as Lavery and Walton had established themselves in London, Sargent enjoyed unprecedented prestige. His background, as several writers have pointed out, uniquely fitted him for the role he came to occupy. His parents were American expatriates on the edge of European society. His close relationship with his master, Carolus Duran, linked him with the second generation realist origins of Whistler's art. Up to 1893, it was regarded as highly risky to submit to Sargent for a portrait commission. His early career had been blighted by the scandal surrounding the display of Madame Gautreau's portrait at the Paris Salon. Two years later in 1886, his 'The Misses Vickers' (Colour Plate 64) was voted 'Worst Picture of the Year' at the Royal Academy by the readers of *The Pall Mall Gazette*. One potential subject regarded it as 'positively dangerous' to sit to him — 'it's taking your face in your hands'. These reservations were sufficient to require assurance from Henry James, who wrote to Mrs. Mahlon Sands in 1894, requesting her to 'trust' the painter. She could not 'collaborate', 'co-operate' or 'assist' the artist; she could only 'cultivate indifference': 'It's *his* affair — yours is only to be as difficult as possible; and the more difficult you are the more the artist (worthy of the name) will be condemned to worry over you, repainting, revolutionising, till he, in a rage of

PLATE 363
John Singer Sargent
*The Wyndham Sisters,
1900*
115 x 84¼ ins.
(292 x 213.5cm)
(Metropolitan Museum
of Art, New York)

ambition and admiration, arrives at the thing that satisfies him and enshrines and perpetuates you'.

The turning point was reached in 1893 when the portrait of Lady Agnew of Lochnaw was exhibited at the Royal Academy (Plate 362). Thereafter Sargent, as Sickert observed, became almost a subject of idolatry in the press, 'he was the Magnetic Pole...towards which the critical needles must all point...' Even impressionism, so maligned and misunderstood by critics was made palatable; '...when Mr. Sargent condescends, in his moments of recreation between the serious and respectable labours of painting proper expensive portraits, to dally with anything so trivial it becomes supreme. . .' It was clear that such a lion could do no wrong. At the Royal Academy his works assumed the prominence which those of Millais and Lord Leighton had done. The great classic images of the Wertheimer suite, the Acheson and the Wyndham Sisters (Plate 363), followed one another to successive Academy shows. Sargent was invited to Blenheim Palace and shown Reynolds's great portrait of the 4th Duke of Marlborough and his family (Plate 197), and commissioned to paint an equally imposing canvas of the present incumbent and his offspring (Colour Plate 65). In all of this he managed to suggest the qualities of a life lived beyond the canvas, in the words of a contemporary critic, T. Martin Wood, of '. . .time given over to wholly social amenities, long afternoons spent in pleasant intercourse, hours well ordered and protected. . .'

So agreeable was this reflection of upper class living that, despite James's advice, strong minded sitters were prepared to tussle with the painter over the effects which they wished to create. This was the case with the ticklish Sir George Sitwell. The proposition here was for Sargent to provide a large portrait group of Sir George and his family which would complement J.S. Copley's portrait of the Sitwell Children (Plate 222) which hung in his country house at Renishaw in Derbyshire. Sitwell considered the commissioning in the same breath as the purchase of two parcels of land and a new billiard table. Sargent refused to paint the picture at Renishaw, so the Copley was brought to London along with the furniture for the setting, which included a large Brussels tapestry, a splendid commode designed by Robert Adam and executed by Chippendale and Haig plus several other items. The Empire table in the foreground was lent by Sargent and, at the last minute, Sir George realised that he had forgotten to bring several pieces of choice porcelain to place upon the commode. These were, however, furnished by Duveen's antique shop in Bond Street. When the sittings began it became evident that, in Sir George's view, the painter's relationship to his patron should be similar to that of 'a bone to a dog'. Faced with Sargent's passivity, Sir George rehearsed his own theories and demanded changes, some of which were conceded and others which were, like the shapes of his and his daughter's noses, not approved! None of the diplomacy which surrounded it was allowed to bring a halt to the picture's progress. The extraordinary discontinuity of Sir George's and his wife's costumes was permitted, even though it provoked one of the elder members of the family to ask the patron why he had not gone 'to an *ordinary* painter?' In the end, however, Sir George was well pleased with the result (Plate 364). Frozen as his family was, in 'cataleptic immobility', it was recognised that this state endured 'only for an instant in time' and that the group would 'presently thaw to life'. Eventually, by 1907, the sheer volume of commissions and the strain of dealing with difficult sitters such as these led Sargent to abandon portrait painting, but his huge popularity in the preceding fifteen years can only be considered as a product of the mushroom growth of portraiture.

PLATE 364
John Singer Sargent
The Sitwell Family, 1900
67 x 76ins.
(170 x 193cm)
(Private collection)

Following the establishment in 1891 of the Society of Portrait Painters, several groups of portraitists were formed. Many of the New English Art Club artists, Steer, Sickert and Tonks among them, turned to portraiture not simply as a means of augmenting their earnings, but because the aesthetic debate initiated by Whistler had proclaimed the importance of the genre. Shannon, Solomon and Bacon were well supported by their clientele. Glasgow School portraitists like Henry, Walton and the Irish-born Lavery established studios in London and by their high profile in the newly formed International Society of Sculptors, Painters and Gravers were looking beyond the traditional client groups. John Lavery (1856-1941) had seasons in Rome and Berlin around this time, and with two notable purchases for the Musée du Luxembourg by 1904, he joined Millais and Watts in a small select band of British artists approved by the French establishment. With the portrait of an Austrian Baroness, Marguerite von Hollrigl, known by its French title, 'La Dame aux Perles' (Plate 365), his work became temporarily rhetorical. The elegant sitter was described by Lavery's biographer, Walter Shaw Sparrow, as 'action in repose...with restful arms that negligently contradict the alert energy that she herself represents, [she] is like an actress who listens with patience and yet prepares for instant movement'. Here again, was a reiteration of the point made on behalf of Shannon, de László and a host of younger aspirants such as Peacock, Jack, da Costa and Furse. For all of these artists, the words used

PLATE 365
John Lavery
'La Dame aux Perles', 1901
54 x 40ins. (137 x 101.5cm)
(Hugh Lane Municipal Gallery of Modern Art, Dublin)

to describe a de László apply: the sitter was found in some 'pleasant converse, or listening to some fascinating discourse', there was 'no stiffness, no constraint — no posing'. In Lavery's case, 'La Dame aux Perles' departed from Whistlerian decorum. The knowledge gained from the experience contributed to a more self-confident *hispagnolisme* which led to *tour de force* full-lengths such as 'Hazel in Black and Gold' (Colour Plate 66).

The international character of portraiture in the early years of the century was enhanced by the presence in London of distinguished foreign artists. Boldini, Blanche, Mancini and others spent seasons with members of the

British establishment. They stalked the same sitters as Sargent and Lavery. In 1906 for instance, Boldini followed Sargent in painting the celebrated portrait of Consuelo Vanderbilt, then Duchess of Marlborough (Colour Plate 67). Sickert hailed him for this and other efforts as the 'non pareil parent of the wriggle and chiffon school'. Blanche's movements are not so easy to document, since his life-long friendships with Steer, Sickert and Rothenstein brought him frequently to London. Contemporary critics regarded him as the ace practitioner of what was known as *le style anglais*. These painters and their British counterparts were regular contributors to International Society exhibitions. The market was so buoyant that this Society spawned a series of 'Fair Women' exhibitions at the Grafton Gallery before 1910. Through them, the values of English portraiture became international as never before.

Describing the ambiance of portraiture in the early years of the century, there is a high-flown rhetoric and rich eclecticism extending to virtual pastiches of Van Dyck, Reynolds and Gainsborough. The language of the seventeenth and eighteenth centuries was reinvented to produce such exuberant displays as Furse's 'Diana of the Uplands' (Plate 366) and Steer's portrait of Mrs. Violet Hammersley (Plate 367).

At the same time there were emergent young painters such as Rothenstein, Nicholson, John, Orpen and McEvoy who, adhering to Whistlerian precepts, sought to simplify portrait painting. These were artists who discounted Sargent. In works like Rothenstein's 'The Browning Readers' (Plate 368) they saw themselves distilling an abstract essence. In this stark modern interior, there is none of the flourish of the Sitwell Family. The intimate calm which connects the sisters, Alice and Grace Knewstub, is as much a product of Rothenstein's stage-craft, as it is of their pensive activity. This picture, it has been pointed out, led to a series of 'English' interiors in which there is a suggestion of melancholy. Its ascetic quality pervades Orpen's 'A Window in a London Street', McEvoy's 'The Convalescent' and various early pictures by Gwen and Augustus John. The emphasis upon formalism, upon dramatic shapes, upon spacing and interval, equally characterises the work of Nicholson whose portraits of W.E. Henley and Max Beerbohm (Plate 369) avoid the flashy paint techniques of Sargent. In most instances, the portraits produced by this group are testaments to friendship. Augustus John cites the difficulty he had with an early portrait of an old lady who bored him as much as he bored her. Yet a little later, in the splendid series of pictures of W.B. Yeats (Plate 370), there is an appropriate suggestion, beyond the poet's features, of romantic reverie.

The early portraits of William Orpen (1878-1931) have a similar restraint. It was only after 1905 that the volume of commissions led to a much greater confidence in handling people. Even here, the best results were often portraits of friends and pupils, given generalised titles. His teaching commitments in Dublin brought Orpen into touch with the Celtic Revival and its associated nationalism. As an Irish painter, he was swept along by the demand for a

PLATE 367
Philip Wilson Steer
Mrs. Violet Hammersley,
1906-7
84¼ x 60½ ins.
(214 x 153.5cm)
(Art Gallery of New
South Wales, Sydney)

distinctive cultural identity and in the portrait of his republican student, Grace
Gifford, he endeavoured to capture the spirit of 'Young Ireland' (Colour Plate
68). The result is one of the most extraordinary images of the Edwardian years,
drawing the spectator into direct confrontation with a young woman whose
features differ markedly from those of the conventional Edwardian beauty.
The critic, Frank Rinder, described the work as an 'exuberant essay' in which

PLATE 368
William Rothenstein
'The Browning Readers',
1900
30½ x 38¼ ins.
(76 x 96.5cm)
(Cartwright Hall Art
Gallery, Bradford)

'candour...mingled with a measure of delight in freedom from responsibility...'

Such pictures were authentically modern. They were far removed from the
confections of Boldini and Sargent. They were not dependent upon precedent,
even though at the level of technique there were residual echoes of Whistler
and Velazquez. Faced with a commission for a large family group in the
summer of 1907, Orpen revealed, however, the full depth of his dependency.
Sir Augustus Vere Foster of Glyde Court, County Louth, was to be shown
returning from a shoot, accompanied by his wife and two daughters. His figure
was modelled upon Velazquez's 'Philip IV Dressed for Hunting', while his
elder daughter, leading a donkey, looks across towards the spectator, in a pose
reminiscent of Whistler's 'Miss Cicely Alexander' (Colour Plate 61). The
whole ensemble contains unmistakable recollections of Van Dyck and Snyders
(Colour Plate 69).

A range of similar sources could be advanced for Lavery's large studio
interior painted between 1910 and 1912. Here, too, is a work which overtly

PLATE 369
William Nicholson
Max Beerbohm, 1905
19¾ x 15¾ins. (50 x 40cm)
(Private collection)

PLATE 370
Augustus John
W.B. Yeats, 1907
30 x 20ins. (76 x 51cm)
(Manchester City Art
Gallery)

courts comparison with a notable precedent — this time Velazquez's 'Las Meninas'. The ability of the most celebrated portraitists of the age to challenge in its entirety a great tradition, may be taken as an indication of the supreme self-confidence from which true originality sprang.

At the same time as these painters pitted themselves against ever more demanding tests of skill, they were being overtaken by those for whom it was more important to absorb the outside influences from post-impressionism. Technical innovations in the European avant-garde were rooted more in the landscape tradition than in portraiture. Those head studies which were produced by the young Camden Town and Bloomsbury painters were seldom commissions. As exercises in radical art styles, they challenged portrait conventions and the society which supported them. Sickert's preference for portraying those of an inferior social position and for the *jolie-laide* has been noted by a number of writers. His portraits of 'The Blackbird of Paradise' (Plate 371) and of his charwoman, Mrs. Barrett, insist upon the pictorial worthiness of the lower orders. His younger colleagues in the Fitzroy Street group, when they painted head studies, tended to use one another as models.

381

PLATE 371 (above)
Walter Sickert
*'The Blackbird of
Paradise',* c.1896-97
26 x 19ins. (66 x 48cm)
(Leeds City Art
Galleries)

PLATE 372 (right)
Harold Gilman
Mrs. Mounter, 1916-17
36¼ x 24⅛ins.
(92 x 61.5cm)
(Walker Art Gallery,
Liverpool)

Only Gilman, in the numerous reworkings of his redoutable landlady, Mrs.
Mounter, arrived at an imposing rendition of an English type (Plate 372). The
Cézannist experiments of the painters of the Fry circle were more concerned
with form than features, and the obliteration of the familiar and the
recognisable was seen as a deliberate flaunt to convention. Here again, types
rather than individuals were preferred. Whilst these works cannot be easily
summarised, they should not be dismissed. Wyndham Lewis's 'Architect with
a green Tie' (Plate 373) for instance, led to the evolution of a language
deployed in many inter-war portrait commissions. There are also works which
for their uniqueness hold important places in any survey of painting prior to
the Great War. Henry Lamb's portrait of Lytton Strachey (Plate 374) and
Gerald Leslie Brockhurst's 'Ranunculus' (Colour Plate 70) are two examples.

Yet such pictures are at a tangent to the mainstream tradition of portraiture.
This had much to do with the demands of a social stratum which was heedless
of the massive changes in the British way of life. Portrait painters were
purveyors of fashion whose style should reflect the contemporary *vie moderne.*
Ambrose McEvoy (1878-1927) is an interesting instance of a painter who
abandoned the spartan interiors of his youth to be lionised by debutantes. His

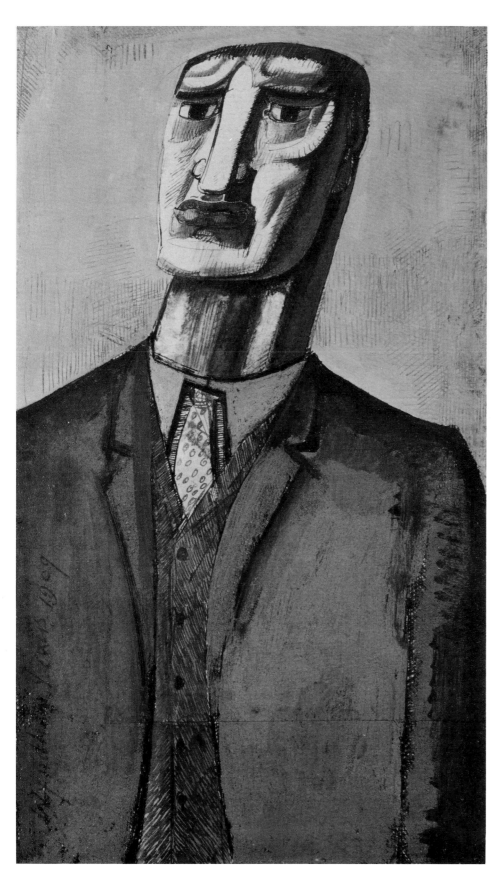

PLATE 373
Wyndham Lewis
'Architect with green Tie',
1909
16 x 12ins.
(40.5 x 30.5cm) gouache,
pen and ink on paper
(Metropolitan Museum
of Art, New York)

vaporous watercolours carry the ether in which the social butterflies of the 1910s and early 1920s tested their wings. One such was the ravishing Lady Diana Manners (Plate 375). McEvoy was to her what Shannon had been to her mother. Her husband-to-be, Alfred Duff Cooper, declared that if he had been a millionaire, he would have founded a gallery to contain portraits of her in every dress she ever owned. Within a few years, such hyperbole dissolved in the shell craters on the road between Arras and Bapaume.

It is impossible, even given the frenzy of pre-war government collapses,

PLATE 375
Ambrose McEvoy
Lady Diana Manners, c.1915
16¼ x 11¼ins. (41 x 28.5cm), watercolour on paper
(Private collection)

imperial rumblings, Irish nationalism, the rise of the labour movement and women's suffrage, to avoid the view, supported by the canvases of Sargent, Lavery, Orpen and McEvoy, that the Edwardian era was a decadent flowering. The writers of the 1920s looked back upon it, both puzzled and bemused. The young John Rothenstein, writing in 1929, regarded the current reaction to the 1890s as more than just a change of taste. The 'strident challenge' of the age '...to conventions appears to us unnecessary: its individualism cannot seem otherwise than preposterous to a generation, which crushing economic pressure and greater knowledge of Eastern philosophy is making increasingly collectivist in outlook'. Rothenstein was reflecting upon his father's aesthetic individualism, and at the same time, taking in a society which, as a consequence of its supremacy, had sustained that individualism. As Clutton Brock ruefully remarked after the war, it was necessary now 'to cut down on expenses'. The eloquent swan song of the high Edwardian years was, however, provided by James Laver, describing in 1925, close to the moment of Sargent's death, the age which he had dominated:

> The upper classes, that plutocracy whose court painter Sargent became, envisaged life as a voyage in the first-class saloon of an ocean liner. The murmurs of labouring multitudes were nothing to them but the just audible throbbing of the engine, the heaving of the ocean came to them as a hardly perceptible roll. They were sceptical of storms; confident that no wandering iceberg, sunken reef, nor sudden tempest, could ever bring disaster to a ship whose stewards were so silent and so efficient. Was there darkness? Switch on the lights! Fog? Counfound it! Blow the sirens! Danger? Let the captain look to it! We pay him, don't we?

This bleak response to spectacle is coloured by the grey facts of maturity. Its sharp invective nullifies attempts at objective evaluation. It should not be quoted. Through the eyes of the 1920s' commentators it was impossible to regard the Edwardian era without being blinded by its supreme self-assurance and its 'apparently unshakable prosperity'. The efflorescence of portrait painting during the period was proof of that prosperity. Its painting should not just portray individuals, it should also capture the assurance which sat upon their shoulders.

KENNETH McCONKEY
Historical and Critical Studies
Newcastle upon Tyne Polytechnic

Chapter 7
The Modern Face
1918-1960

During the period discussed in this chapter portraiture underwent a marked increase in informality. Many outstanding portraits were not officially commissioned, but done by people whom the artist either knew well or admired. As a result, twentieth century portraiture is often the product of a creative meeting: the artist, instead of following custom or accepted style, expresses a very personal slant on the sitter's character. David Piper once described portraiture as a bargain between two people — sitter and artist; but in this century there has often been little compromise: the two-way exchange is more equal, less mediated by tradition and more direct. Sometimes, as in the case of Graham Sutherland's portrait of Winston Churchill, which the sitter disliked and his widow had destroyed, the independent or forthright viewpoint can startle or offend. Always it throws an interesting light on art and society, proving that, despite the increasing multiplicity of imagery through photography and other means, the portrait has remained a vital artistic and social document.

Another significant difference with previous periods is that many of the best portraits have been produced by artists for whom portraiture has been an occasional occupation rather than a professional practice. Good portraits can be found in every decade. Nevertheless, as the annual illustrated catalogues of the Royal Society of Portrait Painters reveal, the portrait industry sank into a rut during the inter-war years and did not show signs of recovery until the 1970s. By the 1960s, the marked lack of invention in so much official portraiture had resulted in a loss of confidence on the part of commissioning authorities. In some instances firms and colleges, needing a portrait of an outgoing chairman or principal, resorted to photography and a gilt-framed colour photograph was hung beside paintings of previous boardroom and academic dignitaries.

After the First World War the accepted style of portraiture remained that of the Edwardian period, and the names of John Singer Sargent, John Lavery and William Nicholson were still dominant. Sargent, however, had privately declared, 'No more mugs', and up until a few months before his death in 1925 he was largely preoccupied with his murals for Boston Public Library. But his virtuoso, apparently nonchalant handling of detail — especially the glint of light on silk, satin, silver or pearls — was still admired and imitated, for in his hands it had become a superb vehicle for the expression of aristocratic ease. His influence is evident in the portraits of the New Zealand born artist Sir Oswald Birley (1880-1952) who settled in England after travelling Europe and painted many eminent men and women, as well as in the work of Philip de László (1869-1937). László outstripped all others in the sheer number of portraits he produced. Born in Budapest, he had begun as a sign painter's apprentice, moved on to work for a photographer but finally entered the Budapest School of Arts and Crafts. A scholarship for foreign study took him to Munich, after which he undertook further training at the Académie Julian in Paris. His reputation as a portrait painter was first established in Bavaria, Austria and Germany. He visited Britain in 1898 and two years later married into the Guinness family. This helped extend his clientele to Ireland and England, though he did not finally settle in London until 1907, in the same year holding a highly successful one-person exhibition at the Fine Art Society in Bond Street. The following year he visited America and painted Theodore Roosevelt. In 1914 he was granted British citizenship and his career seemed unassailable. But during the First World War he suffered from British xenophobia, was suspected of spying and imprisoned in Holloway jail. After the war he retrieved his position as a leading portraitist but he remained a controversial figure and often had his pictures rejected by the Royal Academy.

Like Sargent, de László aspired to the commanding elegance of eighteenth century English portraiture, that of Reynolds and Gainsborough in particular. His stated aim was to show 'the spirit by which the human form is vitalised'. He brought to his work a sure grasp of essentials and technical mastery, also an attractive personality and prodigious industry. His portrait of Sir William Flanders Petrie (Plate 376) displays his authoritative rendering of likeness and character. When painting women his handling is often lighter, more flirtatious and capable of vivacious effects. He had a vivid appetite for people and by the end of his life could boast that he had painted around 2,700 portraits, including two popes, four presidents of the United States of America and innumerable royalties, dukes, diplomats, generals, politicians, scientists, scholars and figures of distinction.

It is, however, William Orpen (1878-1931) and not de László who is generally regarded the finest portraitist working in the years immediately after the First World War. He, too, was highly productive, executing nearly six hundred portraits in just over thirty years. He had made his reputation in the Edwardian period with some boldly experimental interior and conversation pieces, but after the war the pressures created by market demand began to diminish his capacity for originality. Born in Ireland, he had trained at the Slade where he met his friend and rival Augustus John, with whom for a brief period he founded and ran the Chelsea Art School. In 1899 the Rembrandt exhibition held at the Royal Academy had made on him an unforgettable

impact, though his love of clear tonal oppositions owed more to the example of Manet. The portrait that secured his reputation in high society was that of the Countess of Rocksavage (Colour Plate 71); during the 1920s he was capable of earning up to £35,000 per annum. Like de László he adopted a lighter and often more superficial style when painting women. His portraits

COLOUR PLATE 71
William Orpen
The Countess of Rocksavage, later Marchioness of Cholmondeley, 1913
48 x 37½ ins. (122 x 94.5cm)
Orpen clearly lightened his style when painting the female sex, and with this portrait secured his reputation in high society
(Private collection)

COLOUR PLATE 72
Percy Wyndham Lewis
'Portrait of an Englishwoman', 1914
22 x 15ins. (56 x 38cm), graphite and gouache on paper
This portrait could be interpreted as an ironic riposte to the received notions of female
beauty associated with the title. Though a schematic rendering of the face can be read
into the bars and rectangles, the picture's more immediate impact is that of a spare,
architectonic abstract design
(Wadsworth Atheneum, Hartford, Connecticut)

PLATE 377
William Orpen
'The Chef', *1921*
50 x 41ins.
(127 x 101.5cm)
(Royal Academy of
Arts, London)

also vary in quality and can be dull. At his best, as in 'The Chef', with its
incisive rendering of character, he sought to uncover, in the words of
Shakespeare that he quoted, 'the mind's construction in the face' (Plate 377).
He also favoured the square, or almost square, format, and after 1918
arranged the light in his studio so that it struck the sitter from both sides,
thereby eliminating all heavy shadows.

Augustus John (1878-1961) never established himself as a practising
portraitist in the way that Orpen did, in part because, though he needed the
money his sitters were prepared to pay, he was discomforted by the
professional relationship between artist and sitter that accompanied any

PLATE 378
Augustus John
Madame Suggia, 1922-23
73.5 x 65ins.
(186.5 x 165cm)
(Tate Gallery, London)

commission. When asked to paint Queen Elizabeth (now the Queen Mother) he dithered, invented numerous delaying procedures, cancelled appointments or pleaded illness and for many years kept the end result hidden away. But he exceeded Orpen in the reputation he amassed. The legend that grew up around his name began at the Slade. During one vacation he dived into the sea, struck his head on a rock and, as the incident was reported by a Brooke Bond tea card (one of a series on Famous People), 'emerged from the water a genius'. Certainly some alteration had been affected: whereas during his first two years at the Slade, Professor Tonks had described his work as 'methodical', John now displayed such wizardry at draughtsmanship that students snatched up the drawings he intended for the waste paper basket. Everything he did set a new code for artistic behaviour. He became especially renowned for his bohemianism, his sexual prowess and his admiration for gypsies.

COLOUR PLATE 73
Vanessa Bell
Iris Tree, 1915
48 x 36ins. (122 x 91.5cm)
The overriding concern seems to be not likeness nor imaginative characterisation, but a desire to create form through hue rather than tone. Even the shadows on the face and arms have been translated into patches of pure colour, the brilliance of the whole contrasting strangely with the sitter's passivity
(Private collection)

COLOUR PLATE 74
Meredith Frampton
Sir Charles Grant Robertson, 1941
47¾ x 43¼ins. (121.5 x 109.5cm)
As in many of Frampton's portraits, the objects surrounding the sitter have been
chosen to denote his personal and professional interests: a nearby globe and maps on
the desk allude to Robertson's publication of historical atlases; volumes of music,
flowers and a can of weedkiller indicate his fondness for music and gardening
(Scottish National Portrait Gallery, Edinburgh)

His fluent naturalism, which combined assured draughtsmanship with a fresh and direct use of paint, made portraiture a natural outlet for his talents. His clientele was more colourful and less establishment than Orpen's. Undoubtedly his best portraits are of his own family or people he admired. They signal, among other things, his pleasure in female beauty, as can be seen from his likenesses of his second wife, Dorelia, of the actress Tallulah Bankhead and of the Marchesa Casati, society hostess and mistress of d'Annunzio. Once, when given a list of twenty rich prospective sitters, he crossed off all the names except one, that of an exceptionally pretty girl. He was also drawn by creative or powerful personalities. Lady Ottoline Morrell's charged presence and prominent facade, her red hair, pearls, teeth and jutting chin, perfectly suited his bravura. Equally memorable is his portrait of the famous Portuguese 'cellist, Madame Suggia, who played uninterrupted Bach throughout some eighty sittings (Plate 378). Though the relationship between the musician and her instrument in John's portrait is unconvincing, it matters little, for the portrait is sustained by an energetic painterliness and by the sweep and verve of the artist's conception.

John extemporised but did not innovate. As the critic Frank Rutter has observed: 'We admired John, not because he was doing new things, but because he was doing old things superbly well'. For evidence of the modernist practices that had radicalised the English art world after Roger Fry's two post-impressionist exhibitions, in 1910 and 1912, we must turn to the work of Percy Wyndham Lewis (1882-1957). He had been the chief protagonist behind Vorticism, founded in 1914, and the magazine *Blast,* both of which had promoted a machine aesthetic that banished all inessentials and replaced organic form with harsh geometry. In 1914 Lewis painted 'Portrait of an Englishwoman' in a Vorticist style, perhaps as an ironic riposte to the received notions of female beauty associated with the title (Colour Plate 72). Though a schematic rendering of the face can be read into the coloured bars and rectangles that compose this picture, its more immediate impact is that of a spare, architectonic abstract design, in which geometrical elements are held in taut relationship with the picture surface.

The Vorticist movement did not survive the First World War. When Wyndham Lewis attempted to create an avant-garde, forming 'Group X' which held its first and last exhibition in March 1920, his attempts were not successful. He himself had lost confidence in the aesthetic he had earlier upheld. 'The geometrics which interested me so exclusively before', he admitted, 'I now found bleak and empty. They wanted *filling'.* Nevertheless the imprint of his earlier concern with abstraction remained in his work, and when he began to concentrate on figure and portrait drawing his whiplash line displayed a clipped stylisation. Lewis's best portraits, whether drawn or painted, are of literary figures: Naomi Mitchison, Rebecca West, Stephen Spender, T.S. Eliot, Ezra Pound and Edith Sitwell. They are forceful and precise, but in most cases the likeness presented is little more than a carapace, coldly unilluminating. The defect probably lay in Lewis's personality which was circumscribed by paranoia and a deep-seated hatred of privilege. It is instanced in his dealings with the Sitwell family.

Soon after he met the Sitwells he solemnly informed them at dinner: 'Remember! I'm thirty-seven 'till I pass the word round'. He developed a particular liking for Edith and she sat to him every Sunday for a period of ten months, in whatever clothes he suggested. The drawings that resulted evince a variety of mood, from the sad and withdrawn to the hieratic and majestic. He also began a portrait of her in oils, the sittings for which were abruptly terminated when the relationship between sitter and artist became strained. Edith Sitwell later recalled that Lewis had developed a *schwärmerei* for her to which she had not responded. This alone would not explain the cruel caricature of the three Sitwells that Lewis later incorporated into his novel *The Apes of God*. Another cause of ill feeling may have been his collar. Lewis was a man 'born without relations but with a collar', Edith Sitwell wrote, and 'one had only to add up the rings on it (made by time). . . to arrive at some estimate of his age'. On a visit to the Sitwell family home, Renishaw, Lewis mislaid his collar, which had probably been removed by the butler for laundering, and would not emerge from his room until it was found. The discomfort he endured fanned in him a malicious but respectful hatred: Edith, especially, became for him 'one of my most hoary, tried and reliable enemies'.

When he flitted with his portrait of Edith (Plate 379) the hands and arms were left unfinished, but were completed later, in 1935, with faceted areas of bright colour which stylistically jar with the rest of the portrait. Earlier she had been painted in a rainbow jacket by Nina Hamnett (1890-1956) and given, one critic noted, 'kaleidoscopic breasts'. Undeterred by such criticism, she sat willingly to a great range of artists, including Sargent, Roger Fry, Rex Whistler, C.R.W. Nevinson, Alvaro Guevara (Plate 380), Stella Bowen, Pavel Tchelitchew, Frank Dobson and Feliks Topolski and never tried to influence the proceedings. Only once did she complain at the result and that was when Topolski, in his bold expressionist style, emphasised the curvature of her spine and reawakened in her childhood memories of being incarcerated in a metal contraption which her parents and a family doctor had believed would straighten her back.

'If one is a greyhound', Edith Sitwell once asked, 'why try and look like a pekinese?'. Undismayed by her lack of conventional beauty, she had turned her back on prevailing fashion and dressed eccentrically, in heavy brocades, barbaric jewellery and extravagant (and sometimes unfortunate) hats. Her extraordinary appearance partly explains why she has probably inspired a larger body of portraiture than any other sitter outside of the royal family. With some justification, she derogated most English women for dressing 'as though they have been a mouse in a previous incarnation'.

Another sitter popular with artists was the poet and actress, Iris Tree. She sat to Alvaro Guevara, Augustus John, Jacob Epstein, Duncan Grant, Roger

COLOUR PLATE 75
Gerald Brockhurst
'By the Hills', 1939
30 x 25ins. (76 x 63.5cm)
In this portrait of Lady Marguerite Strickland, Brockhurst uses a low horizon line to
enhance the drama supplied by the lifted face. His strong colour and painstakingly
photographic technique helped give his sitters film-star appeal
(Ferens Art Gallery, Hull)

COLOUR PLATE 76
Ruskin Spear
'Strawberry Mousse', 1959
21¾ x 19¾ins. (55 x 50cm)
Spear's portraits often tend towards the satirical, continuing a tradition that looks back
to Hogarth and Rowlandson. He had a particular fascination with the grinning or
gaping mouth, and often made it, as here, the focus of expression
(Private collection)

PLATE 379
Percy Wyndham Lewis
Edith Sitwell, 1923-35
34 x 44ins. (86.5 x 111.5cm)
(Tate Gallery, London)

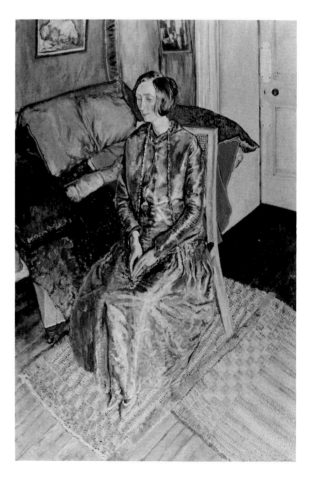

PLATE 380
Alvaro Guevara
Edith Sitwell, 1919
72 x 48ins. (183 x 122cm)
(Tate Gallery, London)

PLATE 381
Roger Fry
J. Maynard Keynes, c.1917
20½ x 24ins.
(52 x 61cm)
(Fitzwilliam Museum,
Cambridge)

Fry and Vanessa Bell. Arguably the most outstanding is that by Vanessa Bell (1879-1961). She accurately portrays Iris Tree's plumpness, pale flesh, blue eyes and daringly bobbed hair, but in this instance the sitter becomes secondary to the artist's style. The overriding concern is not likeness nor imaginative characterisation but the desire to create form through hue rather than tone. Even the shadows on the face and arms have been translated into patches of pure colour, the brilliance of the whole contrasting strangely with the sitter's passivity (Colour Plate 73).

Behind Vanessa Bell's painting lies the example of Matisse. Like Roger Fry and Duncan Grant, with whom she was closely associated, Vanessa Bell was influenced more by French art than by British. Gradually, however, her bold experiments with colour settled into a more naturalistic form of post-impressionism in which colour and form, though still regarded as abstract entities in their own right, are held in closer relationship with the representational requirements. A similar loss of inventiveness is noticeable in the portraits which Roger Fry (1866-1934) painted at intervals throughout his life. These reflect tellingly on his wide-ranging interests, for, owing to friendship with his sitters, he was able to catch informal likenesses of André Gide, Arthur Waley and J. Maynard Keynes (Plate 381) as well as more formal likenesses of Bertrand Russell and Clive Bell. Of these three Bloomsbury artists, it was Duncan Grant (1885-1978) who, once the initial

COLOUR PLATE 77
Francis Bacon
'Study of Henrietta Moraes Laughing', 1969
14 x 12ins. (35.5 x 30.5cm)
As if testing his sitters, Bacon pushes likeness to
the edge of dissolution before pulling the image
back by the introduction of a recognisable feature
or look
(Private collection)

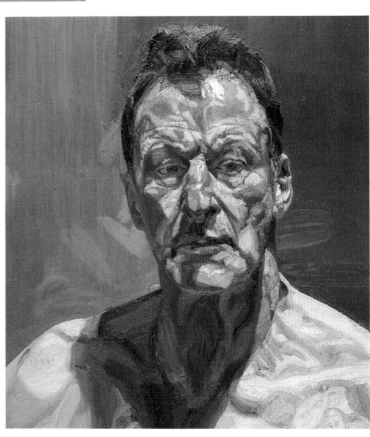

COLOUR PLATE 78
Lucian Freud
'Reflection' (self-portrait), 1985
22 x 20ins. (56 x 51cm)
As the expression in this portrait suggests,
Freud's gaze is sharp and remorseless. As
a painter of flesh he is unsurpassed
(Private collection)

COLOUR PLATE 79
Suzi Malin
Baron Home of Hirsel, 1980
44 x 29 ¾ ins. (112 x 75.5cm)
The technique, that of tempera on white ground, and the meticulous attention to detail
are reminiscent of the Pre-Raphaelites. Nevertheless the sensibility informing every
idiosyncratic tuck and crease is modern
(National Portrait Gallery, London)

PLATE 382 (above)
Duncan Grant
Bea Howe, 1926
32 x 22ins.
(81.5 x 56cm)
(Sheffield City Art
Galleries)

PLATE 383 (right)
Henry Lamb
Pernel Strachey, 1925
44 x 30ins. (112 x 76cm)
(Newnham College,
Cambridge)

excitement concerning post-impressionism had evaporated, best sustained a satisfying relationship in portraiture between formal and representational demands. In his portrait of Bea Howe (Plate 382) is found an unforced vivacity, both in the likeness portrayed and in the jubilant handling of paint.

The most famous Bloomsbury portrait is, however, that by Henry Lamb (1883-1960) of Lytton Strachey in which the lassitude of the sitter's pose is imitated in the branches of the trees seen through the window and mocked by his tightly furled umbrella (Plate 374). Less well known is Lamb's portrait of Strachey's sister, Pernel (Plate 383). As an artist Lamb changed his style according to his current allegiance: at one time he was closely associated with Augustus John, at another with Stanley Spencer. As a result it is difficult to detect in his work as a whole any pronounced artistic individuality, though what does emerge is a sensitive grasp of tonal harmonies. In his portrait of Pernel Strachey, painted during her time as Principal of Newnham College, Cambridge, his uninflected style allows a very direct statement of character, conveyed through pose and expression, which if further underlined would have taken this portrait to the verge of caricature.

PLATE 384 (left)
Stephen Tomlin
Lytton Strachey, 1928-30
10⅞ ins. (27.5cm) high,
bronze
(Anthony d'Offay
Gallery, London)

PLATE 385 (above)
Frank Dobson
Sir Osbert Sitwell, 1923
12½ ins. (32cm) high,
polished bronze
(Tate Gallery, London)

The Bloomsbury intellectuals were also well served by the sculptor, Stephen Tomlin (1891-1937), who produced memorable bust portraits of Virginia Woolf (National Portrait Gallery) and Lytton Strachey (Plate 384). Better known was Frank Dobson (1888-1963) whose more classical style was capable of subtle inflection. His bust portrait of Osbert Sitwell (Plate 385), cast in polished bronze, has a suave fluency and a haunting stillness, leaving the impression that the sitter's attention is focused on some point beyond time. More rooted in the particular are the bust portraits Jacob Epstein (1880-1959) executed during the inter-war years. Though he had been associated with the Vorticists during the years immediately preceding the First World War, Epstein after 1918 abandoned the machine aesthetic and replaced it with an obsessive pursuit of the human. Though he still turned to carving for his experimental pieces, he led the revival of interest in modelling, producing bust portraits and figures which were subsequently cast in bronze (Plates 386 and 387). The vitality that he brought to bust portraiture set a standard that has rarely been surpassed, even though his lively effects were sometimes achieved through exaggeration, especially in his treatment of eyes, and through an emotionalism that can border on vulgarity.

In that portraits attempt to arrest time it is not surprising that this fast-changing century has produced a style of portraiture which suggests an almost

PLATE 386 (above)
Jacob Epstein
Lady Gregory, c.1910
15ins. (38cm) high,
bronze
(Leeds City Art
Galleries)

PLATE 387 (right)
Jacob Epstein
Albert Einstein, 1933
17½ins. (45.5cm) high,
bronze
(Fitzwilliam Museum,
Cambridge)

surreal timelessness. It ignored the vagaries of artistic fashion and encouraged the use of a meticulous realism. Leonard Campbell Taylor (1874-1969) achieved a widespread reputation through coloured reproductions of his portraits and interiors which, with their deliberately calm compositions and soft realism, hung harmoniously in many drawing rooms. Their stillness imitated that found in Vermeer, an illusion only disturbed by the slightly banal sentiment conveyed by his figures. He painted with such technical precision and control that the quality of paint is virtually eliminated.

A more brilliant practitioner of this style was Meredith Frampton (1894-1982). His portrait of Sir Charles Grant Robertson (Colour Plate 74) was commissioned by the University of Birmingham following the sitter's retirement as Vice-Chancellor in 1938. As in all Meredith Frampton's portraits the sitter is surrounded by clues as to his profession and interests: a nearby globe and maps on the desk allude to his publication of two historical atlases; the framed pictures of buildings on the wall behind refer to the sitter's work for Birmingham University and a nearby hospital; elsewhere, volumes of music, flowers and a can of weedkiller indicate his fondness for music and gardening. The can of weedkiller proved so controversial that, on Varnishing Day at the Royal Academy in 1941, Frampton added the label that semi-obscures the imprint on its side. The intensity of the illusionism in his work

PLATE 388
William Coldstream
Inez Spender, 1937-38
30 x 40ins.
(76 x 101cm)
(Tate Gallery, London)

is remarkable, and stories were told of flies in one of his pictures that onlookers had tried to flick off. But it is not the only reason why his portraits have such compelling fascination. The design of each is minutely calculated and every detail is fashioned with the same evenness. The result is weirdly disquieting: clarity of definition makes everything immediately present and yet, in its marmoreal perfectionism, simultaneously strangely remote.

A different kind of realism was introduced into portraiture in the late 1930s by painters associated with the Euston Road School. More artistically conceived, it derived from the brushwork of Degas and the searching analysis of Cézanne, and was fostered by a reaction against recent developments in modern art, especially the move into abstraction. The School, led by William Coldstream, Graham Bell, Victor Pasmore and Claude Rogers, placed sober emphasis on 'observation'. It encouraged an unemphatic, objective appraisal of the subject, and became associated with a subdued, lyrical realism, reticent yet poetic. It is evident in the portrait of Inez Spender (Plate 388) by William Coldstream (1908-1988), and shares an affinity with the quiet realism of Percy Horton (1897-1970), an artist not associated with the Euston Road School, but who proceeded from the belief that 'one must paint from reality and with a human concern'. His 'Unemployed Man' (Plate 389) achieves dignity through restraint, its status as a social document equalling Orpen's society portraits.

In 1944 Alfred Munnings (1878-1959) was elected President of the Royal Academy, in recognition of the success he had achieved as a painter of equestrian portraits as well as landscape and rural subjects. During the inter-war years he had won acclaim with his portraits of members of the royal family

PLATE 389
Percy Horton
'Unemployed Man', 1936
17½ x 14ins.
(44.5 x 35.5cm)
(Sheffield City Art
Galleries)

and aristocracy, shown either riding or with their horse in a landscape setting. No small degree of self-satisfaction motivated his painting 'My Wife, My Horse and Myself' (Plate 390) in which his wife, Violet, is seated on the bay horse Master Munn which the Munningses bred themselves in Suffolk. The picture is posed in front of the Regency façade of Castle House in Dedham, Suffolk, acquired by Munnings in 1915. Munnings, at his best, painted with brio. He was also a volatile personality, fond of provoking highbrows and in 1949 resigned from the Presidency of the Royal Academy after making a controversial speech in which he vituperatively attacked modern art, its protagonists and advocates.

PLATE 390
Alfred Munnings
*'My Wife, My Horse and
Myself', c.1935*
39¼ x 49¼ ins.
(99.5 x 125cm)
(Sir Alfred Munnings
Art Museum, Dedham)

Munnings's position at the Academy passed to Gerald Kelly, who four years earlier had been knighted after painting state portraits of King George VI and Queen Elizabeth (Plates 391 and 392). He had exhibited at the Academy since 1905 and was a highly respected portraitist (Plate 393), but the vitality of his work lessened as his increasingly orthodox career progressed.

A more consistently successful artist was the academic portrait painter Gerald Brockhurst (1890-1978). 'By the Hills' (Colour Plate 75), a portrait of Lady Marguerite Strickland, daughter of the 3rd Earl of Darnley and also a professional actress, uses a low horizon line to thrust attention upwards towards the lifted face. Brockhurst's strong colour and painstakingly photographic technique made his work highly popular, and in 'By the Hills' they give the sitter a Hollywood gloss. Brockhurst moved to New York in 1939, the year that this picture was shown at the Royal Academy, partly in order to escape scandal as he had left his wife for his favourite model, Dorette, whom he married in 1949.

PLATE 391
Gerald Kelly
George VI, 1949
107 x 68ins.
(271 x 172.5cm)
(Royal Collection)

PLATE 392
Gerald Kelly
Queen Elizabeth (now the Queen Mother), 1949
107 x 68ins.
(271 x 172.5cm)
(Royal Collection)

Further outlet for portraiture during the Second World War was provided by the War Artists' Advisory Committee, chaired by Sir Kenneth Clark. Laura Knight (1877-1970) was one whose gift for characterful likeness was harnessed by the Committee. Her early leaning towards sombre harmonies, reminiscent of Dutch art, had gradually given way to a liking for strong colour. In the inter-war years she had specialised in studies of theatrical and circus folk; some of her gypsy paintings were done from a borrowed Rolls Royce, the inside of which she found made an excellent portable studio. Her work for the War Artists' Advisory Committee took her into factories and R.A.F. stations. Her particular brand of realism — detailed and prosaic — had demotic appeal. It also allowed for accurate depiction of mechanical equipment. In 1943 she was invited to paint a female celebrity in the engineering world. The result — 'Ruby Loftus screwing a Breech Ring' (Plate 394) — showed the screwing of a Bofurs breech ring, one of the most highly skilled jobs in the Royal Ordnance Factory. It was normally attempted by a man after eight or nine years training: Ruby Loftus, at the age of twenty-one, had mastered the art after only two years. Because of her skill, Ruby could not be spared from the factory and Laura Knight had to go to Newport to paint her. The painting was so popular

PLATE 393
Gerald Kelly
Jane (the artist's wife), 1924-26
76½ x 36¼ ins. (194.5 x 92cm)
(Fine Art Society, London)

PLATE 394
Laura Knight
'Ruby Loftus screwing a Breech Ring', 1943
34 x 40ins. (86.5 x 101.5cm)
(Imperial War Museum, London)

in industrial circles that the W.A.A.C. made a poster of it which was widely distributed. With regard to this and other paintings done for the W.A.A.C. Sir Kenneth Clark wrote to Laura Knight: 'The pictures you have done for us have been an immense success from every point of view'.

Another artist who achieved eminence through portraiture during the Second World War was Rodrigo Moynihan (1910-90). After serving with the Royal Artillery for three years, he was appointed a war artist. His 'Private Clarke' (Tate Gallery), a portrait of an A.T.S. girl in uniform, is as direct and fresh-faced as Hogarth's 'Shrimp Girl'. When the Queen was persuaded to

PLATE 395
Rodrigo Moynihan
*'The Staff of the Painting
School at the R.C.A.',
1951*
84 x 131¾ins.
(213.5 x 334.5cm)
(Tate Gallery, London)

PLATE 396
John Minton
Nevile Wallis, 1952
48 x 60ins.
(122 x 152.5cm)
(Art Gallery and
Museums Brighton)

412

choose Moynihan as the portraitist of Princess Elizabeth she wanted the same quality as that found in 'Private Clarke'. The following year, 1948, Moynihan was appointed Professor of Painting at the Royal College of Art and soon after taking up office he began work on an eleven foot long group portrait of his staff in the Painting School (Plate 395). The scale of this canvas, and the ambitiousness of its composition, is reminiscent of the group portraits by Hals and Rembrandt. As Lawrence Gowing has commented, it is a picture not only of individuals (John Minton, Colin Hayes, Carel Weight, Rodney Burn, Robert Buhler, Charles Mahoney, Kenneth Rowntree, Ruskin Spear and Moynihan himself) but also of relationships and the unrelated. In a subsequent group portrait, 'After the Conference: The Editors of Penguin Books' (1961), Moynihan again made use of the tensions and uncertainties that arise from the comings and goings created by a loose gathering of individuals.

During the early 1950s a growing interest in realism encouraged John Minton (1917-57) to abandon a Picasso-inspired stylisation in favour of a more direct response to appearances. There is little trace of his former neo-romanticism in his portrait of Nevile Wallis (Plate 396), an objective but also affectionate homage to his friend who, as art critic to *The Observer,* was widely respected. Many artists regarded portraiture at this time as a viable choice of subject. Not until the late 1950s, when the impact of American Abstract Expressionism hit Britain, was there a sudden loss of confidence in portraiture, and indeed in any art form that was centred on the individual, in content or scale. Nevertheless once the fashion for large scale abstract art had passed, it was possible to see that the painterly realism employed by Moynihan, Robert Buhler, Lawrence Gowing and others in their portraits of the early 1950s was to have lasting influence.

One artist in a category entirely his own was Ruskin Spear (1911-90). His portraits often tend towards the satirical, continuing a tradition that looks back to Hogarth and Rowlandson. In addition he had a particular fascination with mouths, be it the royal grin that enlivens his portrait of Princess Anne or the red open gullet in 'Strawberry Mousse' (Colour Plate 76). Spear's style is characterised by brusque, sometimes heavy-handed observation. In 'Stawberry Mousse', swirling impasto serves to describe the woman's costume jewellery and overblown buttonhole, and in general contributes to the glutinous effect. Pungent and jocular, Spear had a journalist's eye for telling detail and turned his attention mostly on public figures, politicians and film stars, the decorated and overtly seen.

Significant for post-1945 developments in portraiture was the practice Walter Sickert (1860-1942) had adopted in the inter-war years: the substitution of information acquired through drawing with that provided by the ready-made photographic image. Sickert saw in press photographs a greater degree of intimacy than the sitter, posed in front of the artist, would normally reveal. His portrait of King Edward VIII (Plate 397), based on a newspaper photograph, is the only one of him done during his brief reign. He is shown

PLATE 397
Walter Sickert
Edward VIII, 1936
72½ x 36¾ins. (183.5 x 92cm)
(Beaverbrook Art Gallery,
Fredericton, New Brunswick)

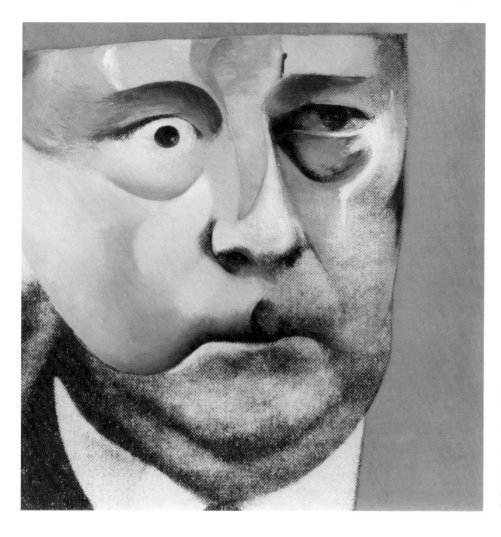

PLATE 398
Richard Hamilton
*'Portrait of Hugh Gaitskell
as a famous Monster of
Filmland', 1964*
24 x 24ins. (61 x 61cm)
oil and photomontage
on panel
(Arts Council
Collection)

in the uniform of the Welsh Guards arriving at the Guards' St. David's Day
service on 1 March 1936. At the time it was painted it was the most daringly
informal portrait of royalty yet produced. It is also one of the most perceptive,
for in the scissor-like movement of the King's legs and in his face his vacillation
is revealed.

Not until the emergence of Pop Art in the 1950s and 1960s were the
implications of Sickert's incorporation of non-fine-art sources into portraiture
taken further. Richard Hamilton (born 1922) merged paint and photography
(screenprinted on to the canvas) in his 'Portrait of Hugh Gaitskell as a famous
Monster of Filmland' (Plate 398) in 1964. In this an image of Claude Rains
as the Phantom of the Opera, taken from the cover of *Famous Monsters of
Filmland* (no.10), is combined with a newspaper photograph of Gaitskell. The
portrait was occasioned by Hamilton's anger at Gaitskell whom he regarded
as the main obstacle to the Labour Party's adoption of a reasonable nuclear
policy.

Another blurring of categories at this time occurred in the work of Peter
Blake (born 1932). He drew upon low-art sources, such as publicity stills, when

PLATE 399 (above)
Cedric Morris
Lucian Freud, 1941
28¾ x 23¾ ins. (73 x 60.5cm)
(Tate Gallery, London)

PLATE 400 (right)
Lucian Freud
John Minton, 1952
15½ x 10ins. (40 x 25.5cm)
(Royal College of Art, London)

painting his portraits of the Beatles, but in other instances turned to the designing of magazine covers, thereby returning his fine art skills to popular culture.

From the late 1950s Francis Bacon (born 1909) began working on portraits based on photographs, finding he preferred these to the sitter's actual presence. Initially his portraits were only of his friends and were often presented in triplicate, like the front and side views found in criminal records. He also began contorting appearances, frequently using a savage sweep of the brush as if to suggest a sudden movement of the head. As if testing his sitters, he pushes likeness to the edge of dissolution before pulling the image back by the introduction of a recongisable feature or look. The onlooker is left edgily aware of an ambivalence, between order and chaos, the presence of a particular individual and the bruising anonymity of the painter's marks (Colour Plate 77).

Like Bacon, Lucian Freud (born 1922) for many years would only paint those he knew well. 'If you don't know them', he has said of the artist in relation to his or her sitter, 'it can only be like a travel book'. Freud studied for a period under Cedric Morris (1889-1982) at the East Anglian School of

PLATE 401 (left)
Stanley Spencer
'The Psychiatrist', 1945
29½ x 19½ ins. (75 x 49.5cm)
(City of Birmingham Museum and Art Gallery)

PLATE 402 (above)
Derek Hill
The Earl of Longford, 1977
24 x 20ins. (61 x 51cm)
(Private collection)

Painting and Drawing. Morris's anti-academic approach liberated his pupils from habitual ways of looking and recording, and his own portraits, almost child-like in their uncircumscribed vision, reveal a shrewd and affecting grasp of idiosyncracies (Plate 399). Freud also makes use of emotive distortion to bring out, as in the case of his portrait of John Minton (Plate 400), the sitter's innate melancholy and desperation. Here, and in his portrait of Francis Bacon (Tate Gallery), also painted in 1952, Freud used a miniaturist's technique. In the second half of the 1950s he abandoned sable for hog's hair brushes and instead of building up form through glazes began using paint, made dense and opaque by the addition of Kremnitz white. The psychological penetration that makes his portraits of Minton and Bacon so outstanding is now replaced by a relentless probing of physical detail. Freud is on record as saying he wants his portraits to be *of* people, not *like* them. The rawness of the facts, portrayed in the artist's particularisation of veined flesh and wrinkled skin, arouses in the spectator his or her own sense of physical existence: whilst capturing an individual, Freud also provides a universal statement on the human condition (Colour Plate 78).

A precedent for Freud's intense analysis of appearances can be found in the work of Stanley Spencer (1891-1959). Best known for his biblical subjects set in the streets of Cookham, the village where he was born and grew up, Spencer produced relatively few portraits. The most notorious are the nude portraits which he painted of his second wife, Patricia Preece. In these he wanted to give the point of view of an ant crawling over the skin. The result is a frank intimacy, made all the more compelling by close-up views. As in Freud's portraits, Spencer's unexpected poses and cropped compositions create the impression that we are looking at raw life and not posed art. His 'The Psychiatrist' (Plate 401), a portrait of Mrs. Charlotte Murray who, with her husband, befriended Spencer whilst he was working on his 'Shipbuilding on the Clyde' paintings, is bunched and crowded. It was not painted from life, but based on drawings of the sitter's head and hands. The rest was done from towels and cushions stuffed inside a dressing gown belonging to Mr. Murray which Spencer greatly admired.

As portraiture became more and more diverse in the second half of the twentieth century there was a noticeable move towards a lighter and more

PLATE 404 (left)
John Ward
*H.R.H. Princess Anne,
1987-88*
74 x 38ins.
(188 x 96.5cm)
(National Portrait
Gallery, London)

PLATE 405 (above)
Graham Sutherland
Somerset Maugham, 1949
54 x 25ins.
(137 x 63.5cm)
(Tate Gallery, London)

graphic touch. In the work of Derek Hill (born 1916) an almost sketch-like approach, as in his portrait of the Earl of Longford (Plate 402), enables him to convey a warm responsiveness. It is as if the gap between the sitter and artist has been closed by friendship and the artist is now on terms of equality with the subject he or she paints. Even with royalty it is nowadays fairly usual for the artist to supply a sense of immediate access to the sitter through casual presentation. In Bryan Organ's portrait of Prince Charles (Plate 403) we see the Prince sideways on, posed against a fence, dressed for polo and relaxing

PLATE 406
Maggi Hambling
Dorothy Hodgkin, 1985
36¾ x 30ins. (93.5 x 76cm)
(National Portrait Gallery, London)

cross-legged in a canvas-backed chair, his head turned towards the spectator in such a way as to suggest that his attention has suddenly been arrested. Organ's spare and original compositions have earned him much acclaim, to the extent that, with the commission to paint Mitterand, he became the first British artist to commemorate a French President.

A more romantic view of royalty is found in the portrait of Princess Anne commissioned from John Ward (born 1917) in 1987 (Plate 404). On leaving the Royal College in 1947, Ward worked initially as a fashion illustrator for *Vogue.* Surprisingly, this skilful recorder of feminine grace has become well known as a portraitist of academic dignitaries, especially at Oxford and Cambridge. He exhibits regularly with the Royal Society of Portrait Painters and frequently makes use of drawn rather than painted detail. The setting for his portrait of the Princess Royal was a room in Buckingham Palace decorated with chinoiserie. Ward saw in this the ingredients for an exotic background composed of birds, snakes, flowers and dragons which elegantly offsets the sitter's white evening dress.

A similar graphic emphasis characterises the portraiture of Graham Sutherland (1903-80) which became an important aspect of his *oeuvre* almost by chance. Having become acquainted with Somerset Maugham in the south of France, he told a mutual friend that had he been a portrait painter Maugham's face and personality were of the kind that would have fired his imagination. Hearing of this, Maugham invited him to undertake his portrait. Sutherland at first refused but then agreed on the understanding that the end results should be regarded 'purely as an experiment'. When it was first publicly exhibited in 1951 the portrait (Plate 405) had a startling, and for some, shocking originality. Maugham, compressed within an unusually narrow format, is seen from below, this viewpoint creating a rising movement that culminates in the sardonic facial expression which makes this portrait at once so striking and memorable.

In the course of the next thirty years Sutherland painted just under fifty portraits. He would not accept a commission unless the prospective sitter's appearance or personality intrigued him. He responded most readily to those with power and therefore under pressure. Occasionally elements in his portraits are derived from past conventions in European painting, but his debt to others does not detract from the brilliance with which he coined fresh and authoritative statements of character. Owing to the extreme clarity of his conception, his portraits can, at first sight, seem harsh. However, as this harshness lessens with familiarity, insights into the sitter's personality are revealed that are often subtly flattering.

Painters and sculptors apart, the single eye of the camera has made a major contribution to portraiture during this period. But it would require a much more extensive study to do justice to this other discipline and to such names as Cecil Beaton, Felix H. Man, Bill Brandt, Fay Godwin and Jane Bown among many others. Nor is it possible to deal adequately with the renaissance in portraiture that has taken place over the last two decades. Never before has the practice of portraiture been so liberated from convention, making each new contract between artist and sitter an exploration without ground rules. The camera has not released the portrait painter or sculptor from the need for the closest scrutiny and analysis of externals. In Suzi Malin's portrait of Alexander Frederick Douglas-Home, Baron Home of Hirsel (Colour Plate 79), the technique, that of tempera on white ground, and the meticulous attention to detail are reminiscent of the Pre-Raphaelites. Nevertheless the sensibility informing every idiosyncratic tuck and crease is modern. Equally viable is the more interpretative approach adopted by Maggi Hambling in her portrait of the Nobel prize-winner Dorothy Hodgkin (Plate 406), whose mental energy is conveyed by the crowded composition and by the artist's decision to give the sitter four hands. These are two of many outstanding works in the National Portrait Gallery's modern collection which attracts crowds of visitors, for portraiture has once again become a vital arena within contemporary art and it is here that we encounter some of the most inventive minds operating in the art world today.

FRANCES SPALDING

Select Bibliography

Chapter 1: Lely to Kneller 1650-1723

Beckett, R.B., *Lely,* 1951.
Contains the largest number of illustrations of Lely's work to date, together with a brief biography and list of known works.

Buckeridge, B., 'An Essay towards an English School of Painting', in Roger de Piles, *The Art of Painting,* 2nd edn., 1744.

Collins Baker, C.H., *Lely and the Stuart Portrait Painters,* 2 vols., 1912.
The first serious attempt to construct an *oeuvre* for Lely, with particular emphasis on his colour and technique. The appendix to the second volume also prints some documentary material relating to Lely and some of his contemporaries.

Collins Baker, C.H., *Lely and Kneller,* 1922.

Douglas Stewart, J., *Sir Godfrey Kneller,* exhibition catalogue, National Portrait Gallery, London, 1971-2.

Douglas Stewart, J., 'Pin-Ups or Virtues? The concept of the ''Beauties'' in Late Stuart Portraiture', in *English Portraits of the Seventeenth and Eighteenth Centuries,* University of California, 1974, pp.3-43.

Douglas Stewart, J., *Sir Godfrey Kneller and the English Baroque Portrait,* 1983.
The most comprehensive account of the artist and his life yet published, with a large number of illustrations, including engravings, and a checklist of works, though not very detailed.

Edwards, E., *Anecdotes of Painters,* 1808.

Foskett, D., *Samuel Cooper,* 1974.

Foucart, J., 'Peter Lely, Dutch History Painter', in *Hoogsteder-Naumann Mercury,* vol. VIII, 1989, pp.17-27.

Houbraken, A., *De Groote Schouburgh der Nederlantsche Konstchilders en Schilderessen,* 3 vols., Amsterdam, 1718-21, reprinted P.T.A. Swillens, Maastricht, 1953.
Probably the most important early printed account of Lely's career.

Kerslake, J., *National Portrait Gallery: Early Georgian Portraits,* 2 vols., London, 1977.

Killanin, Lord, *Sir Godfrey Kneller and his Times 1646-1723,* 1948.

Maccubbin, R.P., and Hamilton-Phillips, M. (eds.), *The Age of William III and Mary II: Power, Politics and Patronage 1688-1702,* exhibition catalogue and reference volume, published in conjunction with the exhibition at the Grolier Club, New York, and the Folger Shakespeare Library, Washington D.C., 1989.

A comprehensive review of political and artistic life of the period, though with only a brief section on painters and patronage.

Millar, O., *Tudor, Stuart and Early Georgian Pictures in the Collection of Her Majesty the Queen,* 2 vols., 1963.

An invaluable source of reference, comprehensively illustrated, with a very thorough catalogue of works produced at the most important centre of artistic patronage and activity throughout this period.

Millar, O., *The Age of Charles I — Painting in England 1620-1649,* exhibition catalogue, Tate Gallery, London, 1972.

Millar, O., *Sir Peter Lely 1618-1680,* exhibition catalogue, National Portrait Gallery, Carlton House Terrace, London, 1978.

An outstanding monograph, and by far the most up to date and instructive account of Lely's career to date.

Millar, O., *Van Dyck in England,* exhibition catalogue, National Portrait Gallery, London, 1982.

An outstanding introduction to the artist and his work in this country.

Nisser, W., *Michael Dahl and the Contemporary Swedish School of Painting in England,* Uppsala, 1927.

Piper, D., *Catalogue of Seventeenth Century Portraits in the National Portrait Gallery 1625-1714,* 1963.

Rogers, M., 'John and John Baptist Closterman: a catalogue of their work', in *Walpole Society,* vol.XLIX, 1983, pp.224-280.

Royal Academy, *The Age of Charles II,* catalogue of the Loan Exhibition, London, 1960.

Stainton, L., and White, C., *Drawing in England from Hilliard to Hogarth,* exhibition catalogue, British Museum, London, 1987.

Stevenson, S., and Thomson, D., *John Michael Wright, The King's Painter,* exhibition catalogue, Scottish National Portrait Gallery, Edinburgh, 1982.

Vertue, George, 'Notebooks', in *Walpole Society,* XVIII, 1930; XX, 1932; XXII, 1934; XXIV, 1936; XXVI, 1938.

An invaluable source which contains a great deal of information on Lely's works as well as those of his leading contemporaries.

Walpole, Horace, *Anecdotes of Painting in England,* ed. R.N. Wornum, 1862.

Walsh, E., and Jeffree, R., *The Excellent Mrs. Mary Beale,* exhibition catalogue, Geffrye Museum, London, 1975 and Towner Art Gallery, Eastbourne, 1976.

Waterhouse, E.K., *Painting in Britain 1530-1790,* 3rd edn., 1969.

Waterhouse, E.K., *The Dictionary of 16th and 17th Century British Painters,* Woodbridge, 1988.

Whinney, M., and Millar, O., *English Art 1625-1714,* 1957.

Chapter 2: The Age of Hogarth 1720-1760

Burke, J., *English Art 1714-1800,* Oxford, 1976.
One of the best surveys of painting, architecture and sculpture of the eighteenth century.

D'Oench, E., *The Conversation Piece: Arthur Devis and his contemporaries,* exhibition catalogue, Yale Center for British Art, 1980.
Contains an excellent essay on the origins and sustained popularity of the conversation piece in the eighteenth century.

Einberg, E., *Manners and Morals: Hogarth and British Painting 1700-1760,* exhibition catalogue, Tate Gallery, 1987.
Sumptuously illustrated survey of British painting in the first half of the eighteenth century.

Hogarth, W., *The Analysis of Beauty* [1753] *with the rejected passages for the Manuscript Drafts and autobiographical notes,* ed. Joseph Burke, Oxford, 1955.
This edition of Hogarth's much-reviled anti-academic treatise contains a useful introduction to his ideas as well as publishing for the first time the artist's scrappy *Autobiographical Notes.*

Kerslake, J., *National Portrait Gallery: Early Georgian Portraits,* 2 vols, London, 1977.
Fully illustrated catalogue of the national collection of portraits of the first half of the eighteenth century.

Miles, E., and Simon, J., *Thomas Hudson 1701-1779,* exhibition catalogue, Iveagh Bequest, Kenwood, 1979.
The only published work of any substance on Hudson with a useful biographical essay.

Paulson, R., *Hogarth, His Life, Art and Times,* 2 vols., New Haven & London, 1971.
Although a revised edition is in preparation this exhaustive biography has much about Hogarth as a portrait painter.

Pears, I., *The Discovery of Painting: The Growth of Interest in the Arts in England, 1680-1768,* New Haven & London, 1988.
Fascinating investigation of the role of collectors patrons and connoisseurs in fostering the arts during an age of increasing commercialisation.

Piper, D., *The English Face,* London, 1957; revised edn. National Portrait Gallery, 1978.
A substantially revised edition will be published by the National Portrait Gallery in 1992. Still the most readable survey of the development of portrait painting from the renaissance to the early twentieth century.

Richardson, J., *An Essay on the Theory of Painting,* London, 1715.
The first of Richardson's essays which claims a moral seriousness for painting. It became an important textbook for aspiring young artists, like Reynolds, in the eighteenth century.

Shawe-Taylor, D., *The Georgians: Eighteenth-Century Portraiture & Society,*

London, 1990.
Good, well-written attempt to place eighteenth century portrait painting in the wider context of social history.

Simon, R., *The Portrait in Britain and America*, Phaidon, Oxford, 1987.
Lively and readable account of portrait painting on both sides of the Atlantic from the later seventeenth century to early years of this century. Particularly good chapters on poses and studio practice in the eighteenth century.

Smart, A., *The Life and Art of Allan Ramsay*, London, 1952.
Although very poorly illustrated and nearly forty years old this is still the standard biography of Ramsay. A new, revised edition will appear in 1992.

Vertue, George, 'Notebooks' in *Walpole Society*, vols. XVIII, XX, XXII, XXIV, XXVI, XXIX, XXX, 1929-1950.
Easily the most important source of primary information about art and artists in England in the first half of the eighteenth century and earlier.

Waterhouse, E.K., *Painting in Britain 1530-1790*, Harmondsworth, 1953; revised edn. 1978.
The first and still one of the best of the 'Pelican History of Art' series.

Waterhouse, E.K., *The Dictionary of British 18th Century Painters in oils and crayons*, Woodbridge, 1981.
Full of pithy and amusingly prejudiced remarks about minor eighteenth century painters. It is also the best illustrated survey of eighteenth century painting currently available.

Wendorf, R., *The Elements of Life; Biography and Portrait Painting in Stuart and Georgian England*, Oxford, 1990.
Stimulating examination of literary elements in portraiture and inter-relationship with biography.

Chapter 3: The Golden Age 1760-1790

Cherry, D., and Harris, J., 'Eighteenth-Century Portraiture and the Seventeenth-Century Past; Gainsborough and Van Dyck', *Art History*, 1982 (3).

Egerton, J., *Wright of Derby*, exhibition catalogue, Tate Gallery, 1990.

Erffa, H. von, and Staley, A., *The Paintings of Benjamin West*, 1986.

Hayes, J., *Gainsborough; Paintings and Drawings*, 1975.

Hayes, J., *Thomas Gainsborough*, exhibition catalogue, Tate Gallery, 1980.

Johnson, E.M., *Francis Cotes*, 1976.

Kerslake, J., *National Portrait Gallery: Eighteenth Century Portraits*, 2 vols., 1977.

Millar, O., *The Later Georgian Pictures in the Collection of Her Majesty the Queen*, 2 vols., 1969.

Nicolson, B., *Joseph Wright of Derby*, 2 vols., 1968.

Penny, N. (ed.), *Reynolds*, exhibition catalogue, Royal Academy of Arts, 1986.
Includes essays on Reynolds's technique, his place in European art, as well as

the most up-to-date research on the artist.

Prown, J., *John Singleton Copley,* 1966.

Ribeiro, A.E., *The Dress Worn at Masquerades in England 1780-1790 and its Relation to Fancy Dress in Portraiture,* New York, 1984.

Shawe-Taylor, D., *The Georgians: Eighteenth Century Portraiture & Society,* London, 1990.
Among the most recent, and one of the most original, books on eighteenth-century portraiture, with many new insights and observations.

Simon, R., *The Portrait in Britain and America,* 1987.
Excellent introduction to the subject, with a lively text and accompanying dictionary of portraitists.

Smart, A., *The Life of Allan Ramsay,* 1952.

Sunderland, J., 'John Hamilton Mortimer: His Life and Works', *Walpole Society,* 1986.

Taylor, B., *Stubbs,* 1975.

Waterhouse, E.K., *Gainsborough,* 1958.
Still the most complete and authoritative work on Gainsborough, although sadly out of print.

Waterhouse, E.K., *Reynolds,* 1973.
Contains a masterly introductory essay as well as an excellent selection of plates.

Waterhouse, E.K., *The Dictionary of British 18th Century Painters,* 1981.

Webster, M., *John Zoffany,* exhibition catalogue, National Portrait Gallery, 1982.

Wind, E., *Hume and the Heroic Portrait: Studies in Eighteenth-Century Imagery,* 1986.
Compilation of Wind's immensely influential essays on eighteenth-century British art, including the seminal article, 'Hume and the Heroic Portrait', not previously available in English.

Woodall, M. (ed.), *The Letters of Thomas Gainsborough,* 1963.

Chapter 4: The Romantics 1790-1830

Armstrong, W., *Sir Henry Raeburn,* London 1907.
With a list of paintings.

Arts Council, *John Opie 1761-1807,* exhibition catalogue, London, 1962.
The only scholarly modern examination of the artist, but not exhaustive by any means.

Earland, A., *John Opie and his Circle,* London, 1911.

Fletcher, E., (ed.), *Conversations of James Northcote with James Ward,* London, 1904.
Reminiscences about the artist and his contemporaries with a younger artist contemporary.

Garlick, K., *Sir Thomas Lawrence,* Oxford, 1989.
Supersedes the two other books by the author on this artist.

Gosse, E. (ed.), *Conversations of James Northcote R.A. with William Hazlitt,* London, 1894.
Reminiscences about the artist and his contemporaries with another good talker.
Greig, J., *Sir Henry Raeburn,* London, 1911.
With a list of paintings.
Gwynne, S., *Memorials of an Eighteenth Century Painter,* London, 1898.
The only biography of James Northcote of any decent length, and contains a list of the artist's pictures.
Levey, M., *Sir Thomas Lawrence,* exhibition catalogue, National Portrait Gallery, London, 1979.
McKay, W., and Roberts, W., *John Hoppner, R.A.,* London, 1909, Supplement, 1914.
Typical early twentieth century dealer-generated *catalogue raisonné,* with many pictures not by Hoppner. Biographical introduction based on the manuscript life of the artist by his granddaughter.
McLanathan, R., *Gilbert Stuart,* New York, 1986.
Many colour reproductions.
Macmillan, D., 'The Portraiture of Common Sense', *Painting in Scotland: The Golden Age,* exhibition catalogue, Edinburgh and London, 1986.
The only scholarly treatment of any length on Raeburn.
Park, L., *Gilbert Stuart,* 4 vols., New York, 1926.
Roberts, W., *Sir William Beechey,* London, 1907.
Still the only thing on the poor man; includes a list of pictures and some of the ledgers.
Rogers, J.J., *Opie and His Works,* London, 1878.
Skipton, H.P.K., *John Hoppner,* London, 1905.
First attempt at figuring out Hoppner's *oeuvre.* Text rather a list.
Whitley, W.T., *Gilbert Stuart,* Cambridge, Massachusetts, 1932.
Still the best book on Stuart.
Williams, D.E., *Life and Correspondence of Sir Thomas Lawrence,* 2 vols., London, 1831.
Published a year after the artist's death, the work is somewhat biased in its praise of its subject.

Chapter 5: The Victorians 1830-1880

Barrington, Mrs. R., *The Life and Works of Frederic Leighton,* 1906.
Blunt, W., *'England's Michelangelo': A Biography of George Frederic Watts,* 1975.
Burne-Jones, Georgiana, *Memorials of Edward Burne-Jones,* 1904.
Christian, J., *The Paintings, Graphic and Decorative Work of Edward Burne-Jones,* exhibition catalogue, Arts Council, 1975.
Coffey, B., *An Exhibition of Drawings by Sir George Hayter 1795-1871 and John Hayter 1800-1895,* exhibition catalogue, John Morton Morris & Co., 1982.

Cronan, K., *John Linnell: A Centennial Exhibition,* exhibition catalogue, Fitzwilliam Museum, Cambridge, 1982.

Curry, D.P., *James McNeill Whistler and the Freer Gallery of Art,* 1984.

Elzea, B., *Frederick Sandys 1829-1904,* exhibition catalogue, Brighton Art Galleries, 1974.

Heleniak, K.M., *William Mulready,* 1980.

Lambourne, L., and Hamilton, J., *British Watercolours in the Victoria and Albert Museum: An Illustrated Summary Catalogue of the National Collection,* 1980.

Lister, R., *George Richmond: A Critical Biography,* 1981.

Lister, R., *Samuel Palmer and 'The Ancients',* exhibition catalogue, Fitzwilliam Museum, Cambridge, 1984.

Maas, J., *Victorian Painters,* 1969.

Millais, J.G., *The Life and Letters of Sir J.E. Millais,* 1899.

Newall, C., *Society Portraits,* exhibition catalogue, Colnaghi and the Clarendon Gallery, 1985.

Newall, C., *The Art of Lord Leighton,* 1990.

Newall, C., *The Grosvenor Gallery,* forthcoming.

Ormond, L. and R., *Lord Leighton,* 1975.

Ormond, R., *Daniel Maclise,* exhibition catalogue, Arts Council, 1972.

Ormond, R., *Early Victorian Portraits,* National Portrait Gallery, 1973.

Ormond, R., *G.F. Watts, The Hall of Fame: Portraits of his Famous Contemporaries,* National Portrait Gallery, 1975.

Ormond, R., and Blackett-Ord, C., *Franz Xaver Winterhalter and the Courts of Europe 1830-1870,* exhibition catalogue, National Portrait Gallery, 1987.

Ormond R., and Hamlyn, R., *Sir Edwin Landseer,* exhibition catalogue, Tate Gallery, 1981.

Ormond, R., and Rogers, M. (eds.), *Dictionary of British Portraiture — Later Georgians and Early Victorians* (compiled by Elaine Kilmurray), 1979, and *Dictionary of British Portraiture — The Victorians* (compiled by Elaine Kilmurray), 1981.

Ovenden, G., *Pre-Raphaelite Photography,* 1984.

Parkinson, R., *Catalogue of British Oil Paintings 1820-1860* (in the Victoria and Albert Museum), 1990.

Parris, L., (ed.), *The Pre-Raphaelites,* exhibition catalogue, 1984.

Pointon, M., *Mulready,* exhibition catalogue, Victoria and Albert Museum, 1986.

Redgrave, R. and S., *A Century of British Artists,* 1866.

Reynolds, A.M., *The Life and Work of Frank Holl,* 1912.

Rogers, M., *Camera Portraits: Photographs from the National Portrait Gallery 1839-1989,* exhibition catalogue, National Portrait Gallery, 1989.

Stirling, A.M.W., *The Richmond Papers,* 1926.

Story, A.T., *The Life of John Linnell,* 1982.

Surtees, V., *The Paintings and Drawings of Dante Gabriel Rossetti 1828-1882 — A Catalogue Raisonnée,* 1971.

Sutton, D., *James McNeill Whistler,* 1966.

Watts, M.W., *George Frederic Watts — The Annals of an Artist's Life,* 1912.

Wentworth, M., *James Tissot,* 1984.

Whistler, J.M., *Mr. Whistler's Ten o'Clock Lecture,* 1888.

Whistler, J.M., *The Gentle Art of Making Enemies,* 1890.

Wills, C., *Sir Francis Grant,* unpublished Ph.D. thesis.

Wood, C., *The Dictionary of Victorian Painters,* revised ed. Christopher Newall, 1978.

Yung, K.K., *Complete Illustrated Catalogue 1856-1979,* National Portrait Gallery, 1981.

Young, A.M., et al., *The Paintings of James McNeill Whistler,* 1980.

Chapter 6: 'Well-bred Contortions' 1880-1918

Arnold, B., *Orpen, Mirror to an Age,* 1981.

Blanche, J.-E., *Portraits of a Lifetime,* 1937.
A book of recollections by the principal proponent of 'le style anglais'.

Caw, J.L., *Sir James Guthrie, P.R.S.A., H.R.A., R.S.W., LL.D.,* 1932.

Konody, P.G., and Dark, S., *Sir William Orpen, Artist and Man,* 1933.

Laver, J., *Portraits in Oil and Vinegar,* 1925.
Elegantly written series of critical essays, not all of which are about contemporary portrait painters.

Lavery, J., *The Life of a Painter,* 1940.

McConkey, K., *Edwardian Portraits: Images of an Age of Opulence,* Woodbridge, 1987.

McLaren Young, A., MacDonald, M., Spencer, R., and Miles, H., *The Paintings of James McNeill Whistler,* London and New Haven, 1980.

Moore, G., *Modern Painting,* 1893.
Essential critical study of contemporary painting.

Olsen, S., *John Singer Sargent,* 1985.

Ormond, R., *John Singer Sargent,* Oxford, 1973.

Pennell, E.R. and J., *The Life of James McNeill Whistler,* 1908.

Rothenstein, J.K.M., *A Pot of Paint, the Artists of the 1890s,* 1929, reprinted 1970.
A period piece.

Rothenstein, J.K.M., *Modern English Painters,* vol. 1, 1952.
Penetrating monograph essays, some of which are based upon recollections.

Rothenstein, W., *Men and Memories,* vols. 1 and 2, 1931.
Recollections of sitters and others.

Rutter, O., *Portrait of a Painter, The Authorised Life of Philip de László,* 1939.

Shaw Sparrow, W., *John Lavery and his Art,* 1911.

Sitwell, O., *A Free House! being the Writings of Walter Richard Sickert,* 1947.
Sickert's often penetrating and amusing art criticism.

Steen, M., *William Nicholson,* 1943.

"Wigs", *The Work of Ambrose McEvoy,* 1923.

Chapter 7: The Modern Face 1918-1960

Arnold, B., *William Orpen: Mirror to an Age,* London, 1982.

Arts Council, *William Roberts, A.R.A.,* exhibition catalogue, 1965.

Arts Council, *True and Pure Sculpture: Frank Dobson, 1886-1963,* exhibition catalogue, 1981.

Arts Council, *Late Sickert,* exhibition catalogue, 1981.

Barnes, J., *Percy Horton, 1897-1970,* exhibition catalogue, Sheffield City Art Galleries, 1982.

Baron, W., *Sickert,* London, 1973.

Clifford, D., *The Paintings of P.A. de Lázló,* London, 1969.

Cork, R., *Vorticism and Abstract Art in the First Age,* vol. I *Origins and Development,* vol. II *Synthesis and Decline,* London, 1976.

Gowing, L., *Lucian Freud,* London, 1982.

Hamilton, R., *Collected Works 1953-1982,* London, 1983.

Hayes, J., *Graham Sutherland,* Oxford, 1980.

Holyroyd, M., *Augustus John,* London, vol. I 1974, vol. II 1975.

Leiris, M., *Francis Bacon: Full Face and in Profile,* Oxford, 1983.

Morphet, R., *Meredith Frampton,* exhibition catalogue, Tate Gallery, London, 1982.

Pople, K., *Stanley Spencer: A Biography,* London, 1991.

Shone, R., *Bloomsbury Portraits,* London, 1976.

Shone, R., *Rodrigo Moynihan: Paintings and Works on Paper,* London, 1988.

Spalding, F., *Portraits by Roger Fry,* exhibition catalogue, Courtauld Institute Galleries, London, 1976.

Acknowledgements

The publishers are grateful to the following individuals and institutions who kindly provided or generously gave of their time in locating prints. They are also grateful to copyright owners for permission to illustrate portraits:

H.M. The Queen.

Abbot Hall Art Gallery, Kendal; Abercorn Heirlooms Settlement; Arther Ackermann & Son Ltd., London; Thos. Agnew & Sons Ltd., London; His Grace the Duke of Atholl.

The Barber Institute of Fine Arts, Birmingham University; Baring Bros. & Co. Ltd., London; The Marquis of Bath; His Grace the Duke of Beaufort; Beaverbrook Art Gallery, Fredericton; Birmingham Museums and Art Gallery; Bonhams, London; Bradford Art Galleries and Museums (Cartwright Hall Art Gallery); Royal Pavilion, Art Gallery and Museums, Brighton; Trustees of the British Museum; Mrs. Dorette Brockhurst; His Grace the Duke of Buccleuch and Queensberry; J.E Bulloz, Paris.

National Gallery of Canada, Ottawa; His Grace the Lord Archbishop of Canterbury; The Carnegie Museum of Art, Pittsburgh; Trustees of the Chequers Estate; Art Institute of Chicago (Mr. and Mrs. W.W. Kimball Collection, Plates 180 and 279; Gift of Mr. and Mrs. Denison B. Hull, Plate 233; Gift of Spencer Stuart and Waldo H. Logan in memory of Mr. and Mrs. Frank G. Logan, Plate 257); Christie's, London; Church Commissioners; Cincinnati Art Museum (Bequest of Mary M. Emery, Plate 265; Gift of Mary Hanna, Plate 266); Clemens-Sels Museum, Neuss; Viscount Cobham; Colnaghi, London; Thomas Coram Foundation; Courtauld Institute of Art (Photographic Survey); Viscount Cowdray.

Dallas Museum of Fine Arts (Mrs. John. B. O'Hara Fund, Plate 286); Viscount De L'Isle; Delaware Art Museum (Samuel and Mary B. Bancroft Memorial, Plate 331); Detroit Institute of Arts (Bequest of Eleanor Clay Ford, Plate 255; Gift of Mr. and Mrs. A.D. Wilkinson, Plate 258); Society of Dilettanti; The Ditchley Foundation; The Drapers' Company; Governors of Dulwich Picture Gallery.

English Heritage; J.J. Eyston.

Richard Feigen Gallery, New York; The Fine Art Society, London; Syndics of the Fitzwilliam Museum, Cambridge; The Frick Collection, New York.

Geffrye Museum, London; J. Paul Getty Museum, Malibu; Glasgow Art Gallery and

Index

Page numbers in italics indicate portraits illustrated

442